Introducing Profiling
A Practical Manual

Patricia Broadfoot
Lecturer in Education, University of Bristol

M
MACMILLAN
EDUCATION

For David

© Patricia Broadfoot 1987

All rights reserved. No reproduction, copy or transmission
of this publication may be made without written permission.

No paragraph of this publication may be reproduced, copied
or transmitted save with written permission or in accordance
with the provisions of the Copyright Act 1956 (as amended),
or under the terms of any licence permitting limited copying
issued by the Copyright Licensing Agency, 33–4 Alfred Place,
London WC1E 7DP

Any person who does any unauthorised act in relation to
this publication may be liable to criminal prosecution and
civil claims for damages.

First published 1987
Reprinted 1988

Published by
MACMILLAN EDUCATION LTD
Houndmills, Basingstoke, Hampshire RG21 2XS
and London
Companies and representatives
throughout the world

Printed in Hong Kong

British Library Cataloguing in Publication Data
Broadfoot, Patricia
Introducing profiling.
1. Students——Great Britain——Rating of
2. Education, Secondary——Great Britain
I. Title
373.12′7   LB1117
ISBN 0–333–39788–6

Contents

Acknowledgements v
Introduction 1

Part I Briefing
1 Why profiles? 5
2 Progress to date 15
3 Choices to be made 17
4 A range of experience 22

Part II The attack
5 Establishing a profiling scheme 75
6 Case studies of school-based innovation 87

Part III De-briefing
7 How well are we achieving our goals? 117

References 126

A note about the author

Dr Patricia Broadfoot is Lecturer in Education, University of Bristol. She is co-director of the DES-funded Pilot Records of Achievement in Schools Evaluation (PRAISE) and of a national evaluation of Profiling in TVEI funded by the MSC. A former secondary school teacher and teacher trainer, she has worked since 1973 in the field of educational assessment, particularly on the problems pupils experience with current procedures – notably public examinations – and the pursuit of possible alternatives. She has been solely or jointly responsible for a number of books on assessment including *Pupils in Profile*, SCRE, 1977; *Assessment Schools and Society*, Methuen, 1979; *Keeping Track of Teaching – the role of assessment in the modern classroom*, RKP, 1982; *Selection Certification and Control*, Falmer, 1984; *Profiles and Records of Achievement*, Holt. 1986.

Acknowledgements

This book is the product of more than thirteen years' involvement in the design, development, implementation and evaluation of profiles. In writing it I have sought to share some of this experience with others. I also wish to pass on the many insights I have gained through being involved with those whose self-imposed crusade has been to make the ideals of profiling a daily reality for their pupils. Profiling itself has grown from nothing into a major educational issue in a relatively short time. This is because those involved have been committed and enthusiastic and, at the same time, willing to share their experiences with others who in their turn have been anxious to listen. No one reading this book will be left unaware why this enthusiasm for change is so infectious. Nor will they be left unaware of how many difficulties stand in the path of its successful realisation. In this book I have tried to bring this goal one step nearer by building on the lessons already learned in order to make more widely available such wisdom as now exists. Thus I am grateful to all those who have generously allowed material to be reproduced here and for those who have provided commentaries and case studies. Some are acknowledged by name; others cannot be for reasons of confidentiality. All are making their contribution. I have tried to provide details which are as up-to-date and accurate as possible about individual schemes. Inevitably some things will already be out of date before this book is in print and much more will rapidly become so. Where details of individual schemes are out of date or incorrect I hope those concerned will be tolerant.

I am also greatly indebted to a number of other people for their part over the years in helping me to write this book: to W. Bryan Dockrell, formerly Director of the Scottish Council for Research in Education, and Bill Ritchie, HMDSCI, Scottish Education Department, who first introduced me to profiles and to Ian Morris, then Director of the Research and Intelligence Unit, Scottish Education Department, who provided the funds for initial development work; to the many students who, over the years, have taught me so much and helped deepen my understanding; to Desmond Nuttall and the rest of the DES-funded Pilot Records of Achievement in Schools Evaluation (PRAISE) team for many insights and much support; to my publisher, Brenda Stones, who for thirteen years shared the same classrooms with me and thus understood why this book needed to be written; to Ruth Sutton and Eileen Shaw for their helpful comments on earlier drafts.

As always I have been totally dependent on the good offices and secretarial magic of Sue Cottrell to make this project a reality and I thank her most sincerely for both her skill and her endurance.

To all these and others belongs the credit for this book; the mistakes are my own.

PMB
Bristol
August 1986

Associated Book Publishers for a table from *Keeping Track of Teaching* by Black and Broadfoot, Routledge and Kegan Paul, 1952; Avon County Council for material from the *Avon Student Profile*; City and Guilds of London Institute for excerpts from the Joint Board's publications on profiling in the Certificate of Pre-Vocational Education and from *Profiling Systems* by N. Stratton, 1985; Clwyd County Council for material from the *Clwyd Record of Achievement at 16*; Essex County Council Education Department for material from their *Records of Achievement Scheme* and material from J. McNaughton; Evesham High School for an extract from their Personal Achievement Records; Further Education Unit for material from *Profiles in Action and Computer Aided Profiling*; Harper & Row Ltd for an extract from *Uses and Abuses of Profiling* by Bill Law, 1984; The Controller of Her Majesty's Stationery Office for crown copyright material from the Policy Statement on Records of Achievement, 1984, Department of Education and Science and Manpower Services Commission publications; Institute of Personnel Management for material from papers produced on behalf of the IPM's National Committee for Training and Development; Joint Board for Pre-Vocational Education for material from the CPVE

Handbook; Leeds Education Authority for the Unit Submission and the Statement of Achievement; London Express News and Features Service for the cartoon on page 78; Monkscroft School, Cheltenham for a table from their Personal Achievement Record; NFER-Nelson for an extract from *Records of Achievement at 16* by Burgess and Adams, 1985; Northern Examining Association for material produced by the Northern Partnership for Records of Achievement; D. Nuttall for material from an unpublished paper on Personal communication; PPR Management Group for material from *Pupils' Personal Records*; Joan Rosser for the cartoon on page 83; R. C. Sims for material from his paper on Profiling; SCDC Publications for material adapted from *Profile Reporting in Wales*, 1983; The Scottish Council for Research in Education for material from *Knowing Our Pupils: an outline report of 'Pupils in Profile'*, Edinburgh, 1977 and from *Diagnostic Assessment in Secondary Schools* by H. D. Black and W. B. Dockrell, Edinburgh, 1980; Southway School, Plymouth for material from their pupil profiles; Ron Tandberg for the cartoon on page 77; University of Oxford for an extract from a report to Delegates, May 1984; The Victorian Curriculum and Assessment Board for material from *Guidelines for Descriptive Assessment* by Dahle Suggett, 1985; Colin Wheeler for the cartoon on page 8; T. Wilkes for extracts from dissertation *Pupil Profiling: Demanding Innovation*, 1985; M. T. Williams and D. Johns for extracts from an unpublished report *Pupils Records of Achievement (Profiling) Study* written for the TVEI Unit, MSC.

Every effort has been made to trace all the copyright holders but if any have been inadvertently overlooked the publishers will be pleased to make the necessary arrangement at the first opportunity.

Introduction

Why this manual has been written

This manual has been written to help the various partners in the educational enterprise who are interested in learning more about profiles and records of achievement. Its specific aim is to give practical guidance to those people who may be thinking of initiating such a recording scheme in their own institution or authority. More generally, however, it also aims to give help and encouragement to the many participants in development schemes already underway. The need for such help is increasingly urgent in the light of the recent DES commitment that, by the end of the decade, *all* school-leavers should be provided with such a 'record of achievement'. The DES initiative means that *all* secondary schools, as well as a good number of further education institutions, are likely to become caught up in the profiling movement, even though many feel far from ready to undertake such a commitment.

Who is it for?

This manual has been designed for a 'mixed-ability' audience so that, whether beginner or expert, all readers may find food for thought and practical guidance in it. It is a characteristic of the 'profiles' movement that good ideas have spread from school to school and group to group. Very little development work has been centrally directed or funded and, in consequence, there exists a great diversity of practice. Thus all have something to learn from the experience of others. The manual is written in the same spirit that has characterised the movement so far, in attempting to use a wide variety of examples of current practice to stimulate thinking and discussion about more general issues.

What is it about?

The DES initiative will make enormous demands on teachers' skill and goodwill, as well as institutional resources and ability to change. In return, however, it holds out the possibility of providing young people with quite new kinds of curricular experience and new ways of recognising what they have achieved. This manual exists to help those on whom these new demands are being made; to provide some guidance on the process of implementation and to help teachers themselves work out what is best for their own institution. There are certainly neither magic formulas nor easy options. Experience to date suggests profiling does make new and sometimes heavy demands on staff time and skill. It also suggests, however, that the majority of those who have had experience in some kind of profiling scheme are sufficiently convinced of its value to keep going. Many derive considerable satisfaction from being able to offer their pupils a genuine alternative to the examinations that so many must fail. This manual is thus about maximising success and minimising failure both for the pupils themselves and for the teachers seeking to implement a profiling scheme.

How is it organised?

The major part of this volume – as the title 'manual' implies – is devoted to a consideration of practical issues. These include a discussion of the range of profile approaches available, approaches to implementation within an institution and how profiling might work in practice. However, it is appropriate that the first chapter should review some of the reasons that lie behind this major policy initiative. In this more theoretical discussion, readers are given the opportunity to consider for themselves whether they are convinced of the need for such an innovation and, if so, what form it should take. No innovation can hope to be successful if those responsible for implementing it are confused or doubtful about its value. Thus if you are not convinced by the end of the first chapter you need read no more.

Part I
Briefing

Chapter 1
Why profiles?

To understand fully what profiles are, and why the movement to implement them has grown so rapidly, we need to consider the needs profiles are designed to meet. These needs may be classified in terms of the three main elements with which educational assessment is concerned:
- assessment for curriculum;
- assessment for communication;
- assessment for accountability.

Assessment for curriculum

Within the *curriculum*, assessment has two principal roles to play. Firstly, it has a *diagnostic* function for both teachers and pupils. It should tell the teacher:
 i) what each pupil has learned;
 ii) more general information about a pupil's strengths and weaknesses; and
 iii) how far his or her teaching has succeeded in its aims

Secondly, assessment is concerned with *motivating* learners.

It operates on a 'carrot and stick' principle, rewarding the successful and chastising the unsuccessful.

Assessment for communication

With regard to communication, assessment again has two major roles to play. Firstly, it has a *certification* function which tells the pupil and, if he chooses, the rest of the world, the level of his achievements in a range of activities. Secondly, it has a *selection* function which allows the world outside the educational institution, such as employers, colleges and universities, to choose those pupils with the characteristics they are looking for.

Assessment for accountability

The third element in assessment is that of accountability. An educational institution must increasingly be able to demonstrate to both itself and to the world outside that it is fulfilling the aims that it has set for itself and the ones expected of it by society in general.

It is also possible to break down these general roles of assessment in terms of the different people concerned, as listed in the table on page 6.

Purposes of assessment

For pupils:
  diagnosis of progress, strengths and weaknesses
  guidance – curricular and vocational
  motivation – from a sense of achievement
For teachers:
  decisions about what needs to be taught
  feedback on how effective teaching has been
  feedback on class performance in comparison with other teachers and schools
For 'consumers':
  fair selection and allocation of opportunity (the 'meritocracy')
  feedback about the quality of a particular institution
  monitoring of national standards
  curriculum standardisation and control

Having once identified the major purposes that assessment procedures have to fulfil, this in turn prompts four other questions. These are:
- Who should be assessed?
- What should be assessed?
- When should assessment take place?
- How should it be done?

Figure 1.1, 'A blueprint of assessment concerns', represents the relationship between these questions in a tabular form. When the primary purpose is diagnostic, assessment must take the form of a continuous monitoring of all pupils' strengths and weaknesses in a particular curriculum area, together with an appraisal of their behaviour and attitudes as these impinge upon the learning process. Teachers must be able to identify what has been learned by each pupil in order to decide

	CURRICULUM		COMMUNICATION		ACCOUNTABILITY
	Formative		*Summative*		*Formative and summative*
Why	Diagnosis	Motivation	Certification	Selection	Accountability
when	continuously	frequently	at end of a stage of schooling	where choices have to be made	constant/periodic
who	all pupils	all pupils	all/some pupils	all pupils	all/some pupils all/some teachers
what	what has been learned understanding difficulties non-cognitive influences (behaviour and mastery)	realisable goals progress and mastery	overall subject achievement basic skills non-cognitive qualities experience	skills, knowledge qualities experience relevant to future work/life role	examination results school self-evaluation external inspection informal opinion e.g. sporting success appearance of pupils
how	informal observation questioning diagnostic tests pupil self-assessment	criterion-referenced assessment self-assessment	public examinations teacher assessment externally-moderated school accreditation by external agency standardised tests and item banks records of achievement	personal records profiles references examination results	light-sampling e.g. APU examination results – 'league tables' school self-report staff appraisal

Figure 1.1: A blueprint of assessment concerns

the next curriculum step. They will do this by some combination of informal observation; questioning and discussion; more explicit diagnostic tests and exercises and perhaps through pupil self-assessment.

Where teachers are concerned to use assessment as a means of motivating their pupils, this again will apply to all pupils emphasising for each, short-term, graduated goals in which criterion-referenced assessment procedures allow each pupil to know what he or she is striving to attain and that mastery is likely to reward his or her efforts. Pupils may be asked to participate in the assessment process as teachers seek to show that they recognise the need to take seriously the notion of the pupil as an active partner in learning and to underline that pupils themselves must take a good deal of the responsibility for their own progress.

Thus the '*assessment curriculum*' should provide a positive feedback system in which the emphasis is on:
- assessing mastery of learning objectives;
- assessing a comprehensive range of contributory factors;
- diagnosis of strengths and weaknesses;
- collaboration between pupils and teachers.

This approach to assessment, where the emphasis is on using *assessment as a means to encourage learning*, is generally termed 'formative'. It can also be applied to assessment of the quality of the learning process being provided by the individual teacher and the institution *as a whole*. Procedures such as institutional and curriculum reviews, staff appraisal and school self-evaluation provide for *institutional formative* assessment in the form of positive feedback to improve practice.

Assessment can only be formative when it is part of a process in which there is opportunity for response to it. Of the range of formative assessment techniques set out below, some are much more likely to encourage this than others. These approaches are marked with a *.

In-course assessment techniques available

- written (school) examinations and tests
- oral tests
- graded tests, graduated and staged assessments*
- continuous teacher assessment
- observation
- negotiated assessments*
- student self-assessment*
- peer assessment*

The four assessment approaches marked with a * require pupils themselves to collaborate in the assessment either with each other, with teachers or by themselves. It is this active involvement of pupils which makes these procedures outstanding in their potential for formative impact. It is thus the starred techniques which are most characteristic of attempts to elevate the curriculum aspect of assessment at the present time. Each approach is discussed in more detail later in the manual.

The column headed *communication* in Figure 1.1 shows a very different set of answers to the questions of when, who, what and 'how' to that shown under *curriculum*. In place of the formative emphasis on a continuous process of diagnosis, remediation, feedback and mastery is a *summative* emphasis on assessment at a particular point, curriculum stage or age, not necessarily open to all pupils in which the emphasis is on providing reliable and acceptable information on what has been achieved as the basis for choosing who should be allowed which opportunities where these must be rationed. Such assessment must be as free as possible from personal bias and provide the best possible indication of likely future success. These differences may be listed as shown in Figure 1.2.

Communication

certification : affirmation of achievement
identification of specific inadequacies
documentation of experience

selection : discrimination between candidates
reliability
legitimacy
predictive validity

Curriculum

learning : diagnosis
remediation
feedback

motivation : mastery
self-respect

Figure 1.2: Formative and summative aspects of pupil assessment

Unfortunately, whilst the characteristics of the communication function of assessment are readily understandable in terms of the role such assessment plays as an allocation device, they nevertheless are frequently out of step with more general educational concerns. The procedure that has hitherto been taken to be the most suitable for such purposes is that of public examinations. The elaborate care that goes into their design, administration and marking has been widely assumed to be the fairest way of judging candidates' relative merit in relation to specific areas of achievement. Such examinations provide for very fine 'norm-referenced' discrimination between candidates, and a high degree of reliability and legitimacy in the eyes of the general public which makes them an ideal basis for selection. Yet there are many criticisms that are made of examinations.

1	They can be inaccurate	- perhaps due to marker fatigue or personal preference
2	They can be an unfair reflection of what a candidate is really capable of achieving	- perhaps he has an 'off' day or bad handwriting
3	They only measure a small sample of a candidate's skills and qualities	- such as short-term memory and ability to function under pressure
4	They encourage extrinsic motivation	- working for future rewards rather than the intrinsic pleasure of learning
5	They discourage cooperation between students	- helping each other is specifically disallowed
6	They tend to narrow curricular experiences and constrain teaching	- learning becomes didactic rather than exploratory
7	They tend to conceal in one aggregate grade a candidate's diverse strengths and weaknesses	- practical skills may bear no resemblance to written performance, for example

These examinations, which test knowledge, which sieve people, which look very hard at one side of the human brain, are conducted in a certain way. They are designed to test pupils against each other. They are, in the main, norm-referenced.

If external examinations have such an influence, what methods of assessment do they employ? It seems reasonable to assert that the examination system which the majority of schools use is based on the application of cognitive testing and applies norm-referenced measurements to determine outcome. In other words, a formal paper and pencil test of knowledge recall with the candidates ranked and graded by the use of a normal distribution curve whose aim is to produce a spread of results.

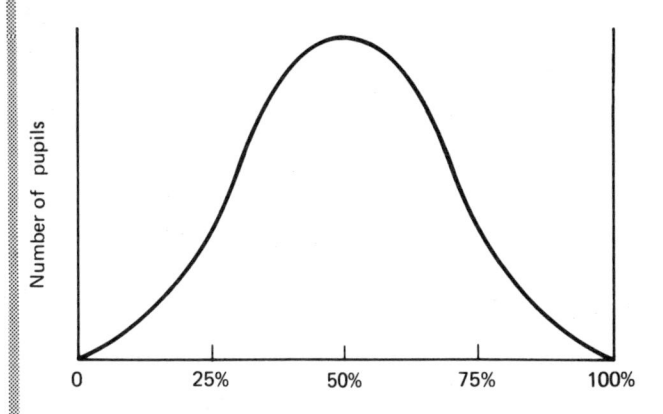

Figure 1.3: The distribution of results norm-referenced assessments aspire to

It is thus arguable that one of the major characteristics of secondary school organisation is still geared to the development of a small number of pupils at the expense of the majority.

If we can relate this system to the aspirations of a typical year group of approximately 250 pupils and illustrate them jumping over hurdles of increasing height, then only 20 of them will clear the 'final' hurdle, but at age 11 245 of them are urged toward it (5 have been diagnosed as having special need so they have been re-routed). At 14 years of age 200 of them are still being urged on (45 have proved to be 'troublesome' in a variety of ways – can't take the discipline of 'sit still, shut up, take notes, listen to me' perhaps). At 15 years, 180 of them are encouraged to leap over a large hurdle called external exams – but a lot haven't trained and others aren't big enough. What do they fall onto or into?

The diagram in Figure 1.4 represents this traditional system. It poses several fundamental questions.

Is it a 'learning' slope or a 'measurement' slope?
What about all the other aspects of learning?
What about personality, social skills, character and behaviour?
Are there 'slopes' available for these also?
This model, of course, needs qualifying.
It does not recognise the advances made in pastoral organisation within schools (even though some of these are still little more than discipline structures).
It does not recognise the efforts of those teachers who have struggled over the years to develop new curricula and assessment techniques with no extra time, few resources and a lot of resistance to change from all sides.

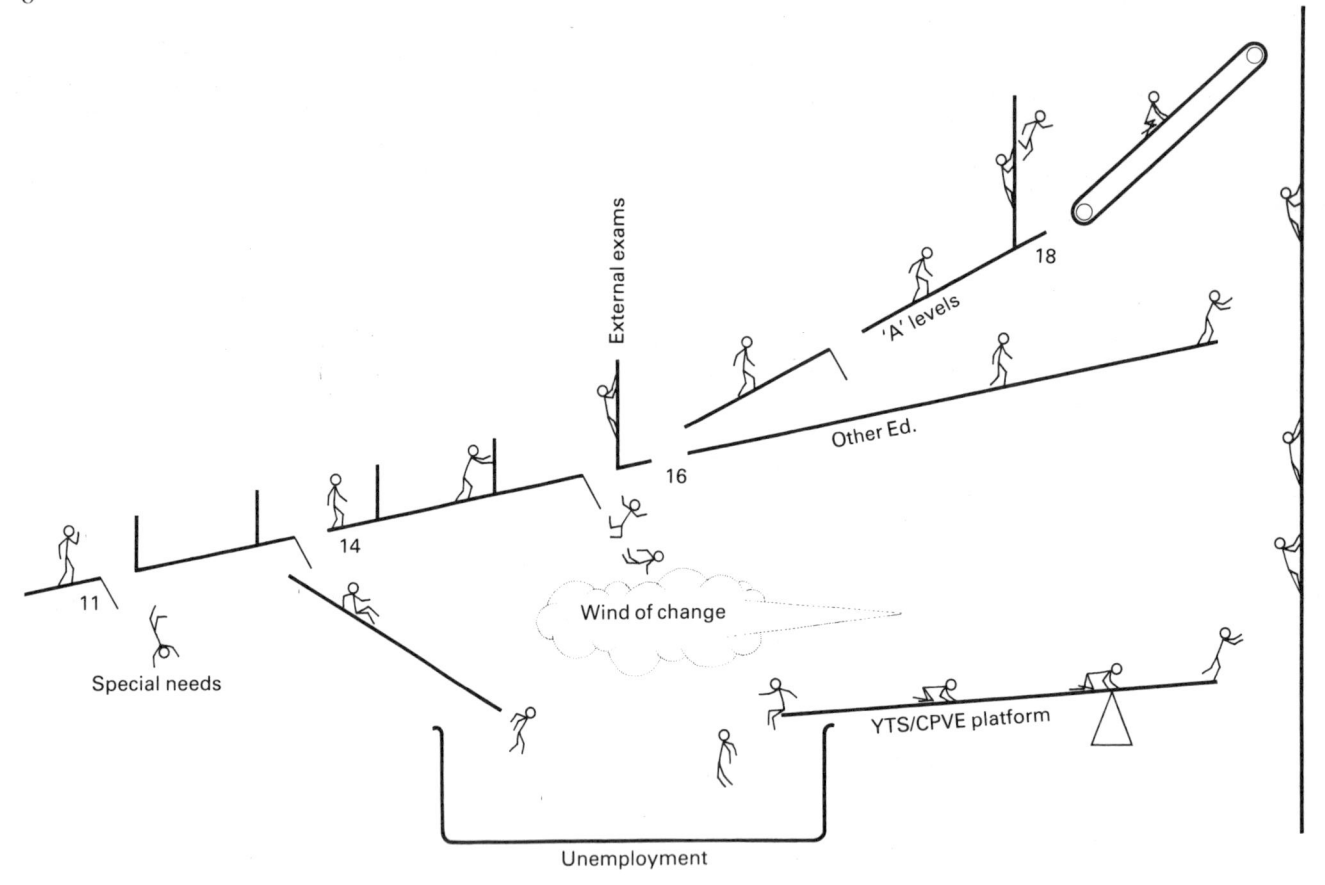

Source: T. Wilkes, *Pupil Profiling: Demanding Innovation*, Diploma in Advanced Studies in Education dissertation, University of Bristol, 1985

Figure 1.4: Assessment pitfalls on the learning slope

It does not fully recognise the quite dramatic developments wrought through YTS, TVEI and CPVE over the last two years.

It does not recognise that many employers have left school behind and now demand qualities other than exam success. But while these advances are not peripheral, they have still done little to counteract the central place of examination-oriented thinking in the secondary school.

(T. Wilkes) *Pupil Profiling: Demanding Innovation*, Diploma in Advanced Studies in Education dissertation, University of Bristol, 1985)

Source: H. MacIntosh, D. Nuttall and P. Clift, *Measuring Learning Outcomes*, Milton Keynes, Open University Press, 1981

Figure 1.5

Given that perhaps only three marks may separate 'B' and 'D' gradings at 'A' level and that many candidates are affected by stress, (1) and (2) (on page 7) must constitute a serious concern. According to a recent report on 'Improving Secondary Schools in the Inner London Education Authority' (ILEA, 1984) (3) is an even more serious concern since it leaves out of account major aspects of achievement as identified by the committee. These are as follows:

Aspects of achievement

1. Written expression, knowledge retention, ability to organise material and select appropriately and effectively
2. The application of knowledge; practical, oral, investigative and problem-solving skills
3. Personal and social skills; communication and relationships; working in groups, initiative, self-reliance, responsibility and other such qualities
4. Self-confidence, motivation, commitment and attitude

Public examinations, it is suggested, hardly assess aspects 2–4 at all. In consequence, such concerns do not often feature explicitly on the curriculum of secondary schools, despite the fact that all four aspects of achievement are likely to form part of any statement of curricular goals. Thus we may contrast quite starkly the mismatch between the intended outcomes of schooling and the actual outcomes. As Burgess and Adams

(1980) suggest, examinations are 'exclusive, trivial, uninformative, expensive, misused and in many ways, anti-educational'. The 1977 DES Green Paper 'Education in Schools', for example, emphasises the fostering of enquiring minds, respect for people, world understanding, use of language, mathematics and other skills and knowledge as well as cultural pursuits. An example follows, taken from another curriculum statement, that of the 1977 Munn Report on the 14–16 curriculum in Scotland as compared to the revelations of several volumes which report what pupils actually felt when they got out of school.

Intended outcomes of school	Actual outcomes
knowledge and understanding of self	- lack of self-awareness
understand society	- failure to connect education with life
interpersonal skills	- destroys confidence
willingness to learn	- creates dependent learners
growing maturity	- inhibits initiative and self-reliance
effective community membership	- pro passivity and apathy, hierarchic view of society
emotional and moral development	- neglects self-discipline
commitment to democracy	- offers authoritarian model of society – stunts decision making abilities
life enrichment	- fails to engage the concerns of young people
1977 Munn Report (Scotland)	- Gow and McPherson (1980), White (1983), Hargreaves (1982)

The final column of the assessment blueprint given in Figure 1.1 refers to the accountability dimension which is both formative and summative. Schools will judge themselves and be judged by others on both the opportunities they offer for pupil learning and the outcomes they achieve in this respect. If they allow the summative to be dominant, consumers are likely to be unhappy at the excessive emphasis on outcomes at the expense of enjoyment, richness and all-round development within the learning process itself. If they allow the formative to be dominant, schools are in turn likely to be accused of having a lack of realism, and not serving their pupils' long-term interests.

All this adds up to a nightmare of conflicting pressures on schools and teachers in which curriculum concerns battle for a place alongside the communication imperatives to which schools are subject. Can such pressures be resolved, and if so, how? Figure 1.1 again gives the clue. It is not the formative/summative distinction itself which is the problem but the lack of continuity between the two. If the summative assessment procedures can be brought more into line with formative concerns so that they too emphasise the whole range of learning objectives as set out in Figure 1.3, the contradiction between the two will be correspondingly reduced. The answer then is a summative assessment procedure that recognises not only the skills and knowledge measured in written examinations but also the practical skills, social attributes and personal qualities which represent the wider aims of education.

The list might be as follows:

General skills	– intellectual	e.g. memory and recall reasoning
	scientific	e.g. observation experimentation
	social etc.	e.g. communication leadership listening
Subject achievement	knowledge understanding etc.	
Personal qualities	– empathy perseverance self-discipline etc	
Attitudes	– interest commitment etc.	
Experience	– school home community	e.g. sporting activities community service work experience residential

This list will be immediately recognisable to many as the ingredients of a typical profile report. By means of a step by step analysis we have established the main reasons behind the profiles movement and the widespread enthusiasm that sustains it, namely:

1. a desire to improve the learning process by elevating the assessment curriculum (diagnosis and motivation) to a proper balance with summative concerns;
2. a desire to recognise the full range of pupil achievements in summative terms;
3. a desire to bring both formative and summative assessment in line with curricular goals and so make the school accountable on its own terms;
4. a desire to increase teachers' professional satisfaction by removing them from a situation of contradictory pressures.

These points are well made by Law in his book, *Uses and Abuses of Profiling*:

Here are some such distillations of possible intentions. They each say something is wrong and improvement is possible.

For changing the *bases on which we present portrayals of students*:
- Traditional methods are too crude and global and mask individual differences. By *making fuller, more detailed use of the information about performance in subjects* that we already have, we can give more recognition to the fact that, at all levels of ability, different students are developing in different ways.
- Subject based methods arbitrarily divide portrayals of our students. By *identifying a range of cross curriculum 'core' characteristics*, which a number of teachers will have an opportunity to portray, we can offer a more rounded and whole impression of each of our students.
- Curriculum based assessments are too limited; people are worth more than performance in the curriculum can demonstrate: particularly the examined part of the curriculum. By *extending the bases on which we portray our students*, beyond the existing curriculum and by

paying attention to more than is traditionally associated with 'doing well' at school or college, we will make it possible for more of our students to show how well they can do.

For changing the *bases for action by students*:
- Traditional methods of reporting and certification offer little incentive to many of our students. By *developing a form of portrayal which is an incentive to all students*, documenting something of real worth concerning each of them, we will provide them with an important motivator to sustained effort during their years at school or college.
- Traditional forms of assessment are addressed, as it were, 'to whom it may concern', they offer little information to the students themselves about how and why they came to be assessed in that way. By *developing a method of portrayal which is addressed to the students, and which gives them useful feedback on how they are being assessed*, we will be offering them bases for changing what they do in order to bring them closer to where they want to be.
- Traditional assessments are part of the procedure by which schooling is given to students; their responsibility being limited to receiving what is given. By *developing a method of portrayal in which they are active participants contributing to the record themselves* we are acknowledging their responsibility for the way in which they are portrayed, and the fact that self portrayal can be an educational experience.

For changing the *basis for action by teachers*:
- Traditional methods of recording and reporting give teachers very little to go on when they are required to give an account of their work with students, to help students with decision points in their lives, or give portrayals of students to people outside the school or college. By *developing a more continuous and comprehensive bank of information about students* teachers will be providing themselves with a useful resource from which to draw impressions of how well the teaching and learning process is going, how to help students take the next step, and how to give a useful account of the student to others
- Traditional methods of assessment are impersonal; students have little opportunity to discuss them. By *developing methods of portrayal which invite discussion in personal contact between teachers and students, and which also offer students the opportunity to discuss the use they are able to make of their experience*, we are mandating and supporting teachers in their role as counsellors and giving them an enhanced opportunity of gaining direct feedback from students on the use students make of experience during their years at school or college.

- Traditional methods have shackled the curriculum by forcing teachers to pay attention to what they know is going to be assessed. By *entering into a process of developing new criteria for assessment* we may release the curriculum from those shackles; we are also presenting ourselves with the task of re-examining the objectives of syllabuses and curricula – and of their relevance to the purposes of education and the lives of our students.

Some intentions may respond to present realities in your school or college more than others. Some may respond to your, and your colleagues' educational ideals more than others.

The first three are useful for *summative* purposes; to seeking better ways of summing up a student at the end of her or his college experience. They could, for example, help employers, and recruiters to training schemes, to make selection decisions in a more informed way.

The middle three are useful for *formative* purposes; to seeking better ways to help students get the best from their learning while still at school or college. They could, for example, help students to become more involved in and responsible for their decisions and experience.

The last three are useful for *catalytic* purposes; to seeking better ways of bringing about changes, not only in the way in which schools and colleges assess students, but also in the way they develop curricula, relate to students, and make themselves accountable. In this sense, such purposes are formative to teachers in school and college – so that they can have a more informed basis for their decisions.

(B. Law, *Uses and Abuses of Profiling*, Harper and Row, London, 1984)

Accountability

Law's extract refers to the last of the three assessment purposes identified at the beginning of this chapter – accountability. It is this aspect of assessment which provides information on the *quality* of the education being provided. This is an extremely complex issue because any assessment of quality is directly dependent on value-judgements about what educational goals should be. Thus, for example, accountability might be based on any one of the following:

- public examination results/university selection
- validated records of achievement
- school reports to parents   } products
- incidence of vandalism, truancy etc.
- employment success

- teacher appraisal/inspection
- open-evenings, newsletters etc.   } processes
- school self-evaluation
- school accreditation procedures

In the past, the tendency has been to judge a school's quality on its visible 'products' such as academic success and pupil behaviour. Much of the debate about the relative merits of comprehensive and grammar schools has been conducted in these terms (see, for example, Gray *et al.*, *Journal of Educational Policy*, 1986). An even more clearcut example is provided by Croydon LEA which in 1986 employed a firm of City management consultants to assess 'school effectiveness' in 'value for money' terms, by comparing a range of 'output measures' with a range of 'input measures'.

Recently, this *product-oriented* 'input-output' model of accountability has begun to change in favour of a more *process-based* approach. Parents, teachers and officials have begun to share the concern which pupils have always had with the quality of day to day experience in school. Government measures to increase parental choice over schools and their voice on governing bodies has put pressure on schools to explain and justify their activities. Official concern about teacher quality has resulted in various highly controversial moves to introduce teacher-appraisal schemes. For their part, many schools and individual teachers have voluntarily engaged in self-evaluation schemes designed to help them improve practice from within.

Just as the more traditional 'product' model of accountability is closely linked to traditional forms of assessment – notably public examinations – so the newer concern with evaluating the quality of the *process* of schooling itself is linked to the new forms of recording and reporting to be found within the profiles movement. In Part III, we shall be looking in some detail at the idea of 'school accreditation' now increasingly being associated with many profiling schemes, in which it is the *school* and not – as with public examinations – the individual *pupil* that is subject to external moderation. In the same way, an externally-validated school-leaver's profile will be a new and much more comprehensive testimony to the range of learning goals aspired to and how far the combined efforts of pupil and school have been able to achieve them.

The arguments of the preceding section may be summed up in terms of the three 'Rs'. What we are looking for is an assessment procedure based on the following principles.

REINFORCEMENT	RESPECT	RELEVANCE
of the	of the	for
LEARNING	STUDENT	ACTION
PROCESS	by emphasising	by emphasising
by emphasising	COLLABORATION	A WIDE RANGE
DIAGNOSIS	MUTUAL	OF
MASTERY	RESPONSIBILITY	CAPABILITIES
CURRICULUM	JUSTICE	AND
INTEGRATION		ACHIEVEMENTS

Profiles and profiling

Such an assessment procedure has become known as 'profiling' – an approach to recording which results in the production of a 'profile' record. A 'profile' is not in itself a form of assessment – a confusion which is frequently made. Nevertheless, the production of a profile depends upon the provision of appropriate assessment information and in practice the two stages are often inseparable. A profile is essentially derived from a separation of the whole of an assessment into its main parts or components. It is thus 'a panoramic representation, numerical, graphical or verbal, of how a student appears to assessors across a range of qualities, or in respect of one quality as seen through a range of assessment methods' (Frith and Macintosh, 1984). It is often used synonymously with the term 'record of achievement', although this is normally used in a narrower sense to describe school leavers' documents which may include the results of a variety of examinations, graded tests and other assessments and information about a student, compiled by teachers and/or students and covering the total educational progress of the student. Most of this manual is about 'profiles', but where appropriate, the term 'record of achievement' is used.

A profile is thus

P
a
ersonal and
ositive record which reflects a
articular
hilosophy of assessment that is both
rocess and
roduct resulting in a **P**ortrait which serves as a
passport

It must not be only a caricature
    a label
    a silhouette
    a shadow
    a 'photograph' for the album

(G. Pearson)

"*Before you look at this, remember it's only a profile and doesn't necessarily show my best side.*"

Source: Times Educational Supplement (Scotland), 1977

Figure 1.6

A profile is 'an outline or representation of separate elements and levels which usually includes information on skills, behaviours, traits or attitudes' (Scottish Vocational Preparation Unit).

Typically profiles are 'a form of teacher-based report designed to be applicable to all pupils; to gather teachers' knowledge of pupils' many different skills, characteristics and achievements across the whole range of the curriculum, both formal and informal; to provide, with the minimum of clerical demands, a basis for continuing in-school teaching and guidance and culminating in a relevant and useful school-leaving report for all pupils' (Broadfoot, 'Pros and Cons of Profiles', *Forum*, 1980).

Thus profiles are typically:
1. descriptive rather than comparative of pupils' achievement;
2. supportive of curriculum intentions rather than dominating them;
3. life-oriented in content and use intended to be relevant to life outside and beyond education;
4. of value as a credential.

The Scottish Vocational Preparation Unit distinguishes between:
- a *record* which provides evidence on which outsiders can make judgements; and
- a *report* which provides judgements which outsiders can take as evidence.

Thus, they suggest, whereas a *record* usually aims to be:

descriptive   reflecting a   self-appraising
personal   negotiated
participative   participative
open   pupil-responsible
assessment   *learning process*

and is therefore *formative* and *curriculum-oriented*, a *report* is:

evaluative   reflecting a   teacher-appraising
standardised   non-negotiable
teacher-dominated   didactic
sometimes confidential   pupil as receiver
assessment   *learning process*

The result, they suggest, is that:
The unilateral control of assessment of students by staff means that the process of education is at odds with the objectives of that process. . . .

Are we then faced with a straight choice between

objective, comparable, teacher-   : assessment for
dominated, systematic and there-   communication
fore high reliability
              versus
subjective, individualised, pupil- : assessment for
involved, 'ipsative'* and there-   curriculum
fore high validity

The answer to this question rests upon the assumption that the characteristics we normally associate with summative assessment are necessarily those which con-

*Comparison against *own* previous standard

sumers look for. But what sort of information do employers, college and training personnel look for?

How do consumers see it?

The evidence seems to suggest that at least as far as the younger sixteen and seventeen year-old school and college leaver is concerned, what matters is:
- basic skills – especially literacy and numeracy;
- specific skills and aptitudes;
- personal qualities.

For example, nearly ten years ago a Manpower Services Commission Survey found that employers' requirements were as set out in Figure 1.7.

	All grades of work %	Skilled manual %	Unskilled manual %	Non-manual %
Willingness/attitude to work	76	80	81	70
Basic 3 R's	50	52	21	67
Good levels of numeracy	39	40	13	55
Good written English	36	21	6	67
Special educational qualifications	23	21	2	38

Source: 'Young People and Work', Manpower Studies No. 1, 1978, Chapter 1

Figure 1.7: 1978 Manpower Services Commission Survey of Employers

In 1985, the Institute of Personnel Managers published a more detailed but essentially similar statement of what employers typically look for.

In most jobs employers look for:
1. Literacy
2. Numeracy
3. Communication
4. Organisation of own work
5. Working with colleagues
6. Working with people in authority
7. Analytical ability and problem-solving
8. Judgement and decision-making
9. Adaptability
10. Responsibility, self-awareness, maturity

(IPM (NCTD), *School and the World of Work: What do Employers Look For in School Leavers?* IPM, London, 1984)

In general terms employers require:
- particular skills to do particular jobs, or, the evidence of potential to acquire skills to do particular jobs after a period of training;
- employees who can cope with, adapt to and manage change; this implies that they must be confident and competent learners and be willing to continue to learn;
- employees who are capable of taking responsibility for themselves, that is, who are self reliant, because employees will increasingly be obliged to find out for themselves what they need to know;

employees who can work satisfactorily with others and integrate their activities in productive work teams, because few products can be made or services offered by an individual employee.

As an attempt to list what we consider should be the end results of what is taught in schools, may we suggest the following as a base:

skills, ability in or awareness of: the learning process, literacy; numeracy; communications; technological appreciation; team work; social 'values'; personal relationships; logical thinking and creativity . . . We are not unrealistic; public examinations are here to stay; however, it does not seem to us unreasonable to investigate new ways of looking at the range of skills, knowledge and attitudes acquired at school and how they are acquired, and at new ways of measuring them – even as a complement to present arrangements [which are] based to some degree on a narrow and inappropriate view of the school curriculum as a collection of single subject disciplines that only had relevance for the days when the twenty per cent most able academically followed a course of secondary education and was a doubtful approach even then.

(IPM (NCTD), *School and the World of Work: What Do Employers Look For in School Leavers*, IPM, London, 1984)

Basic principles

It is therefore not surprising that so many summative 'profiles' are in stark contrast to traditional subject examinations by including information on personal qualities and skills such as

- attendance
- punctuality
- effort
- reliability
- willingness to cooperate
- application
- working with others
- responsibility
- initiative
- leadership
- confidence

The existence of such records is a response to employers' concerns:

1. with *fostering* the all-round development of the student through the 'assessment curriculum';
2. with *receiving* information on a wide range of student achievements through assessment as communication.

The IPM could also have added that the traditional subject examination is also limited in its own terms in that it obscures what may be very significant differences in the levels achieved in the various components of different subjects. Correlations between the structured questions, essay and practical parts of a science examination, for example, can be as low as .3 or .4, suggesting that students vary considerably in the *way* in which they achieve examination success. Knowledge that this is so has led to a number of studies on the profile reporting of examination results (see, for example, Harrison 1983) and a number of countries do now report public examination achievements in this way. How much better, though, to incorporate such profiles into a much fuller record which can also document those achievements far beyond the scope of public examinations to assess, a record that will:

- assess learning achievement across the whole range of competencies;
- identify a young person's strengths;
- diagnose individual problems and weaknesses;
- motivate young people to improve on their own performance;
- supply data for records to inform parents of a young person's progress;
- organise young people in learning groups;
- provide information for educational and employment decisions;
- evaluate the effectiveness of teaching methods or materials;
- assess the effectiveness of the school/college as an institution and the quality of the service it provides.

(EEC, *Policies for Transition, A European Community Action Programme*, March 1984)

It can thus both: recognise achievement (communication) and encourage motivation and personal development (curriculum).

Records which do this are likely to reflect some or all of the following principles. They will:

(i) recognise performance/ability in areas of interest to employers and provide more information than traditional certification;
(ii) be an intrinsic part of the learning package;
(iii) identify cross-curricular skills;
(iv) suit all ability ranges;
(v) facilitate curriculum change;
(vi) involve regular dialogue with pupils in the assessment and recording processes;
(vii) include all pupils from the end of the primary phase onwards;
(viii) enable pupils, their parents and teachers, to examine regularly the progress of individuals and to assess areas where special attention is needed;
(ix) be student centred;
(x) monitor progress through the course as well as report at the end of the course;
(xi) report on positive aspects of development;
(xii) be criterion-referenced.

(Essex Records of Achievement Pilot Scheme)

The list below summarises all these arguments in suggesting that better records require:

JUSTICE	– for all pupils
	– in recognising all types of achievement
	– in a variety of contexts (formative and summative)
RELEVANT INFORMATION for	– pupils
	– teachers
	– parents
	– employers
	– trainers
PRACTICABILITY	– a variety of assessment techniques, as appropriate
	– compatible with teaching purposes
	– minimal clerical and other resources
	– part of each school's overall assessment policy

Summary

The place for profiles

So far in this chapter I have tried to outline:

1. the pressure for change that lies behind the rapid development of profiles;
2. the different purposes that assessment serves in any educational enterprise and the contradictions that are inherent in these different purposes;
3. what profiles are and how they might resolve some of the contradictions inherent in more traditional forms of assessment and certification, by providing a better balance between the *curriculum*, *communication* and *accountability* aspects of assessment;
4. the components of an assessment procedure based on the principles of *reinforcement*, *respect* and *relevance* rather than *competition*, *content* and *control*.

Whilst they may agree with my analysis of the problem and the solution proposed, many readers will remain sceptical that such a major change is possible. Because of this – as I suggested in the Introduction to this book – some will choose to read no more. They will argue that since assessment, and in particular public examinations, are a major controlling force in the provision and practice of education as we know it today, public opinion will not tolerate such a substantial change. At the time of writing, it is still too early to say whether this is so or not but a brief review of the development of profiling over recent years does reveal that change is afoot on a very substantial scale.

Chapter 2
Progress to date

The early years

The first profiling initiatives, such as the SCRE 'profile assessment system' which is described in Chapter 4, were designed to be complementary to existing examination procedures. The emphasis was on providing additional, supplementary ways of recognising achievement which would provide a worthwhile goal for all pupils, not just those for whom the more conventional certification procedures had been designed. At the same time – the mid 'seventies – other initiatives were taking place concerned with personal recording. This very different approach removed the notion of *assessment* from the recording process and replaced it with the idea of pupils' own descriptions of their experiences, achievements, interests and activities, built up and collated over time into an impressive, bound volume. The aim behind this initiative was, however, very similar to that behind profile initiatives based on teacher assessment. This was the desire to enhance pupils' involvement with the learning process and hence their motivation; to encourage personal development and to deal justly with all pupils by recognising officially each one's diverse attainments. Both types of early initiative and some of the 'second generation' schemes that followed, such as the Evesham Personal Achievement Records described in Chapter 4, were nevertheless characterised by being developments *within the status quo*; ideas that individual schools and even departments could take up and develop on their own initiative as they saw fit.

This approach to profiling is still the most widespread despite the changes that have occurred in the status of such initiatives since their early days in the late 1970s. The National Profiling Network for example, which is run by Dorset Local Education Authority, exists to share information between the now substantial numbers of such initiatives. Member organisations – individual schools and colleges, local consortia and even LEA and examination board initiatives – can learn about other approaches and modify their own scheme in the light of such knowledge if they so wish. Many of these schemes still reflect the original *raison d'etre* of profiles in having, as their principal concern, the recording and reporting of a wider and more useful range of achievements.

The middle years

Meanwhile, however, the changing character and clientele of further education, the growing emphasis on vocational preparation as well as academic pursuits in schools, and a national concern with vocational training, schemes such as the Youth Opportunities Programme (YOPS) and more recently, the Youth Training Scheme (YTS) have led to a rather different set of developments within profiling. Following the publication of the Further Education Unit's Curriculum Model, 'A Basis for Choice', and the various associated documents which followed it, many new vocational and training courses were developed which had profiling as an integral and core element. In this context, profiling was no longer an appendage to conventional arrangements but had a key role to play in both the curriculum and communication aspects of the new courses. In addition, several further education examination boards such as the City and Guilds of London Institute (CGLI), the Royal Society of Arts (RSA) and the Business and Technical Education Council (BTEC), began to incorporate a profile as part or all of the certification procedure for their foundation courses. Thus, in this context, profiling was no longer merely a complementary form of recording and reporting but one which, like public examinations, made its own requirements of the way curriculum and pedagogy were practised. From this set of initiatives developed an emphasis on profiling as a formative dialogue in which pupils and teachers together negotiate curriculum objectives and review progress made. This emphasis has now become central to most of the current profiling initiatives in both schools and colleges. But, the impact of the involvement of further education institutions went much further than this. As well as changing the emphasis within profiling from a primary concern with the provision of a summative document in favour of a much greater concern with the institution of formative profiling procedures, the official institutionalisation of profiling on a considerable scale was arguably a major element in its becoming a policy issue for the DES itself and thus providing for a third stage of development.

The present time

The third stage in the development of profiling as a movement is marked more than anything else by the publication of a DES policy statement on 'Records of Achievement' – first in draft form in November 1983 and then in final form in July 1984. This policy statement commits the DES to a programme of research and development which is designed to lead to the identification of national guidelines for 'records of achievement' by the end of the decade. To this end the DES and the Welsh Office have together funded some nine pilot schemes which will be submitted to local and national evaluation for the lessons that can be learned from them.

Alongside the DES initiative are a number of other major initiatives to develop and institute profiles which may be distinguished from early and middle years' developments in the degree to which they involve local education authorities, school examination boards and other institutional elements of conventional academic provision. Major projects such as that of the Northern Partnership for Records of Achievement or the South West Profiles Research Project represent a very much bigger investment of commitment and resources to the development of profiles and associated forms of assessment than any number of individual school initiatives could hope to achieve.

Thus, whilst until recently the profiles movement has been content to co-exist within the *status quo* resulting from more traditional certification procedures, this situation is now changing with implications that are still unpredictable. Certainly the movement's essentially parallel development has been a key factor in the quite remarkable way in which the movement has gathered momentum. Because of it, support for profiles – at least in principle – has been forthcoming from virtually all the sectors of the educational enterprise – pupils, parents, teachers, administrators, politicians and employers. But the combination on the 'stage two' emphasis on formative concerns and the growing involvement of examination boards as potential validators of such new certificates – which is one of the hallmarks of recent developments – are two halves of a pincer movement which threatens the educational status quo. It seems likely that this new approach to recording and reporting achievement will move more and more towards the centre of the educational stage, both in its impact on how teachers and pupils conduct the business of learning and in terms of the relative importance of different certification procedures as Figure 2.1 sets out. As Figure 2.1 also depicts, current developments suggest profiles and pupils' personal records are likely to play an increasingly important role in the certification procedures of the future. Whether this development will continue to receive support from all sections of the community remains to be seen. There seems little doubt, however, that teachers will find themselves caught up in changes of considerable magnitude and challenge. Chapter 4 of this manual thus attempts to give some guidance about the different styles of profile currently being developed and how future users may pick their way through such diversity so that in the end they can come up with a scheme that is most likely to meet those users' particular needs.

For a much fuller account of the ideas set out in this chapter, together with descriptions of some of the more influential profiling and recording initiatives which have helped to define the shape of the movement as a whole, you may read *Profiles and Records of Achievement: a Review of Issues and Practice*, Holts, 1986, edited by the author.

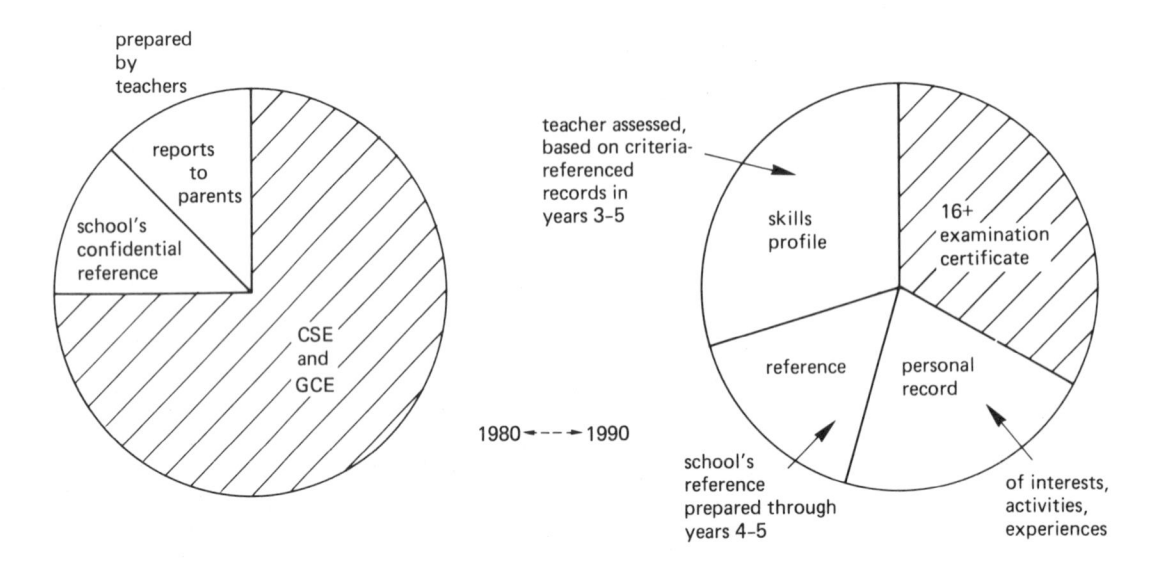

(Adapted from De Groot, 1981)

Figure 2.1: The changing importance of credentials at age 16 during the 1980s

Chapter 3
Choices to be made

Following on the general argument for instituting profiles and Records of Achievement presented in Chapter 1, we now move to a consideration of some of the basic decisions that must be made in designing a profiling system. The first part of this chapter identifies some of these decisions and raises a number of issues in relation to each. The second part of the chapter offers a number of examples of existing schemes in order to illustrate how these decisions are made in practice.

What purposes is the system to serve?

Nearly all the profiles currently being used or developed reflect the same basic intentions. As a reminder, these may be reiterated as:
1. making assessment a much more detailed and constructive activity so that it enhances the learning process; and
2. providing more useful information to potential users and thus a fairer and more efficient basis for selection.

Within these broad principles, however, there is considerable variation between existing schemes. If you are trying to devise your own profile, or simply trying to understand existing practice, the most obvious place to start is with a study of the different intentions profiles have been designed to serve. Within the broad distinction of formative and summative purposes, Figure 3.1 identifies six main intentions.

Style	Intention
FORMATIVE	Negotiation of a learning contract
	Diagnostic
	Pastoral
SUMMATIVE	Reporting to parents
	Recognition of achievement
	Reporting to employers and tertiary education

Figure 3.1: Profiles: all things to all people?

Formative profiles

1. *Negotiation of a learning contract* Some profiles have been specifically designed to provide the basis of a curriculum contract in which teachers and students jointly agree the learning objectives to be pursued for a particular unit of time. At the end of this period of study, the profile contract will provide the basis for a review of what has been achieved and the base line for setting the next set of objectives.

2. *Diagnostic profiles* Curriculum integrated but without the element of negotiation characteristic of 1, these profiles are normally subject-based and are designed to provide detailed monitoring of a student's progress through a course of study. Feedback is provided for both teacher and student as a basis for remedial action.

3. *Pastoral profiles* The opposite of, or rather complement to, course-based profiles, these 'student-based' profiles are used to record a wide range of different items of information – academic and personal – as a basis for effective personal tutoring within the school.

4. *Profile reporting to parents* Following on from 3, it is logical to use such information, where available, as the basis of reports to parents. This can both help save extra work on the part of the school and improve the quality of the information being received by parents.

Summative profiles

5. *Recognition of achievement* One of the original concerns behind the profiles movement was that many pupils have little or nothing to aim for at school and even less to show for the experience when they leave. Many profiles are designed with the primary aim of filling this void in recognising the whole range of achievements, experiences and qualities the student has demonstrated during the educational process. The provision of such a 'certificate' is regarded as a way of improving pupils' motivation and self-respect.

6. *Reporting to the outside world* Although purposes 5 and 6 are often provided for jointly in a profile, different emphasis given to the two intentions will

affect how much concern is shown to avoid negative information being made public. Where the priority is identified as meeting the needs of the outside world, more emphasis is likely to be given to providing a comprehensive and standardised picture of the youngster.

Who is to be assessed?

As has been made clear, the impetus for profiling originally came from those concerned with the need to provide some official summative recognition for young people leaving school, who would have achieved little or no success in public examinations. Associated with this there were fears earlier on in the development that profiling might become the preserve of low-attaining pupils only. In practice, that fear has proved powerful enough to convince the vast majority of those responsible for such innovations that profiling must be for everyone if it is to work at all.

Apart from the obvious dangers of a record of achievement being regarded as a booby prize rather than as a reward, the changes such an approach to assessment impose on schools makes it imperative that a whole-school commitment be made. By the same token, the increasing emphasis on the formative process as well as the summative product of profiling has led to moves for the whole age range of the school to be involved as well as the whole attainment spectrum. These points are well expressed in the 1984 DES Policy Statement on Records of Achievement, which is likely to point the way for developments in this area in the future:

> 14   Records of achievement should be compiled and kept for *all* pupils in secondary education, and summary documents of record should be available to all pupils on leaving school. There should be no question of confining records to pupils expected to leave school with few, if any, examination certificates. Both the internal processes of reporting, recording and discussion and the kinds of achievement and qualities described in the summary records are equally relevant for pupils with greater and lesser talents and gifts. A system of records should be established for pupils with special educational needs, whether in special or ordinary schools, as for other pupils but should take account of their needs. In the view of the Secretaries of State, at least one of the pilot schemes should explore how this might best be done.

> 35   As implied earlier, the Secretaries of State believe that schools should arrange for teachers and pupils to begin the processes of reporting, recording and discussion from the time when pupils enter the secondary phase and continue them on a regular and systematic basis throughout their subsequent time at school. The internal record should begin with an entry summarising achievements by the end of the primary stage.

(DES Policy Statement on Records of Achievement, 1984)

Nevertheless, it is still the case that the continued existence of traditional-type examination courses alongside a range of more novel profiling-based qualifications, such as the CPVE, continues to pose the question of whether such qualifications will have significance equal to that of examinations in the eyes of both participants and consumers.

Who will contribute to the record?

Again, the DES Policy Statement captures the prevailing spirit of current practice in stressing that records of achievement will be a joint effort to which pupils and teachers both contribute.

> 36   The school, and not the pupil, should be responsible for ensuring that records of achievement are maintained. So far as the internal processes are concerned, teachers will need to ensure that the recording activity and the discussions with pupils take place on a regular and systematic basis. It is however essential that pupils should be closely involved in the recording processes so that they can benefit in all the ways discussed earlier. The recording process should be seen not as a judgment by teachers on pupils but as a means of assisting both pupil and teacher. Some pupils may want to contribute elements which are entirely their own.

(DES Policy Statement on Records of Achievement, 1984)

It is little short of remarkable how quickly the idea of involving pupils in their own assessment has grown. In the space of just a few years the old idea that assessment was a prerogative of teachers to be imposed more or less willingly on pupils has been eroded in favour of seeing assessment as a process of mutual negotiation. There is a growing feeling that assessment can be a much more constructive process if pupils are encouraged to take some responsibility for evaluating themselves and diagnosing their own strengths and weaknesses. As will be seen later in this chapter, how pupils are actually involved in this process varies from scheme to scheme. In some cases there is provision for a separate pupil record to be maintained; in others, a mutually agreed check-list. Some schemes only involve pupils at the formative stage; others in the summative report only and still others at both stages. The decision the developers of a particular scheme make in this respect is likely to reflect the relative importance given to:
- assessment as curriculum;
- assessment as communication;
- motivation;
- objectivity;
- diagnosis;
- publicly-defined standards.

In talking about who will contribute to the record, it is quite possible that parents, other pupils, or indeed other members of the community might have a contribution to make in actually supplying information about achievement as well as the more common practice of ratifying the pupil's own record as correct. Progress in involving any of these other parties has so far been limited, but increasingly the intention to do so is very clear, both by schools and by LEAs.

Who will use the record?

Some or all of the following are likely to be involved:
- the pupils themselves;
- the individual teacher;
- the school as a whole;
- parents;
- employers;
- managing agents and training agencies;
- further and higher education;
- the community in general.

It is unlikely that a decision will be made about the audience for the profile independently of the decision about the general purposes it is to serve. Where the priority is a formative one, the prime audience will be the pupils themselves and their parents and teachers. Where the priority is summative, the principal audience will be those outside the school concerned with guidance and selection. While most schemes are likely to have an element of both these purposes, the relative weight given to each will significantly influence the design of the scheme, as will become apparent later in this chapter.

Who will own the record?

Who owns the assessment material on a pupil has always been a grey area. However, the legislative climate now prevailing together with the growing emphasis on giving pupils a say in the process of assessment and recording has combined to make a widespread consensus that profiles will be the property of the pupil. Further it is now widely agreed that pupils themselves will control to a large extent how the profile is to be used in any particular situation. In most cases, schools would agree not to use the information on a profile without the pupil's permission. Again the DES Policy Statement is explicit in this respect.

> **40** The Secretaries of State believe that the final, summary document of record should become the property of the pupil, who would be free to decide whether or not to show it to prospective employers and others. Schools should retain a master copy and meet reasonable requests for duplicate copies by pupils who need them. They should not however supply copies to anyone else without the pupil's permission.
>
> (DES Policy Statement on Records of Achievement, 1984)

Exactly what form this ownership by the pupil will take, however, may vary considerably from scheme to scheme: in some cases, it might be a lavishly bound personal portfolio in which the pupil collects records of particular events, activities and achievements; in other cases, it might be a computer-based system in which the pupil is supplied with a personal code allowing him or her to access their own personal profile in its entirety and no one else. In other cases again, the information may be stored in more conventional records and files where the pupil may have only partial control over what is written. This is certainly likely to be an issue that those embarking on such a scheme will want to address as an early priority.

What will the content of the record be?

From the earliest developments in this area, it has been recognised that a profile would probably involve:
1. a detailed report of aspects of subject achievement;
2. cross-curricular skills;
3. personal qualities;
4. work-related skills;
5. extra-curricular experiences.

More recently, a greater sophistication has entered into the form such assessments might take, with the advent, for example, of graded assessment schemes, modular accreditation schemes, etc. There is now a considerable variety of curriculum provision available to pupils and this is reflected in the potential content of a record. The commonest model is probably one which incorporates information on basic skills, subject achievement, personal qualities and a record of personal experience. How these elements are used in practice, however, varies considerably, according to the techniques used to record the information which is our next heading.

What techniques of recording will be used?

Figure 3.2 offers a visual representation of the options available, which may be combined in different ways in any particular profile.

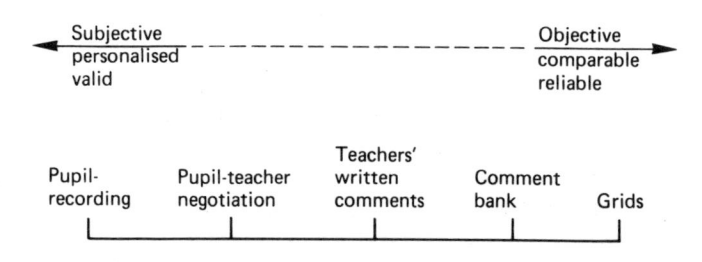

```
Subjective                                    Objective
personalised  ----------------------------   comparable
valid                                         reliable

                              Teachers'
Pupil-        Pupil-teacher   written    Comment
recording     negotiation     comments   bank      Grids
```

Figure 3.2: Types of profile

In this model, schemes can be placed along a continuum which has at one end an emphasis on relatively unstructured, informal and individualised records and, at the other, profiles which make some attempt at providing for comparability and objectivity in the information they provide. The advantage of the individualised record is that it provides a much more comprehensive and valid picture of the individual. The advantage of the more structured variety is that users may need to make such comparisons and distrust lengthy and obviously subjective statements. Most schemes fall somewhere between these two extremes, achieving a compromise according to the way in which they rank their different intentions for the profile. Whilst this choice will be related to the relative emphasis given to formative and summative concerns, it is theoretically possible for formative profiles to be highly structured and objective and for summative profiles to be totally individualised.

Deciding on the technique to be used is probably the most important decision to be made for the institution of a profiling scheme. It is the technique which incorporates the curriculum message of the scheme, whether it is curriculum-centred or user-centred, whether it is pupil-dominated or teacher-dominated, whether it is individualised or standardised. In every case, there will be a trade-off between the greater currency that a more structured, systematic assessment is likely to have in the market place and the greater relevance and educational utility a more idiosyncratic record will have which describes the pupil in a highly individualistic way. Many of the more popular schemes at the present time try to combine both these elements by including evidence of objective assessments such as the results of graded tests, external examinations, etc. and at the same time incorporating a pupil's personal record.

How will the scheme be managed?

This next issue takes the initiative off the drawing-board and into the realm of action. As Brian Goacher reports in his 1983 Schools Council study, many excellent schemes have foundered at the point of being put in to use and there is now considerable evidence accumulated through the painful experience of schools which have tried to institute profiling that careful preparation of the ground is vital if the innovation is to be a success. A number of sub-questions will need to be addressed in this respect.
1 How often are the profiles to be completed?
2 How will this relate to existing recording and reporting procedures?
3 Who will manage these arrangements and provide a timetable which prevents excessive peaks and troughs of activities?
4 How is time to be found to engage with pupils in discussion and to complete the records?
5 Can any existing recording procedures be abandoned to help in this respect?

The complexity and range of the issues to be addressed in managing such an innovation are described in detail in the second part of this manual, and no attempt will be made at this stage to discuss them at length. However, it is important to note that the question of implementation of the scheme needs to figure right from the early stages of discussion and design if the scheme is to be successful.

Where will the resources come from?

Following on closely from the issue of management is that of resources. These are likely to be crucial in a number of respects.
1 Time for teachers to meet with pupils to fill in reports, to engage in discussion with each other, to engage in in-service training, both within and outside the school, to be involved in validation. Other resources apart from time are likely to include computer resources. The provision of suitable hardware and software may greatly cut down the demands made on staff time and facilitate the procedure as a whole.
2 Other clerical assistance, photocopying, off-set litho and materials. In particular, it is important that the summative document be a substantial and impressive folder.

How will in-service training be provided?

The third element in the successful implementation of a profiling scheme is that of in-service training. Studies already conducted of profiling schemes suggest that teachers feel very unprepared to take on the variety of assessment tasks now being asked of them, for example in the assessment of cross-curricular skills, work-related qualities, practical work, etc. Increasing teachers' confidence and skills in these processes is likely to have a positive effect on their support for the scheme as a whole. It is also likely to help teachers see the connection between a number of current initiatives, including graded assessment, records of achievement, GCSE, CPVE, etc., many of which involve the same assessment skills, but which are hitting schools in an uncoordinated way. INSET has an important role to play in helping teachers to see the common ground shared by these various assessment initiatives and thus helping to prevent the erosion of morale that such diversity might otherwise produce.

How will the record be validated?

One of the biggest issues for the profiling movement is its need for credibility in the market place. However enthusiastic the support from those inside schools, the innovation is likely to cut little ice with parents and pupils if it is not seen to have a value as a qualification in the wider world. Thus, in recent years, considerable attention has been given to devising ways of validating such records, so giving them a greater currency than that of a simple school imprimatur. In some cases this has meant an LEA-based initiative, in which the LEA would ensure that the procedure and its ensuing product is working in the way intended in individual institutions. This process is called accreditation. In other cases, a group of schools have bound themselves together for this purpose into a consortium. It is now increasingly common for profiling schemes to cover a wide geographical area and to invoke the services of an examination board to provide additional expertise and kudos. Thus, for example, many of the schemes that the DES is currently supporting in its own pilot initiatives involve several local authorities together with an examination board, who will together accredit individual institutions and give their imprimatur to the subsequent certificates.

The East Midlands Consortium involving four LEAs and the OCEA consortium – also involving four LEAs, the University of Oxford Department of Educational Studies and the Oxford Delegacy – are both typical in this respect. Another major initiative – the Northern Partnership for Records of Achievement involving over 30 LEAs plus all five Boards of the Northern Examining Association – provides another example. Still other models involve using the imprimatur of a national examining body such as the City and Guilds of London Institute, or the Royal Society of Arts. It is possible, in the future when the Government has issued its national guidelines for records of achievement that some kind of national validation procedure will be instituted, but this is still some way off. Meanwhile, there are numerous profiling schemes in individual schools and even subject departments, which have no external accreditation, and there is no reason why these should not continue. However, the issue of external validation is of major importance, since it determines not only the status of any summative report produced by a scheme, but also must be addressed in the initial design stages of a scheme. Many institutions will find themselves caught up in profiling within such a county- or consortium-based initiative, and will have the general shape of the scheme laid down for them in consequence. Others still have the choice to initiate their own scheme independently, and they may choose to do this if they feel strongly that the freedom to pursue their own priorities is more important than any external imprimatur. The case studies reported in this book offer a variety of options in this respect.

The range of options

As a summary of the foregoing questions and to show how complex the issues in designing a profile can prove to be we may usefully consider Figure 3.3 which is taken from the City and Guilds Basic Abilities Profiling System, which we shall be looking at in detail later. Although this table omits some important aspects of profiling, such as the pastoral context and the contribution of pupils' own experience as evidence, it demonstrates very clearly the number of permutations and combinations available.

CONTEXT	Academic	Vocational	Prevocational
FUNCTION	Formative	Summative	Both
SYSTEM	Open	Closed	Tied
PARTICIPANTS	Student	Staff	Both
CONTENT	Attitudes/ dispositions	General abilities	Specific abilities
EVIDENCE	Formal tests	Set work	Observed activities
STANDARD	Non-standard	Local standard	National standard
FORMAT	Free	Pre-specified check-list	Pre-specified grid

Source: N. Stratton, *Profiling Systems*, CGLI, London, 1985
Figure 3.3: A framework for profiling systems

Any school, college or local authority intent on designing a profiling scheme will need to make decisions in relation to each of these dimensions. To facilitate this process, the next chapter describes in some detail examples from the range of procedures being used in existing profiling schemes for recording and reporting achievement, thus illustrating in practical detail what the implications of particular choices of approach might be.

Chapter 4
A range of experience

In the last chapter, I raised a number of the general issues which need to be addressed in the design and implementation of any profiling or record of achievement scheme.

In this chapter we shall consider some of the different ways in which these issues have been resolved in some of the schemes that have already been developed. The enormous variety of existing practice makes it difficult to categorise schemes in any neat way so, in presenting these various examples, I have chosen to adopt a largely historical perspective following the actual development of ideas within the movement itself.

Early prototypes

'Grid-style' records

One of the very first profiling schemes, and one of the most influential, was designed by the Scottish Council for Research in Education in conjunction with the Headteachers' Association of Scotland. Although subject to extensive field trials in the early seventies, the scheme was developed before commitment to profiling had really become widespread in schools and was never implemented on a large scale. Its contribution was rather to provide one of the clearest articulations of the need for profiling and a systematic study of some of the problems involved in their implementation. The publication of *Pupils in Profile* in 1977 attracted considerable publicity and was a major spur to the growth of ing all their pupils:

The study concluded that schools should be encouraged to develop and refine their techniques for assessing all their pupils.

1. These assessments should refer to general skills as well as to specific achievements.
2. Pupil assessments should be recorded for some work-related factors as well as for general skills and specific achievements.
3. Certain procedures for these assessments have been found practicable and should be offered to schools.
4. A common form of school-leaving report incorporating these features for all pupils should be initiated.
5. Further field study should be undertaken in order to produce, for each subject or activity within the curriculum, improved diagnostic profiles.

The profile procedure, developed, evaluated and re-designed to meet these aims allows for teachers to enter on a class assessment form (see Figure 4.1) their assessments of those categories for each pupil, of which they have knowledge, and includes blank optional categories which can be labelled as appropriate for each activity.

If computer collation is used, each teacher's assessments are fed into the computer, which collects together for each pupil the report of all teachers by whom he/she is taught and prints them out against the pupil's name. If the manual system is used the same collation is achieved by having below the teacher's master-sheet a set of overlapping pupil sheets, onto the exposed edges of which the teacher's entries are reproduced by a carbon or similar process. These pupil slips can then be sorted and mounted for each pupil on a peg-board (see Figure 4.2), such that a profile of the pupil is built up from the various teachers' assessments displayed immediately adjacent one to the other.

The pupil profiles, produced perhaps once or twice a year, are designed to provide not only a comprehensive and cumulative basis for within-school guidance but also to provide the necessary information for a leaving report for each pupil, covering basic skills, subject achievements and personal qualities. This school-leaving report – a balance of comment and grades – aims to be brief, accurate, positive and useful to potential users and pupils. The format of the report is summative and does not include all the subject-specific categories useful for in-school purposes. It, too, has been the subject of a continuing process of development and evaluation, resulting in a recommended version, shown in Figure 4.3.

Source: Knowing our Pupils: an outline report of 'Pupils in Profile' [leaflet], Edinburgh: The Scottish Council for Research in Education (1977)

Figure 4.1: Teacher assessment form
The duplicate copy underneath is a single sheet (computer version) or partially overlapping individual pupil sheets (manual version)

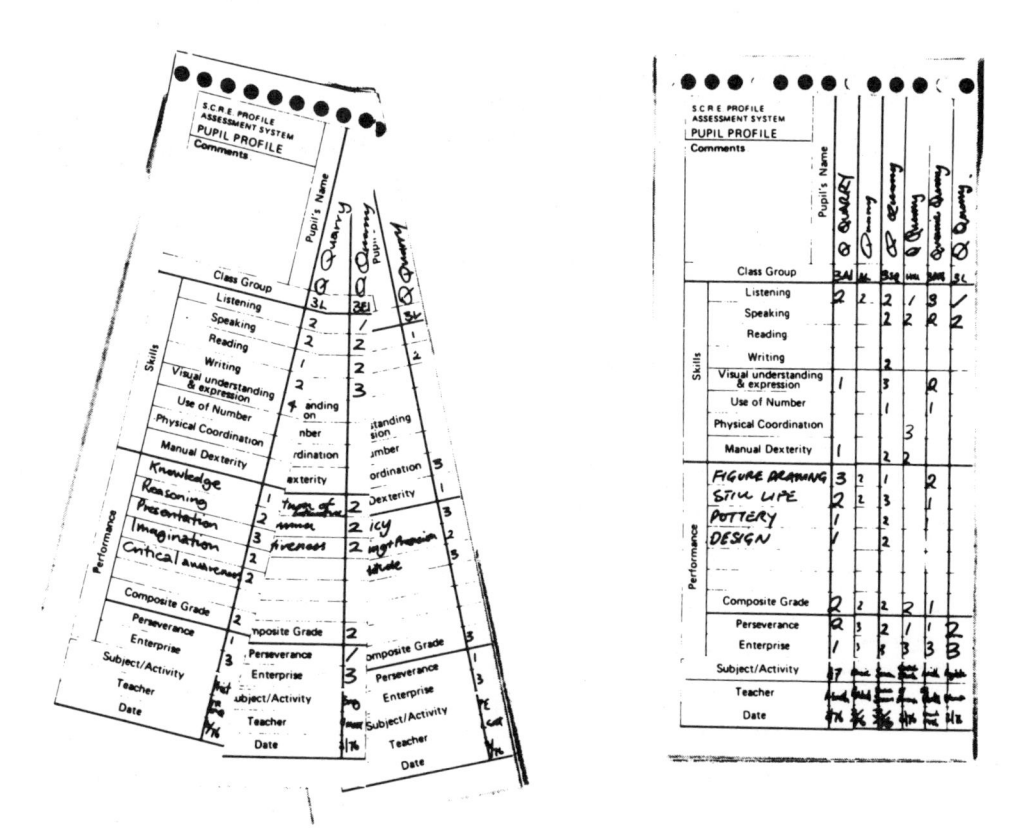

Source: SCRE, *Pupils in Profile*

Figure 4.2: Manual mounting on a peg-board of assessment records relating to a single pupil. Records awaiting mounting are shown to the left. Each slip comes from a different teacher and is a duplicate of a single column of the teacher assessment sheet shown in Figure 4.1.

The report, given to the pupil when he leaves school, will be a summation and abbreviation of the internal assessment data. The contents of such a report will not be unexpected since a pupil will have been frequently advised by his guidance and subject teachers in their encouragement of self-assessment as he has moved up the school. The report has moreover been designed to be readily understood by those concerned with selection for employment or post-school education.

(SCRE, *Pupils in Profile*)

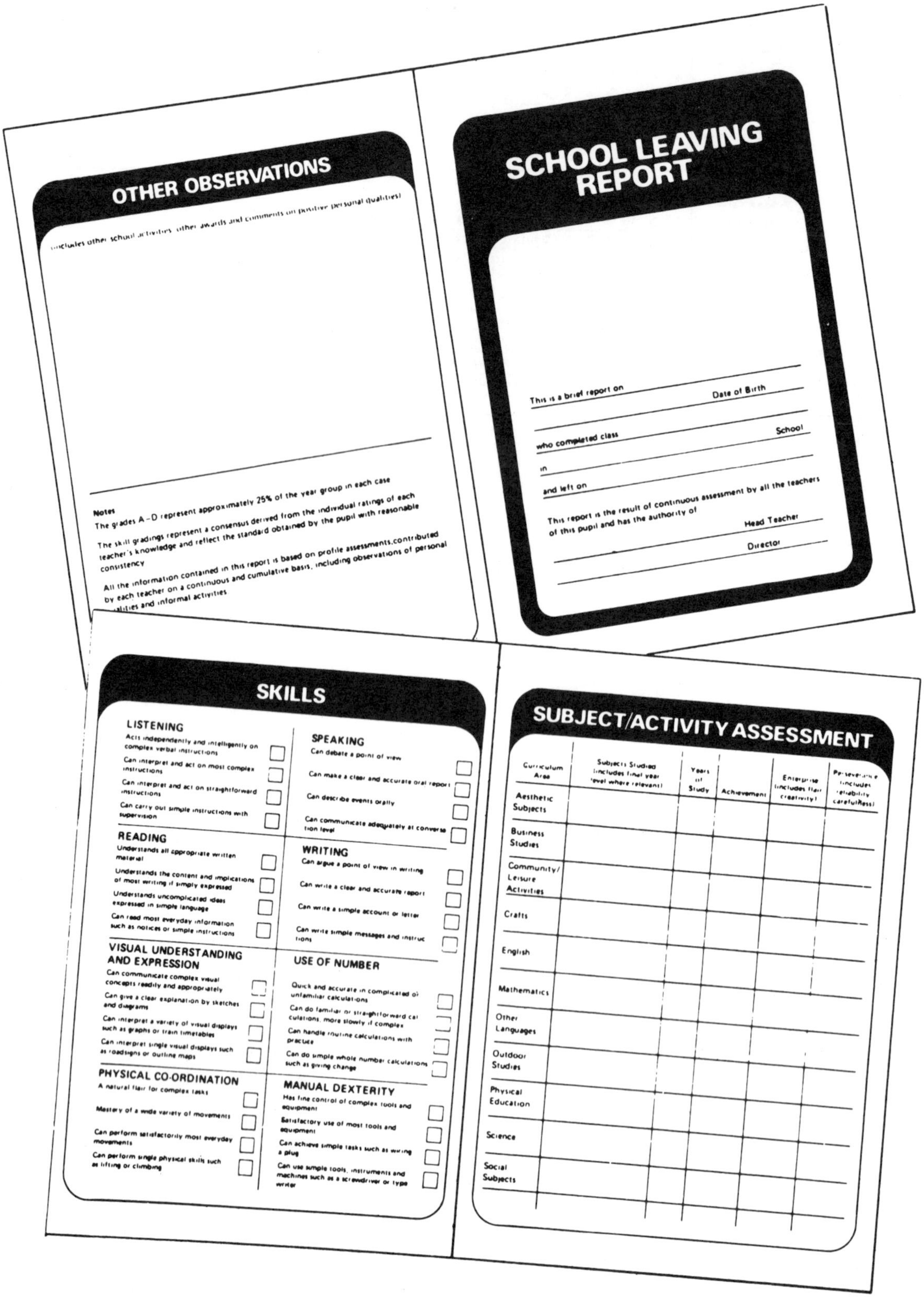

Source: SCRE, *Pupils in Profile*

Figure 4.3: School leaving record (Pages 1 & 4 above, pages 2 & 3 below)
The entries on this record are derived from the series of profile records cumulated during the years preceding leaving.

The SCRE Profile Assessment System has been described in some detail because of the large number of general points about profiling it raises. These include:

1. the different approaches required to meet formative and summative concerns; the former emphasising diagnosis and feedback, the latter, a positive and readily understood record of achievement;
2. the extremely cumbersome clerical task of collating profiles if a computer is not involved;
3. the idea of positive behavioural criteria organised into a 'comment bank' for the reporting of skill achievements, rather than the more traditional grade; and
4. most significant of all, the grid-style profile which has been widely taken up in both formative and summative contexts. It has had particular appeal for individual teachers and subject departments wishing to break down the recording of a pupil's progress in an individual subject into its component concepts and skills. A larger number of such diagnostic profiles are now in use of which the following provide some typical examples.

Subject-based profiling
Diagnosis

Many individual teachers and subject departments have become convinced of the need to institute a profile assessment which can give both student and teacher diagnostic feedback on a regular basis. Such profiles, which may include information on both academic and social criteria, are nearly always designed to be formative. Whilst only a brief summary of the information gathered may eventually find its way onto a summative profile, the formative record may well serve as the basis of reports to parents and feed into the school's pastoral record system.

Figure 4.4 illustrates a typical profile of this kind developed by a group of science teachers.

Notice that no attempt has been made in this example to make all the assessments positive. Some students will even be described baldly as 'incapable'. The emphasis here is on detailing the *criteria* which match the curriculum objectives.

SCIENTIFIC SKILL	ASSESSMENT CRITERIA	GRADE 1	2	3	4	5
Ability to communicate scientific ideas	(a) Writes in good English; concisely, relevantly, and with the correct use of technical vocabulary.					
	(b) Can discuss scientific issues clearly and sensibly.					
	(c) Constructs suitable tables of information with correct headings and units.					
	(d) Accurately plots graphs/histograms/piecharts with correct title/labelled axes/units/use of scale.					
	(e) Draws simple, clear, labelled diagrams, sectional if appropriate.					
	(f) Selects, devises and manipulates formulae; understands the use of standard forms and proportion/ratio; shows accuracy in the use of basic arithmetic and can use chemical formulae and equations.					
Mastery of practical work	(a) Aware of possible sources of danger and acts accordingly.					
	(b) Selects appropriate apparatus and uses it with care and dexterity.					
	(c) Is familiar with a variety of measuring devices and can use them correctly.					
	(d) Is willing to repeat readings and observations and continue with long term investigations.					
	(e) Reliably documents all results.					
Level of scientific understanding	(a) Can devise a procedure to logically investigate a particular problem using suitable apparatus and controlling/eliminating variables as necessary.					
	(b) Can determine the relevance or otherwise of results to a particular problem. Able to identify and suggest explanations for unexpected results.					
	(c) Can infer patterns from either first or second hand observations.					
	(d) Can solve novel problems using principles previously encountered.					
	(e) Shows informed concern for the social consequences of scientific endeavour, recognising the complexity of the issues involved.					

Areas of scientific knowledge encountered

Figure 4.4: A school-based science profile (profile continued on page 26)

Figure 4.4 (contd.)

KEY TO MARK ALLOCATION

Mark	Standard of achievement	In terms of the criteria
5	Excellent	Completely fulfills criteria without fault
4	Good	Reaches a high standard in the criteria indicated.
3	Reasonable	Achieves a satisfactory standard in the criteria indicated.
2	Poor	Fails to fulfill the criteria except to a limited extent.
1	Incapable	Cannot fulfill the criteria indicated.

FURTHER COMMENTS

Teacher's Signature ....

Date ....

Figure 4.5 provides a similar example of a profile grid for physical education and of the kind of subject report that would result.

These two examples do not incorporate the more recent concern that all profile grid descriptors should be couched in positive 'can-do' terms. Opinion is very divided about whether profile statements should be negative as well as positive. In the light of these examples, you may care to reflect upon the following questions:

- How useful are they?
- Do these profiles help the teacher to diagnose the cause of a pupil's achievement or failure?
- What would be the effect of such a profile on the pupil?

Figure 4.6 shows a similar approach for modern languages except that the record provides more of a visual profile of progress over several units of work. It does not, however, specify on the profile itself the criteria for grades 1–5 in each assessment component, although these may be incorporated in the assessment exercises on which the grades awarded are based. Like

CRITERIA FOR ASSESSMENT — PHYSICAL EDUCATION

	1	2	3	4	5
Equipped for lessons A	Is always fully equipped for lessons	Is usually fully equipped for lessons	Occasionally is not fully equipped for lessons	Often not fully equipped for lessons	Rarely fully equipped for lessons
Interest and enthusiasm B	Always works with interest and is a lively and eager participant	Usually shows interest and enthusiasm	Is reasonably interested but without a great deal of enthusiasm	Doesn't show a great deal of interest	Shows no enthusiasm or interest in this subject
Ability to work with others C	Can work extremely well with others and always makes a positive contribution	Usually works well in a group. Is able to share and contribute to the group	Can work well in a group but occasionally has difficulties	Tends to opt out when working with others	Does not contribute in any way in a group. Is a nuisance and disrupts others
Attitude to authority D	Relates very well to authority and accepts decisions	Usually responds well and accepts decisions	Can respond well but finds difficulty in accepting some decisions	Does not often respond well and has difficulty accepting decisions	Resents authority and does not accept decisions
Creative movement E	Produces creative and imaginative work to a high standard	Produces creative imaginative work to a reasonable standard	Can produce creative work but has difficulty expressing ideas	Can copy movements but has difficulty expressing movement ideas	Is unable to express ideas or copy simple movement patterns
Games F	Has a high level of skill, understanding tactics and runs well	Has a good skill level and understands and applies rules	Is able to play a game with reasonable skill and applies the rules with guidance	Understands simple rules and has a limited skill level	Is unable to understand or apply rules and has difficulty with co-ordination
Athletics G					
Swimming H					
Comment:	personalized – each member signs				
Pupil effort S	Always tries as hard as possible	Usually tries hard	Doesn't always make the necessary effort	Does not make much effort and often gives up during difficult work	Does not try at all
Fitness T	Can keep up with physical activity and takes regular exercise	Can keep up physical activity but doesn't take regular exercise	Is not as fit as could be and sometimes has difficulty in keeping going	Cannot keep up with activity for long. Tires easily	Is very unfit

Figure 4.5a: A physical education profile in its design stage

THE MARY ROSE SCHOOL
PHYSICAL EDUCATION Profile/Report on Neil AHTOW OF 1MID

Written by MR SKINSLEY on 17TH NOVEMBER 1985

EQUIPPED FOR LESSONS:- Neil is always well equipped for lessons.
INTEREST AND ENTHUSIASM:- Neil shows interest and enthusiasm.
ABILITY TO WORK WITH OTHERS:- Neil can work well in a group but often has difficulties.
RELATIONSHIP WITH TEACHER:- Neil constantly seeks attention
CREATIVE MOVEMENT/GYM/DANCE:- Neil is unable to express own ideas simple movement patterns.
GAMES:- Neil understands simple rules but has a limited skill level.
EFFORT:- Neil only puts in as much effort as is required.
FITNESS:- Neil can usually sustain physical activity but does not take regular physical exercise.

Figure 4.5b.

Source: H. D. Black and W. B. Dockrell, *Diagnostic Assessment in Secondary Schools*, Edinburgh, Scottish Council for Research in Education, 1980

Figure 4.6: The diagnostic profile recording sheet used in a modern languages department

the other two examples just reviewed, however, this profile is still essentially 'norm-referenced', in that pupils are ranked in relation to each other as much as in relation to some defined criterion of achievement. The basis of the grades given is largely on the basis of having 'more' or 'less' of a given quality or skill rather than on some clear criterion or 'cut-point'.

Figure 4.7 represents yet another variation on this theme in that the grades given – still essentially norm-referenced – are recorded in relation to a matrix that relates skills to content. Thus the teacher can see at a glance which skills are consistently posing problems across a range of content. Equally he or she can see where strengths lie. Thus the profile is more explicitly diagnostic than the previous examples shown.

Comment

Thus whilst none of the profiles illustrated above really provide more than a reporting system, they are still significant in bringing one of the fundamental principles of profiling – breaking down assessment into its component parts – into the daily life of the classroom. At the same time, the implications for the teacher, the pupil and the school of what may appear to be a relatively minor change are considerable.

For the *teacher*, subject profiling requires:
1 clarity of purpose;
2 assessment procedures which are diagnostic in approach;
3 teaching strategies that can provide the information required;
4 teaching strategies that allow a teacher to *act* on the information generated.

For the *student*, subject profiling requires:
1 a willingness to see assessment as an aid to learning and not always a judgement;
2 seeing assessment as a competition with himself or herself rather than with other students;
3 that students take more responsibility for their own learning.

For the *school*, subject profiling requires:
1 a willingness to depart from traditional examinations as the criterion of student achievement;
2 a willingness to make a genuine commitment to 'continuous assessment';
3 that school reporting procedures do not contradict the spirit of subject profiling;
4 that teachers are helped with the necessary training, resources and support to sustain such new approaches to assessment.

Negotiated records

Dialogue

Many teachers are not content just to change the way they record student progress or even their own teaching. More and more departments have come to recognise the benefits to be gained from instituting an assessment *dialogue* as well. Taking their cue from developments in pastoral care procedures, many

Name ....   Form Tutor ....

Form ....   Science Tutor ....

| | SKILLS ||| PRESEN-TATION | ATTAIN-MENT % GRADE | CONDUCT | EFFORT |
	PRACTICAL	ORGANI-SATION	INTER-PRETATION				
CLASSIFICATION							
WATER I							
WATER II							
MEASUREMENT							
REPRODUCTION							
ANNUAL ASSESSMENT							

General Comment :-

Source: H. D. Black and P. M. Broadfoot, *Keeping Track of Teaching*, Routledge, Kegan Paul, 1982

Figure 4.7: a diagnostic science profile (Grades are awarded on an A–E basis)

departments have instituted self-assessment procedures which are designed to help students reflect on their participation in the learning process and give some feedback to the teacher on this. Figure 4.8 shows an example from a religious education department which requires the pupils to keep their own record of their work, behaviour and achievement. Properly done this exercise has clear merit in educational terms in constantly reminding pupils that learning is a two-way process. Figure 4.9 illustrates a slightly different approach where half-termly, rather than after every lesson, students are asked to review their progress. Interestingly, however, in this case, they are also invited to express their satisfaction with the course!

Question: Is it fair to ask pupils to take on such responsibility if they are given no say in the content and organisation of the learning process itself? Can self-assessment without genuine responsibility bring about the desired effect?

Not all teachers may be able to bring themselves to the exposure involved in allowing pupils a real say in the curriculum itself. However, the advantages of even a limited self-assessment are now widely agreed.
1 It reminds students that they, as much as the teacher, are responsible for progress made.
2 It helps students to develop powers of reflection and self-criticism.
3 It encourages students' self-respect by implying that their opinion matters.
4 It provides the teachers with much otherwise unobtainable information on how pupils feel.
5 It provides the teacher with essential feedback on how his or her teaching has been received.
6 It emphasises the notion of partnership in the learning process.

Pupil–teacher negotiation
The most recent development in this aspect of profiling recognises the limitations of instituting self-assessment without ceding any real responsibility. More and more schemes are instituting the idea of negotiation, dialogue or review in the assessment process – with the aim of providing an active, on-going partnership between teacher and pupil.

This category of profile needs to be further subdivided between
1 those schemes in which negotiation covers curriculum as well as assessment, and
2 those where the negotiation is primarily about what is to be recorded, rather than about what is to be learned as well.

Negotiating the curriculum
This sort of approach is most likely to be found where curriculum provision can respond to such individual programmes. One such scheme was initiated by Don Stansbury who pioneered personal recording as 'The Diamond Challenge Programme'. In collaboration with their tutors, students make plans, set completion dates, carry their plans out and record results. They present the outcomes as 'evidence of independent enterprise and initiative'.

At the other end of the scale, such negotiation may be in terms of an officially sponsored policy change such as that following the 1983 publication '16s-19s in Scotland: An Action Plan', where the majority of non-advanced further education and eventually perhaps the bulk of post-16 school provision including the 'Higher' Scottish Certificate passes needed for university entry will be provided in a series of forty hour, internally assessed modules. In consultation with their tutor, students will plot their own unique path through

NAME .... SET .... TUTORIAL ....

DATE	Aim/Theme of the lesson	Listened carefully?	Read silently?	Read aloud?	Contributed to discussions?	Written work?	Illustrated work?	Has anything puzzled me? Have I wondered about anything?	Grade awarded by teacher for work.

At the end of each lesson, the pupil should complete one line of this sheet, recording the aim of the lesson and *ticking* the appropriate columns. The grade column can be completed when the work has been marked.

Source: Southway School, Devon

Figure 4.8: RE department – pupil profile

NAME: _____

Write down your honest opinion about yourself under the headings which follow, in relation to the first half of term.

PROGRESS

A   In writing English

B   In speaking and listening

C   In reading and understanding literature

DIFFICULTIES   Mention any you have come across

EFFORT   How much have you made?

INTEREST AND ENJOYMENT of the course

SUGGESTIONS for changing or improving the course

TEACHER'S COMMENTS

Source: P. Broadfoot, 'Communication in the Classroom: The Role of Assessment in Motivation', 1977

Figure 4.9: Self-assessment in English

nearly 2000 course modules currently available according to the objectives they have set for themselves.

In England, several schools are currently piloting such an individualised learning programme with the support of the Gulbenkian Foundation. The scheme is based on an officially validated negotiated curriculum which culminates at the end of two years in a summative record of achievement. This record is given the imprimatur of a school 'Accrediting Board' specially convened for this purpose and including both school and community representatives.

The activity of 'validation' – of confirming that an educational programme has worth – is familiar in higher and further education, but not so familiar in schools. This book describes how a school's governing body can establish a Validating Board to reassure all concerned that what is proposed is worthwhile. This activity of the governing body is directly in line with its legal responsibility for the conduct and curriculum of the school.

It is also important to reassure all concerned that a record of achievement has been properly prepared, and that any of its claims about achievements or standards are honest and reliable. The record must be accurate and just, and known to be so. This book suggests that each local authority should therefore establish one or more boards, of professional educators, to give public assurance that a school's records have been properly prepared and can be depended upon. This activity of 'accreditation' is at present confined to securing, through the exchange of examiners, that the practices of external examining bodies are comparable. In further and higher education, too, the accreditation of examination and other results is secured by the use of external examiners. This function can be fulfilled, for records of achievement produced by individual schools, if a local authority establishes a professional Accrediting Board.

This book argues that it is very important to keep the school's Validating Board and the authority's Accrediting Board separate. Their functions are different. In the past, one of the chief complaints about education has been the way in which examinations and assessment have come to dominate the curriculum instead of serving it. Assessment and recording should depend on an educational programme, not determine it. A student needs the assurance that an educational programme is worthwhile, and this he will get from knowing that it has been validated by a body of substantial people. Standards that he reaches on successfully completing his programme will be entered into his record, and the record will be professionally accredited. Any further 'results', in external examinations, will be additional to and separate from the properly accredited record.

There is one final task: to secure the credit of each local authority's Accrediting Board. It is widely recognised that even long-established examining boards require this kind of national approval. A new system, like records of achievement, requires it all the more. This book proposes, therefore, that there should be established an Accrediting Council for Education, to oversee the work of local boards and to secure their probity and credit.

(T. Burgess and E. Adams, *Recording Achievement at 16+*, NFER Nelson, 1985)

Although most schemes are still at a relatively early stage of development, the idea of using profiles as an integral part of this kind of curriculum development is becoming more and more characteristic of the profiles movement as a whole. Much more widespread, however, is the idea of teacher–pupil dialogue in assessment.

Negotiating assessment
Although little mention can be found of this idea before the start of this decade, the notion has grown like wildfire to the extent that pupil–teacher dialogue has been officially incorporated into government policy for records of achievement as the following extract from the 1984 DES Policy Statement shows.

12 If the first three purposes are to be properly fulfilled, schools will need to set up internal arrangements for the compilation of records throughout a pupil's period of secondary education
which will involve all the teachers concerned and allow for appropriate discussion between teacher and pupil. Arrangements will also be needed towards the end of a pupil's time at school for preparation of the short summary document of record envisaged in purpose *iv.* above.

16 The Secretaries of State believe that the internal processes of reporting, recording and discussion between teacher and pupil should cover a pupil's progress and activities across the whole educational programme of the school, both in the classroom and outside, and possibly activities outside the school as well. Regular dialogue between teacher and pupil will be important for the fulfilment of the first three purposes of records discussed in paragraph 11.

(DES Policy Statement on Records of Achievement, 1984)

The Avon Student Profile
The Avon Student Profile exemplifies current thinking in this respect. Figure 4.10 shows an extract from the draft Avon Student Profile which is now being piloted in a number of schools within the Authority. The Avon Student Profile contains four sections.

1 *Personal achievements*
Here the student is encouraged to 'write about all the things you do in or out of school, where you feel you have achieved something worthwhile'. The student is asked to write something about the achievement and then ask an adult to comment upon it. The purpose of the adult validation is to give the entry status in the eyes of others.

2 *Personal qualities*
Here the student is asked to look at a list of personal qualities with a question by the side of it. The student is being asked to think about his or her own personal qualities in any given area. The students are asked to write down some of the qualities that they think they possess, and then to ask an adult to comment on it. The aim behind this exercise is said to be to help the student to build up a self-assessment of his or her own strengths and weaknesses. It is different to conventional reporting systems in this area, in that it is initiated by the student, and is not meant to be judgemental.

3 *Basic skills*
This section of the profile has been positively influenced by development work in Wales – it is dealing with what might be termed cross curricular skills and covers three areas:
a) communication – oral, written, graphical;
b) numerical;
c) practical.
The approach to this section of the profile is that of the Comment Bank. The tutor selects key statements which he feels to be descriptive of the individual. Here the school has to decide which departments are to comment on which area.

4 *School subjects*
form the final section of the profile, but it is 'assessment' with a difference. The pupil makes a list of subjects, and of subject objectives (gained from the teacher). The student then comments on how well he thinks objectives have been achieved. The teacher then comments, and makes an assessment of how well the objectives have been achieved.

Perhaps most interesting of all is section 2 on personal qualities, which is illustrated in Figure 4.10. Here the student is provided with a list of 12 personal qualities (such as carefulness, energy and enthusiasm,

```
┌─────────────────────────────────────────────┐
│ NAME : ..............  TUTOR'S NAME : ............  │
│                                             │
│               QUALITY                       │
│                                             │
│ ┌──────────┐         ┌──────────┐          │
│ │STUDENT'S │         │ TUTOR'S  │          │
│ │ COMMENT  │         │ COMMENT  │          │
│ └──────────┘         └──────────┘          │
└─────────────────────────────────────────────┘
```

PERSONAL QUALITIES

Self Reliance, Resourcefulness, Independence
    How much an I able to do things for myself without expecting others to show me or help me?

Initiative, Leadership
    How willing am I to take the lead or think of things to do?

Responsibility, Reliability
    How much do I take on something to do, and do it as well as I can without being checked up on?

Perseverance, Determination
    How much do I stick at something even if it is difficult?

Carefulness
    How much am I able to do something carefully and well rather than in a hurry and badly?

Originality, Creativeness
    How much do I think of things for myself and not copy other people?

Adaptability, Flexibility
    How good am I at changing my mind or my attitude when things around me change?

Energy and Enthusiasm
    How much energy and enthusiasm do I show when I take on something to do?

Relationships with authority, parents, adults and own age group
    How do I get on with other people in different circumstances?

Co-operation
    How willing am I to work with other people and to fit in with them?

Awareness of others
    How much am I able to listen to, understand and sympathise with other people and their needs?

Appearance
    What do I look like to other people in the way I dress and keep myself clean?

Source: Avon Student Profile

Figure 4.10: Avon Student Profile: personal qualities

appearance, initiative, co-operation, awareness of others) and some indication of their meaning. The student is asked to select a number of these qualities which appear relevant or desirable to him or her, and say briefly how the quality contributes to a true self-picture. This is then discussed with a teacher who knows the student well and the teacher's comment is added. This approach differs from conventional reporting in that it is initiated by the student and is not meant to be judgemental. The novelty of this approach is that not only are youngsters free to contribute their perspective, they are also free to choose what to comment about; to reflect upon what personal qualities are most relevant for them. In so doing, this scheme goes a long way towards avoiding some of the potential hazards of value judgement and stereotyping currently causing concern to many.

The rationale for this approach is well expressed in the following extract written by a teacher involved in the scheme.

> Here we observe a Profile which would include subjects, skills, interests, and personal qualities, and certainly would aim at presenting a fuller picture of the pupil than conventional reporting and certificating could hope to give. The profile is not just an adult commenting on student performance, etc., but the student is to be involved in all the assessment processes by a series of negotiations with significant adults. The aim is to give a more balanced and fairer picture, in that it comments on areas which traditional techniques leave alone.
>
> One problem with this new system is that it requires a new approach not only to assessing and recording that assessment, but for many it will require a new, more dynamic approach to teaching and learning as well. Much more emphasis will need to be put on the interactive basis of these twin activities. For some teachers brought up in a more traditional mode this may require a change of direction.
>
> If schools/teachers and students are to assess and report on some of these areas, then the school will need to make sure that it provides learning experiences that will enable students to demonstrate competencies in these areas. This is not a system that can be fitted comfortably into the existing organisational structure. For this to work, it will need to be backed up by a careful programme of INSET, which will help teachers to reorganise what they do and the way that they do it.
>
> It is clear that profiling is not just a collection of assessments. Profiling has to be linked inextricably not only with assessment modes, but also with the very design of curricular activities.

(R. Sims, The Strengths and Weaknesses of Profiles, 1985.)

Comberton Village College

> Comberton Village College has been producing Records of Achievement since 1984. The College is now a member of the Cambridge Partnership for Records of Achievement (CPRA) which is organised jointly by Cambridgeshire Local Education Authority and the University of Cambridge Local Examination Syndicate (UCLES).
>
> Comberton Village College's scheme of Records of Achievement is designed primarily as a formative process to supplement and extend existing methods of assessment. We are, therefore, concerned with recording achievements in areas which traditionally have not been part of school assessment procedures. In doing so, we are concerned with the achievements

that have occurred both in and out of the classroom and in 'academic' and non-academic contexts. We believe that the process of recording these achievements is as valuable as the final outcome, because the process itself is an education one for those engaged in it, the pupils and the teacher. . . . Pupils self-assessment and the discussion of that self-assessment with tutors are the central elements of the process. . . . The outcome of the process is a Record of Achievement which has been written jointly by both pupil and teacher. . . . The Record of Achievement consists of statements written by pupils under the following headings:

1) *The Record of Personal Experience* is designed to encourage students to keep an account of a range of achievements, experiences and activities in which they engage both in and out of school time. Form Tutors are responsible for overseeing the students recording of these experiences.

2) *Personal Qualities*. The aim of this section is to help the student develop a description of his or her personal qualities. The student is assisted in this task by
   (i) the activities of the Tutorial programme
   (ii) various 'prompt' sheets and
   (iii) interviews and discussion with the form tutor.

3) *Work skills*. This section is compiled as part of the work of the student in their specialist subject areas. There are four elements
   (a) a course outline, identifying the key skills being developed
   (b) the student's account of progress, difficulties and achievements
   (c) the teacher's view of progress in key skills and other aspects of the pupil's achievement in the subject
   (d) an agreed target for the future.

Within this framework, departments develop their own particular process for recording work skills.

The *Final Summary document* is about four sides of A4 paper. The front cover is similar to the cover of this booklet. It contains
   (a) personal details about the student
   (b) a summary of the 'Personal experiences' section written by the student
   (c) a final statement written by the student about their Personal Qualities
   (d) a summative statement on work skills, compiled by the tutor, commenting on certain core work skills, and other highlights of the student's work, as revealed in the formative documents.

Process
Most of the work of recording the Personal Experience section and the Personal Qualities section occurs in Tutor time. This work forms part of the tutorial programme, and is linked to other activities timetabled for this period.

In addition, each tutor is allocated an extra one hour non-teaching time to enable them to withdraw students for interviewing and discussions, particularly in connection with the Personal Qualities section of the Record.

The recording of the work skills section occurs in subject time, as part of the assessment procedures of the course.

Thus for a subject like mathematics, the profile would include the following:

FRONT OF PROFILE
Course Details
An outline of the courses offered in the 4th and 5th years which will include reference to the aims of the course, to the examinations and certification and to the form of the assessment.

Achievements
A space in which achievements can be recorded. These may be marks in tests and examinations, details of coursework assignments or outstanding pieces of classwork. There are many ways in which this can be used and it may vary from school to school or from set to set within a school. Where coursework tasks form part of the scheme of assessment, titles of these could be printed on the proforma.

BACK OF PROFILE (and continuation sheets) (See Figure 4.11a)

Student/Teacher Comments
The frequency of commenting is something which needs to be decided by the department. Sensible times to comment would seem to be after a review test or at the completion of a topic or unit of work. For courses based on a text book this could be at the end of a group of chapters.

The teacher comment will consist of:
1. Subject specific statements linked to text books, schemes of work or coursework assignments. Key skills could be agreed on by the staff and form a departmental list. Comment will need to be selective and focus on those ideas which the student has mastered particularly well and those in which specific improvements can be made.
2. Additional comments focusing on the core work skills:
    * Listening and contributing to discussion
    * Expressing ideas and views
    * Working independently
    * Problem solving (including investigations)
    * Organising work and materials

   Any one formative statement could include reference to only some of the above skills but over the two year period each one should be mentioned at least once so that the summative statement may summarize all of them.
3. Other comments as appropriate, e.g. on teamwork, decision making etc.

Students will need to be given guidance in making appropriate statements. The target for future performance will be recorded by the student after consultation with the teacher. An agreed 'menu' could be presented by the teacher to assist choice.

STUDENT'S COMMENT:

TEACHERS COMMENT:

AGREED TARGET:

Figure 4.11a The student/teacher comments section of the mathematics workskills profile
These short summary comments would be entered as regularly as the Department fell appropriate to units of work undertaken.

Rob Pepper, Head of Mathematics, Bretton Woods School. Copyright UCLES, Cambridge Partnership for Records of Achievement 1985.

Personal Qualities

For their own personal recording, students are provided with the following guidance and are invited to comment on qualities such as determination, taking responsibility, enthusiasm, being reflective, co-operation, carefulness, reliability, and self-image.

> In this section of your Record of Achievement, you have the chance to create a picture of the kind of person you feel you are. Everyone is a special person, with different interests, enthusiasms, and ideas: it is these things which make you unique, an individual quite unlike anyone else.
>
> To help you start thinking about how you want to describe yourself, you will find a list of different qualities which people have. Under each heading there are some questions to ask yourself, and examples of the kinds of activities or views we think of when we use a word such as 'co-operative' or 'caring'.
>
> Start by making notes in the blank spaces of your OUTLINES sheets beside each of the qualities. All sorts of information is useful here – activities you enjoy, things you believe are important in your life, the way you try to treat other people, issues you care about. All of this information helps build up a unique picture of you – as you think you are.
>
> When you start to make your notes and think about what you want to say, there is one thing, above all, which is important. Being honest. Nobody is perfect, and probably none of us would much like a person who was! Our friends like us in spite of our funny habits, and sometimes because of them. But one thing you need to remember about this part of your Record, is that it gives you the chance to write down the good news and the bad news; the person you are, and a bit about the person you'd like to be.
>
> After you've worked for a while on your outline, you'll have the chance to explain your ideas to your group tutor, who may be able to help you add bits you hadn't thought about before. You will have the chance to meet with your tutor on your own several times in the coming year. When you go to see your tutor, he or she will encourage you to talk about the things you're interested in at the moment and help you build up the written picture of yourself that you want to include in your Record of Achievement.
>
> Try to include some aims to work towards – you may want to become a better listener, or the opposite – better at speaking up for yourself in a group. Becoming more clear in your own mind about what you're good at and what you find difficult is half the battle towards becoming more confident. It's a step towards being able to use your personal strengths to achieve what you want from life.
>
> Above all, have fun working through the various sections. Try to bring yourself to life on the page, to draw a portrait which is a good likeness. After all, there's nobody quite like you, anywhere!

Source: Cambridge Partnership for Records of Achievement: Comberton Village College: Information Booklet

Notes to students on completing their personal qualities statement, Comberton Village College

Students are encouraged to set targets for themselves about how they would like to develop and improve in the future.

Pupils' own records

One of the original and still among the most influential currents in the profiling movement has been the idea of students' personally-compiled records. Originating with the work of Don Stansbury and others in the late sixties, the earliest prototype – the Record of Personal Achievement (RPA) – was designed principally to cater for the new population of pupils to be created by the Raising of the School-Leaving Age.

Essentially, it was for tutors to encourage pupils to make factual records of their achievements in and out of school. A declared aim was the development of personal qualities; the main objectives were to provide pupils with (a) an organising principle for their work; (b) motivation; and (c) a tangible record of achievement for school leavers. It was a procedure and not a course. From RPA, Don Stansbury developed the Record of Personal Experience which gives greater emphasis to the development of personal qualities through individual experience.

Another flourishing offshoot from this early work is Pupils' Personal Records (PPR). After a three year pilot stage which started in 1980, the scheme is now widely available and attracts much interest. In its own words:

Philosophy

Pupils Personal Recording does not provide a Profile. It aims to offer all pupils the opportunity to declare themselves on their own terms. The record is a chronicle of personal interests, experiences and activities recorded in the pupils' own words and style. It blends evidence drawn from inside and outside the school environment and is made without imposition of ranking, rating, marking or censure. The record may be organised under nineteen card Titles with the help of sensitive tutoring. Successful PPR experience provides the bedrock for pupil participation in the compilation of Records of Achievement and the pupil may use the written entries as the basis for an interview.

(Pupils' Personal Records [PPR])

The procedure is briefly described in these extracts from the PPR handbook:

KEY CRITERIA FOR THE OPERATION OF PPR THROUGHOUT SECONDARY EDUCATION

All schools will not necessarily follow the same working pattern or use the same materials but it is vital to assume that the school will wish to place real decision-making and responsibility within the grasp of the recorder. Respect for individual needs and pupil autonomy are fundamental to the process of PPR.

1. *PPR is a process not a course of study*
   A personal record is an important tool in Personal and Social Education and pupils need time to discuss entries with and, as necessary, seek support from their Tutor.

   The opportunity/expectation of engaging in this process could start at any stage during Secondary Education but ideally is available from year 1.

2. *PPR is not a diary*
   Pilot schools and experienced tutors acknowledge that the record provides a reflective reference for the pupil which can, in turn, form the basis of Pupil Tutor dialogue.

3. *Entries are pupil-decided*
   Pupils use their own judgement and exercise their own choice in deciding which experiences/activities they wish to record.

4. *Entries are pupil-controlled*
   The language, style and pattern of an entry are determined and made by the recorder in person. Tutors should be supportive *not* prescriptive.

5. *Records are pupil-controlled*
   The Personal Record is essentially a private document during preparation and on completion. Public access to the record must be agreed by the Recorder beforehand.

6. *The opportunity to keep a Personal Record shall be available to all pupils*
   Record keeping is not restricted to any academic ability range. Its advantages are for all.

7. *Materials are of good quality*
   Schools must ensure that cards, files and any other support materials are attractive, durable and of good quality.

8. *Personal Recording is elective*
   All the above criteria assume that pupils create a personal record from choice but schools are obviously free to project the scheme vigorously to pupils, parents, professional colleagues and the local community.

9. IF PUPILS ARE TO REGARD PERSONAL RECORDING AS A THOROUGHLY WORTHWHILE UNDERTAKING THE SCHOOL MUST BE SEEN TO PLACE A HIGH VALUE ON THE PROCESS AND STRIVE TO ENSURE THAT IT IS UNDERSTOOD AND SUPPORTED BY ALL CONCERNED PARTIES.

ORGANISATION

1. *Co-ordinating Tutor*
   Experience has shown that the appointment of a co-ordinating tutor at middle or senior management level not only ensures coherence but emphasises the importance that a school places on the process.

2. *Groups*
   Most Tutor Groups are appropriate for PPR. Although it is not difficult for a tutor to support individual recording with a normal class group. Ideally the work favours smaller groups.

3. *Time*
   Every student needs at least forty minutes each week in a single block to engage in the process and keep the record up-to-date. Time should be divided by the pupil into:

   (i) thinking and planning
   (ii) preparing draft entries (if desired)
   (iii) making actual records

   Discussions between pupils about entries is a matter for the tutor's discretion. Discussion between Tutor and individual recorder is *vital*.

   Pupils should be encouraged to work at home on drafts and final entries. The use of a jotter diary is often appropriate.

4. *Materials*
   These should be of a high quality and comprise a) a hardback ring file with PPR Logo on front cover, b) suitable blank cards, c) list of suggested headings as guidelines for pupils.

5 *Access to Materials*

A systematic filing system should be maintained, from which cards and reference material can be retrieved. From the start pupils must learn to locate and collect the materials themselves.

Firm disciplined use of materials is imperative. All materials should be kept in a locked place and the actual files are always in the custody of the tutor. The files are not intended to be taken home or indeed, to other parts of the school.

(PPR Handbook)

Pupils' instructions are simple, as the extract in Figure 4.12 from the PPR Pupils' handbook shows.

WHAT do I actually write down?

i) Why did you do "whatever" you've recorded.
ii) How did you go about it, and could you improve next time.
iii) How you felt about it afterwards – did you enjoy it, was it worthwhile.
iv) If it was a group project – what was your responsibility.
v) Did you learn anything? What was most difficult?

Here are two sample entries.

P.P.R.

DATE	DETAILS	SIGNED
10/11/87	I took the motorbike apart, cleaned the engine and frame and reassembled it. It goes well now.	C. Jour.

P.P.R. Helping at Home

DATE	DETAILS	SIGNED
23/1/87	On sat. my mother was not so well so I did the shopping and cooked the meals. Both my brothers and my father said they enjoyed the meals especially the roast	

Source: PPR Handbook

Figure 4.12: Instructions to pupils engaged in PPR

The experience of one participating school is reproduced below.

School 13–19

Westwood St. Thomas's Salisbury is a ten form entry 13 to 19 mixed comprehensive upper school taking over 1000 pupils from the west side of Salisbury and Wilton. We have used Personal Records since being selected as one of the Schools' Council pilot study schools in 1980. We have now expanded the use of Pupils' Personal Records and over 300 pupils participate. All our intake year pupils, over 250, are given the opportunity to keep a Record during a part of their two forty minute tutorial lessons. We provide pupils with an A5 size hard back two-ring file and with as many PPR cards as required. Last year the cost of each file was 95 pence and they will, of course, be the property of the pupil when he/she leaves school. We have found that pupils of all abilities benefit from and enjoy the process of recording their experiences. Our development over the last four years has emphasised the need for tutor commitment to the idea and a weekly allocation of time to enhance the place of PPR on the pastoral programme.

(C. E. Whiteley, p. 7, *Pupils as Partners*)

PPR is also in operation in Southway School, Devon, but here it is used in a slightly different way, bringing in the idea of negotiation once again, and of teachers as participants in at least part of the recording process. At the end of their school career, pupils will receive a record of achievement.

Pupils are invited from the first year onwards to keep records of their own achievements and involvements. In the third year the PPR folders are used as the foundation from which pupils can negotiate with their tutors a summative statement in terms of Records of Achievements statement (1) 'Information, other than academic successes, which throws light on personal achievements and characteristics'. This agreed statement is normally updated, deleted and improved on the subsequent years four and five when it can eventually form the final statement (albeit a 'snap shot in time') which pupils can take with them from school. The pupils maintain the right of ownership and are naturally incorporated into a process of self examination which in its formative mode serves them well in developing good and positive notions of self. The materials we use are cheap; folders and stationery are normal County Supply Issue with the addition of Logos printed in school.

(PPR Newsletter, PPR Devon)

The instructions to pupils ask them to:
i) Write a record about yourself which will help someone else reading it learn something of you as a person and your achievements. (You need not make reference to academic achievements – since evidence of this will be provided by the school when you leave.)
ii) Only state positive things about yourself, there is no need here to mention any failure or defect.
iii) Wherever you can give evidence – for example if you would like to say that you are a good swimmer, mention that you have 'swum the channel' or for example if you would like to describe yourself as persistent say that you have tried to

learn 'hang gliding' even though you have crashed several times. The evidence ought to come from your PPR file!!

iv) If you are stuck for a start think about these words – enthusiasm, enterprise, adaptability, persistence, punctuality, willingness and capacity to accept responsibility, ability to participate constructively in group activity, ability to work independently.

You may not understand what these words or phrases mean, but you could discuss them with your parents, your teachers or other people as a start to help you think how you could describe yourself.

v) Include examples of your interests and involvements both in and outside school.

REMEMBER – BE POSITIVE
INVOLVE OTHER PEOPLE IN HELPING YOU THINK OF WHAT YOU WRITE, BUT DO NOT LET ANYONE ELSE WRITE *YOUR* RECORD.

(Letter to parents: guidelines for first draft records of achievement, Southway School, Devon, 1985.)

Personal recording has attracted much interest and support in schools. Its influence has gone far beyond the initiation of specific schemes in helping to establish as a generic principle the idea that students know things about themselves that no-one else does and that the act of reflecting or recording this experience can be of major educational benefit. The legitimacy such recording schemes have given to students' involvement in what used to be the exclusive preserve of teachers has been vital to the development of the profiling movement into a coherent educational philosophy rather than being confined to the domain of assessment and recording.

Trainee-centred reviewing
is one recent offshoot of this philosophy which embodies very similar principles, albeit in a very different learning context. In its 1979 report 'Making Experience Work', the Manpower Services Commission suggested that trainees would benefit if they 'logged' their experience as they progressed through the various elements of a scheme. This log, along with parallel records kept by the careers office and tutors, would:
1 'serve as a basis for discussion between the young person, tutors and careers officers';
2 'be a record of personal achievement for the trainee' (MSC, 1979)

As a result of development work by the Counselling and Career Development Unit at Leeds University and the Industrial Training Research Unit at Cambridge, 'Trainee Centred Reviewing' was devised. A basic principle is giving trainees responsibility for their own learning and to help them learn from their experiences. TCR also aims to help trainers evaluate the scheme as a whole. It has five elements:

Step one : Describe what you do already.
Step two : Describe what you are trying to achieve.
Step three : Make it happen.
Step four : Test out your new method.
Step five : Develop and modify your reviewing methods.

Trainee Centred Reviewing is more concerned with the learning or personal development of the student than with assessment and has more in common with the Record of Personal Achievement (RPA) and similar schemes of personal recording. It helps the student to feel more valued and to take a greater responsibility for individual learning. A Diary kept by the student and a simple Personal Profile is often the starting point. The primary focus and outcome of profiling is the widely based assessment of a young person which will help in making decisions about that person. (NPN)

'Reviewing' has now become an integral and often definitive part of many, more assessment-oriented trainee-profile schemes, as we shall see later in this chapter.

Personal achievement records
Another of the early approaches to profiling drew its inspiration jointly from the idea of:
1 defined levels of achievement in a range of skills as pioneered by the SCRE profile assessment system;
2 pupil-initiated and controlled recording as pioneered in the RPA/PPR approaches.

The approach, which was first developed at Evesham High School in Worcestershire (Figure 4.14), is now used in many other schools. Figure 4.13 shows part of the PAR currently in use in Monkscroft School, Gloucestershire. Apart from information on examination results and personal achievements and interests, the bulk of the record is taken up with some 64 criterion-referenced statements of practical, language, maths, and personal and social skills. Students control the completion of the PAR, initiating an assessment by the appropriate member of staff when they feel they are ready. If they are successful, their achievement is recorded with an official stamp.

Designed in close collaboration with local employers, the advantage of this scheme is that it gives all pupils who choose to take part the possibility of achieving a worthwhile record of achievement whilst being relatively simple to operate. The criteria for most of the skills such as 'can type accurately at 25 wpm' are laid down, although others such as 'shows good artistic skill' are clearly still ambiguous.

The disadvantage of the scheme is that it is essentially summative, confined to pupils in the last year or two of schooling and impinging relatively little on the main educational work of the school. However, combining as they do some of the principles of personal recording with an attempt to introduce a measure of

PRACTICAL SKILLS

	Staff	Stamp	Date
1. Has used simple tools safely			
2. Can select appropriate tools			
3. Has used basic machine tools safely			
4. Can understand simple scientific terms			
5. Can make and record accurate measurements or observations			
6. Has read a meter and wired a three-pin plug			
7. Has shown an understanding of the various types of kitchen equipment			
8. Has planned, prepared and served a meal to a guest			
9. Has an understanding of the importance of a balanced diet			
10. Can type accurately at 25 w.p.m.			
11. Can express ideas in sketch or diagram form			
12. Can work accurately from a drawing or pattern			
13. Shows good artistic skill			
14. Can choose and follow a route on a map using a prismatic compass			
15. Can produce guidance and a sketch map to assist a visitor who does not live in Cheltenham			
16. Can use a sewing machine			

Figure 4.13: Extract from Personal Achievement Record, Monkscroft School, Glos. (adapted from High School, Evesham)

PERSONAL AND SOCIAL SKILLS

Staff   Stamp   Date

1. Is normally punctual
2. Understands and can supply simple first aid
3. Can receive and escort school visitors
4. Has been pleasant and well-mannered

LANGUAGE AND MATHS

Staff   Stamp   Date

1. Can convert British to foreign currency using a table
2. Has coped with areas and perimeters of a square, rectangle, circle, triangle
3. Regularly borrows from school library
4. Can make a spoken report

Source: Personal Achievement Record, Evesham High School, Worcs.

Figure 4.14: Extract from Evesham High School Personal Achievement Record

comparability and information on specific skills, the personal achievement records have been highly significant in reinforcing some of the main guiding principles that underlie the contemporary profiling movement.

Comment banks and computers

Comment banks

Comment banks are a relatively recent development among the approaches to profiling. They have received particular support in Wales but are now widely used. Their appeal is that they can cut down the clerical task involved in teachers actually having to write down their comments. Instead, teachers can simply select the appropriate descriptor from an agreed list of appropriate comments. These are then entered into a computer and the resultant profile, when printed out, looks very much like a specially composed report. Three examples are described here to illustrate this approach.

Former Schools Council WJEC* pilot profiles

As a result of field trials of a number of profile models between 1981–83, a draft national profile for Wales was prepared for further development. It involves:

1. The name of the school and the LEA, together with a brief introduction to the underlying philosophy.
2. Individual comment by the Head or Tutor.
3. A prose record on each of three aspects of personal qualities, derived from a comment bank of prepared sentences:
   - Attitude to People
   - Attitude to Activities in School
   - Attitude to Work in School
4. A prose description of communication skills (oral, written and graphic) derived from a comment bank.
5. A prose description of Practical Skills derived from a comment bank.
6. Assessment of various Numerical Skills by five grades.
7. A voluntary contribution by each pupil concerning non-scholastic activities.

Main Considerations

(a) This profile was intended for all pupils at 16+ and should supplement any examination results.
(b) Several teachers should contribute to each profile by use of comment banks.
(c) Only positive statements should be made.
(d) There should be regard for the best use of teachers' time – particular consideration was given to the use of computers with the 'human touch'.
(e) There should be a regular review of the comment banks and in-service training of teachers.
(f) The role of the WJEC to ensure 'national currency' was important.

(SCDC Publications, 1983)

* The Welsh Joint Education Council

Figure 4.15: Comment-bank produced specimen profiles taken from Welsh draft national profile

NAME OF PUPIL .... SIAN THOMAS ....
ATTENDANCE – Year 4 ...... 97% ...
         – Year 5 ...... 89% ...

Tutor's Comments

Sian has shown a very good response to her school courses and to the varied situations she has encountered in school. She has demonstrated a degree of initiative and some self-assurance when these have been required and encouraged. When undertaking school work and extra curricular tasks she has shown application and the capacity to work independently without being supervised. Not a natural extrovert by disposition Sian has, nevertheless, maintained very good relationships with fellow pupils and with staff, respecting their viewpoints and showing understanding. She has a number of varied and impressive interests which can be extended with great profit and we are grateful for the extent to which she has participated in school and community activities. Her community work is most impressive.

Sian has a very pleasant nature and is always cheerfully friendly in conversation. We wish her every success in her continuing efforts.

Signature of Tutor ....

Communication Skills

Sian speaks readily in a small group but is more reluctant to contribute orally during class. She speaks clearly and usually correctly.

Sian can research and organise most information effectively and most written material can be read and understood. She has a feeling for language and uses an appropriate style of writing. Her command of vocabulary is good and she spells and punctuates with acceptable accuracy for most purposes.

Sian can interpret intricate plans, maps, patterns and diagrams. She can select the appropriate form of representation and is able to draw simple diagrams accurately.

Figure 4.15 reproduces some of the original examples used for this scheme in order to illustrate the kind of product that can be produced.

The Clwyd 16+ Profile

Clwyd is one part of Wales where development work has continued most enthusiastically since the publication of the Schools Council for Wales/WJEC document in 1983. Its current scheme, heavily based on comment banks, has now been in use in schools for a number of years. Essentially summative in focus, the profile contains:

● overall comment;
● courses followed in years four and five;
● attendance and punctuality in years four and five;
● numerical skills;
● personal skills and characteristics;
● record of personal interests and achievements;
● school and community service.

Part II of this manual provides a case study of its use in practice.

Most of the comment banks are organised in terms of A 'unqualified praise', B 'qualified praise', C 'some reservations', and D 'more serious reservations',

NAME OF PUPIL .... HUW JONES ...
ATTENDANCE – Year 4 ...... 72% ...
         – Year 5 ...... 79% ...

Tutor's Comments

Though not exceptionally shy Huw has a quiet and reserved nature which at times restricts him expressing his views and opinions. With encouragement he does display some self confidence, and is capable of independent thought and action as his achievements in Autograss racing show. He can adapt to new demands which do not require any drastic change of approach, but he does need assistance and clear guidance if tasks are set in an unfamiliar context. He gets on well with his peers but is often a passive member of the group.

Huw's limited number of CSE entries reflects his academic ability but does not do justice to his diligent effort. We wish him well for the future.

Signature of Tutor ....

Communication Skills

Huw speaks readily in a small group but is more reluctant to contribute orally in class.

Huw can read and understand most simple written material. He can look up information using an index and can extract straightforward facts. His vocabulary is basic but adequate for everyday communication and he can spell and punctuate simple sentences.

Huw can interpret simple plans and diagrams and is able to sketch simple diagrams which do not call for accurate use of scale.

Personal Skills and Characteristics

The method of assessment will be by reference to pre-selected comments (See separate book). The comments are coded and are grouped accordingly. The codes *will not appear* on the final document; the groups are simply for ease of reference by staff and to assist internal communication. They are not grades, and should not be communicated to pupils as if they are. It is possible for teachers to select more than one comment, and from more than one group.

Personal Skills
1. *Numeracy* skills will be assessed by teachers of Mathematics.
2. *Literacy* skills will be assessed by teachers of English, and by any other teacher who wishes to make an assessment.
3. *Oral* skills. These can be commented on by all subject teachers.

Practical, Creative and Physical Skills These should be commented upon by teachers as appropriate, for example:
4. *Practical.* Design subjects, Science, Music, etc.
5. *Creative.* Art, Music, English, etc.
6. *Physical.* Design subjects, Drama, P.E./Games, etc.

The Banks of comments cannot, of course, include every possible talent displayed by pupils. If a skill is not referred to in the bank, the teacher should choose the most appropriate sentence and substitute the required word(s) for the one(s) used in the example.

Personal Qualities

All staff are asked to comment on three areas in which pupils' personal qualities may be observable. These are: Response to Others; Response to work in School and Response to Activities in School. Using the Banks of Comments provided, staff should select *a range* of comments under *each* of *the three headings* and enter the appropriate codes on the group assessment sheet to be handed in to the Form Tutor as required.

Source: adapted from *Profile Reporting in Wales*, SCDC Publications, 1983

Numerical Skills

NAME: JOHN JONES

1.	Whole number	Addition of whole number of any size.	B
		Subtraction of whole numbers of any size.	B
		Multiplication of whole numbers up to 100.	B
		Division of whole numbers by number up to 10 remainder as a fraction.	B
2.	Decimals	Place value	B
		Addition	B
		Subtraction	B
		Multiplication by 2 significant figures	B
		Division by 1 significant figure	B
		Conversion between measures	C
3.	Mental Arithmetic	Simple addition and subtraction	B
		Multiplication tables and multiplication and division of a number with just one non zero digit.	B
4.	Estimation	Multiplication and division	B
		Money	C
		Length	C
		Area	C
5.	Applications	Interpretation of graphs and pictorial data solving problems in percentages and fractional quantities.	C
		Costing problems, calculating bills and earnings.	C
		Practical measure.	C

Explanation of Codes

A. Complete mastery of the process. Can tackle problems in this area.

B. Understands the process. With little help can produce work containing few errors.

C. Generally understands the process but needs help if errors are to be limited.

D. Uncertain grasp of the process. Without considerable help is liable to make numerous errors.

E. Does not show understanding of the process and needs constant help and supervision. Even then errors are numerous.

Source: Clwyd 16+ Profile: Handbook

Figure 4.16a: Comment-bank produced specimen profiles for numerical skills, Clwyd

PERSONAL SKILLS AND CHARACTERISTICS

NAME: JOHN JONES

PERSONAL SKILLS

Practical   John's presentation of practical work is usually neat
              and tidy, and he is able to find appropriate solutions
              to most problems encountered in practical work.

Creative   John's design work is competent and well produced but
              does not display sufficient originality.

Physical   He is well co-ordinated in his movements and has a
              particular interest in and talent for football.

Oral Skills   His natural cheerfulness is very apparent in his
              readiness to communicate socially, though he is less
              fluent in more formal situations.

Literacy   John can sometimes adopt the appropriate style for his
              writing, can organise his work according to a given
              plan and can achieve a degree of accuracy in
              spelling, punctuation and grammar when assisted. He
              can read and understand simple written material and with
              help he can locate and use appropriate sources of infor-
              mation. He can appreciate the work of a writer when it
              appeals directly to him and listens effectively when the
              subject is frequently changed.

PERSONAL SKILLS AND CHARACTERISTICS

NAME: JOHN JONES

PERSONAL QUALITIES

John consistently tries to present his work neatly, and he is usually
able to persevere with a task but has to be actively encouraged to go on
in the face of difficulties. Homework tasks are generally completed
satisfactorily.

He knows when to seek support from adults in resolving conflict situations
and he has proved himself to be generally trustworthy and responsible.

During the last two years especially, his increasing maturity has enabled
him to make a most praiseworthy contribution to school life without diverting
his attention from the pursuit of academic qualifications.

Source: Clwyd 16+ Profile: Handbook

Figure 4.16b: Comment-bank produced specimen profiles for personal skills and characteristics, Clwyd

although 'personal qualities' are covered by a straight list of comments, and numeracy is graded on a five-point scale according to a specific level of attainment achieved in pre-defined operations. The extracts given in Figures 4.16a and 14.16b show what the end product of this approach looks like for John Jones.

The North Warwickshire College of Technology and Art Profile

This scheme, reported in the Further Education Unit publication 'Computer-assisted Profiling' (FEU, 1983) offers another example of the use of comment banks and of how the computer can profitably be involved in the compilation of both formative and summative profiles. The scheme is based on a

... 'master profile' which would cover all, initially low-level, courses across the college.

1 Staff were approached and asked to contribute profile 'grids' for their specific subject areas.

2 Subjects were to be split into their component parts and skills, and, for each 'objective', four levels of achievement were to be defined by a concise statement of what a student could reasonably be expected to do at each of these levels. Four levels were chosen rather than three or five or any other number because it was felt three would not give a sufficient range of achievement while five or more would make the project unwieldy.

3 Staff were asked to write the descriptors in positive terms emphasising what *could* be done by the student at each of the four levels. The levels of achievement were designed to be cumulative so that students would build on each level to reach the next and a statement that, for example, level 2 had been reached would automatically imply that the implicit 'knowledge' for levels 3 and 4 had been achieved (level 1 is high, 4 is low).

4 The descriptors were to be expressed in language understandable to the students concerned as they would be major participants in the process. The distance between the levels of achievement were not to be too large, otherwise real progress in the student's view would be too difficult to achieve.

The descriptors, while defining hoped-for practice, in no way dictate the methods by which subject content should be taught and the profile cannot be regarded simply as a substitute syllabus.

While, for each teacher, assessment is a continuous, on-going process, ideally involving the student in a meaningful dialogue about progress made, it is intended that this should be formalised at regular intervals – perhaps monthly – and, through a process of consultation and negotiation between the teaching team and the student, the progress of each student on each objective be recorded on the documents shown in Figures 4.17a and 4.17b.

In Figure 4.17a, the list on the left-hand side describes the subject areas chosen to be included on the course. Each subject area can be split into 20 sub-sections or 'objectives'. Those squares which are shaded represent objectives not being used on this course.

Each member of staff has one of these sheets for each student, and the member of staff fills in an assessment (numbered 1–4 to match the descriptors) for each objective which he/she feels an interest in. Hence, several staff might fill in assessments for literacy (or some aspects of literacy) while only one member of staff might fill in the Home Economics section.

The course tutor can then collate the grades on to one sheet (as in Figure 4.17b) and transfer these to the computer which will then translate the numbers back into descriptors and display them when required.

There are some subjects like Literacy which go across the curriculum and several staff would therefore have a legitimate claim to contribute to literacy assessment. This has the result of making the student more aware of the interdependency of subject areas which are too often presented as being mutually exclusive. Staff also become much more aware of the content of other subject areas and the way in which their particular discipline may contribute to them.

(FEU, *Computer-assisted Profiling*, 1983)

As in the previous example, there is always a possibility that two or more staff may disagree on the level of achievement of a student on a particular objective. This could be caused by a variety of factors – suitability of teaching methods, relationships between tutor and student or the subjective element in the assessment process. Where the difference cannot be resolved by discussion, the student is given the benefit of the highest level of achievement recorded. Nevertheless this problem – inherent in all the grid-style profiles which include the assessment of cross-curricular skills – has yet to be properly resolved.

The student is also given the opportunity to question the staff's evaluation of his work and to clarify his own self-assessments where these differ from those of his tutors.

Supervisors on work placements also have a very important part to play as members of the assessment team.

The information accumulated from regular assessment meetings is transferred to the computer, and, when required, this can be reproduced on a VDU or a printout of that information. An example of an extract of such a printout is shown in Figure 4.17c.

If the institution is running a course for which the knowledge and skill requirements are already known, then the course outline can be defined prior to the start of the course. If the course is vocationally specific then the course tutor should have a very good idea of what the course content should be and what standards are required of the students by the end of the course. In this situation, the course tutor, in consultation with the teaching team can select from the master profile those subject areas and the specific objectives from within those subject areas which need to be covered on the course (any areas which may be lacking can then be compiled by the relevant 'specialists'). The course tutor then has a complete outline of the course content and can allocate areas to particular staff noting where there are overlaps of subject matter (where two or more staff are concerned with the same content) and where there are marked interdependencies of subject matter. Each member of the course team also has a much clearer idea of what is going on in the other subject areas and how their work contributes to the overall scheme.

The profile also has a valuable role to play in informal learning situations or courses of which the content is not pre-determined. After an initial induction or orientation phase, during which a student may be sampling opportunities, deciding on possible options and settling into the institutional

NWCTA Profile Assessment Scheme

COURSE UPDATE DOCUMENT.

COURSE TITLE: PRE-CARING.

STUDENT:

DATE:

Teacher's Name:

Date:

COURSE SYLLABUS:	1	2	3	4	5	6	7	8	9	10	11	12	13	14	15	16	17	18	19	20
1. Literacy.																				
2. Numeracy.																				
3. SLS.																				
4. Job Seeking.																				
5. Personality.																				
6. Physical Education.																				
7. General Practical Skills.																				
10. Home Economics.																				

COURSE TUTOR: R.225 Int. Tel: 11.

Source: FEU, *Computer-assisted Profiling*, 1983

Figure 4.17a: An individual's assessment sheet: NWCTA profile assessment scheme

NWCTA Profile Assessment Scheme

Teacher's Name:

Date:

COURSE UPDATE DOCUMENT.

COURSE TITLE: PRE-CARING.

STUDENT: A. N. Other

DATE: May 7th 1982

COURSE SYLLABUS:

	1	2	3	4	5	6	7	8	9	10	11	12	13	14	15	16	17	18	19	20
1. Literacy.	1	2	2	3	2	2	2	2	3	3	3	2	2	2	2	2	3	3	2	3
2. Numeracy.	1	1	2		4		1	3		4										
3. SLS.	2	2	3	3	3	3	2	4	3		N/A	3	3	3						
4. Job Seeking.	2	2	2	3	2	2	2													
5. Personality.	2	2	2	1	1	1	1							1	2					
6. Physical Education.						2														
7. General Practical Skills.	2				2	2	1	2												
10. Home Economics.	1	2	2	1	2	2	2	3	2	2	3	2								

COURSE TUTOR: R.225   In. Tel: 11.

Source: FEU, *Computer-assisted Profiling*, 1983

Figure 4.17b: A collated assessment sheet: NWCTA profile assessment scheme

framework, an individual learning agenda can be compiled through negotiation and then student and staff can 'key-in' to the substructure provided by the profile, to chart progress, provide a basis for counselling and give an up-to-date statement of achievement whenever required.

The profile may, therefore, be utilised from an institutionally-determined course approach or from a completely student-centred approach.

(FEU, *Computer-assisted Profiling*, 1983)

This profile scheme is thus very flexible, providing, where desired, a readily accessible and detailed picture of a student's *curriculum*, as well as his or her progress. It lends itself readily to student–staff discussion and negotiation. It is also clearly a stereotyped assessment. Some would argue that this is a more acceptable use of comment banks than the approach developed in Wales which may make many readers think that the assessment they are reading is idiosyncratic and extempore when it is not. The pseudo-personalisation this implies is deeply offensive to some people. Yet others regard it as the best possible compromise between objectivity and subjectivity, creativity and convenience. Certainly the North Warwickshire approach does not produce a picture of the whole person in the way that the Welsh approach does. Rather it is closely modelled on the earlier 'grid-style' approach to profiling which has been adapted to provide for curriculum negotiation and assessment review.

The advent of external validation

Up to this point we have been concerned with 'home-grown' developments, what individual teachers and institutions can do who support the arguments for profiling outlined in Chapter 1 and who aspire to the implementation of them in their own work. But, just as it is difficult, if not impossible, for a teacher to introduce diagnostic and collaborative assessment without the support of the department and the school as a whole, so frustrations will inevitably set in if some way is not found of balancing the public examination system's total dominance of certification procedures by giving summative profiles a measure of their external currency.

Even if many teachers, despite all the problems of time, resources and lack of recognition, continue to maintain their existing enthusiasm for profiles, parents and students are less likely to give their support unless they are convinced that profiles are of value in the market place where qualifications are traded for training and employment. The DES is anxious to introduce national guidelines for such 'records of achievement' by the end of the decade. Many people currently involved in development feel that the imposition of such guidelines will kill the enthusiasm currently inspiring the movement and that the search for a profile with a wider currency is best conducted at a more regional level where local authorities and examination boards can together develop schemes which meet their own priorities.

STUDENT PROFILE ASSESSMENT

Course Title: PRE-CARING

Student:

Date: 07-Jun-82

LITERACY

1.01 READING
Reads fluently without hesitation, and in an intelligent manner, a wide variety of reading material including books, newspapers etc.

1.02 INTERPRETING WRITTEN MATERIAL (PROSE)
Can understand a variety of written material if written in straight-forward manner.

1.03 INTERPRETING DIAGRAMMATIC MATERIAL
Understands most forms of diagrammatic presentations, but unsure about the more complex systems.

1.04 DRAWING DIAGRAMS
Can produce simple sketch maps or diagrams.

1.05 HANDWRITING
Handwriting is clear and easy to read in joined script. Fluent in execution.

1.06 PRESENTATION AND APPEARANCE OF WORK
Work usually shows care in presentation – some room for improvement

1.07 VOCABULARY
Some attempt at developing range of words used. Fluent but limited.

1.08 GRASP OF CONVENTIONAL LETTER LAYOUTS
Can write an acceptable letter observing most of the conventions of letter layout.

1.09 SIMPLE DESCRIPTIONS
Can describe with help how to perform simple operations.

1.1 SIMPLE FACTUAL REPORTS
Can give in a reasonably ordered fashion an account of straight-forward events. May omit points.

1.11 FORM FILLING
Can cope with most forms in a legible and accurate manner.

1.12 USE OF DIRECTORIES, ALPHABETICAL LISTS, INDEXICES etc.
Shows good grasp of alphabetical arrangement and has some knowledge of where to begin to look for information.

1.13 LISTENING
Listens well under ideal conditions – needs reinforcement on instructions.

1.14 PERSONAL ORAL COMMUNICATION
Can cope with most one-to-one encounters. Needs encouragement to sustain interchange.

1.15 GROUP ORAL COMMUNICATION
Will take part if encouraged.

1.16 USE OF TELEPHONE
Can use public and private telephone effectively in most situations.

1.17 SYNTAX
Writes inaccurately constructed simple sentences. Limited use of relative clauses.

1.18 PUNCTUATION
Can use most punctuations accurately.

1.19 SPELLING
Can spell most words accurately.

1.2 ORGANISATION OF IDEAS
Can organise familiar ideas in coherent fashion.

NUMERACY

2.01 FOUR RULES
Can perform a range of skills – perhaps using a calculator for more difficult examples.

2.02 TABLES
Can utilise most tables up to 12 times with acceptable degree of accuracy.

2.03 PLACE-VALUE
Grasps place value significance in most straight-forward examples.

2.05 FRACTIONS–FOUR RULES
Can cope with very straight-forward calculations. May have difficulty in transferring the principles to situations.

2.07 STANDARD UNITS
Conversant with units–can compare imperial with metric and work with some ease in all modes, read timetables etc. Reasonably accurate in estimating. Measures accurately with variety of instruments.

2.08 RATIO AND PROPORTION
Can deal with more straight-forward relationships eg. scaling up a half to a whole number relationship.

2.1 PERCENTAGE
Can cope with most straight-forward examples. Can apply basic ideas to situations under supervision.

SOCIAL AND LIFE SKILLS

3.01 BUDGETING
Can draw up a personal budget sheet and has realistic ideas on possible expenditure.

3.02 PRICE/VALUE–ADVERTS
Can make straight-forward comparisons between sizes and/or prices. Susceptible to forceful advertising.

3.03 BANKS AND BANKING SERVICES
Understands most bank functions but may be reluctant to use them.

3.04 POST OFFICE SERVICES
Understands most of the services offered by the GPO.

3.05 BUILDING SOCIETIES
Has a basic understanding of how a Building Society functions. Could open a savings account or apply for a mortgage with a bit of help.

3.06 INSURANCE
Understands purpose of insurance and how to go about obtaining insurance for various purposes.

3.07 CONSUMER LAW
Is fairly conversant with consumer law and could establish rights in most of the probable instances. Usually demonstrates a constructive and helpful attitude to preservation of law and order.

3.08 LOCAL AUTHORITY SERVICES
Is aware of the main services offered by the local authority. Would know where to get advice if needed eg. CAB.

3.09 LIBRARY SERVICES
Is familiar with the workings of at least one local library, can find information usually without help and knows some of the available ancillary services.

3.11 LEGAL AID
Is aware of rights regarding bail arrest. Knows where to get help eg. Citizens Advice Bureau.

3.12 ACCOMMODATION
Is aware of the main sources of information concerning accommodation. Possesses some of the skills necessary for maintaining property and is aware of major differences between renting and owning.

3.13 FURNITURE/HEATING
May need help in selecting suitable furniture etc.

3.14 EDUCATION SERVICES
Has an incomplete knowledge of the educational facilities in the area. Attitude towards continuing education is ambivalent and easily influenced by peers.

JOB SEEKING

4.01 EMPLOYMENT ASPIRATIONS
Has begun to look at requirements of some job areas, and has begun to make some connections between these and own self-assessment but needs much help and guidance.

4.02 JOB SEEKING
Needs help in exploring sources of situations vacant. Needs help to reach realistic assessment of own preferences, qualities and qualifications, and in selecting an appropriate job.

4.03 APPROACH TO JOB APPLICATIONS
Creates a favourable impression through some preparation and some awareness of the importance of appearance and presentation.

4.04 JOB APPLICATIONS BY 'PHONE
States reason for phone call and takes down basic information accurately. Gives personal particulars accurately.

4.05 JOB APPLICATIONS BY LETTER
Letter reasonably neat with acceptable layout, on adequate stationery. Reasonable structure, spelling and punctuation adequate.

4.06 JOB APPLICATION FORMS
Completes items of factual information accurately but answers other questions only shallowly. 'Undersells' self. Produces a reasonably neat and attractive application.

4.07 INTERVIEWS
Presents self at interview in good time and reasonably well-groomed and dressed. Speaks reasonably well and answers questions adequately. Asks questions of interviewer when given the opportunity.

PHYSICAL EDUCATION

6.06 GROOMING AND HYGIENE
Understands the need for personal hygiene and grooming and can achieve this with some guidance.

Source: FEU, *Computer-assisted Profiling*, 1983

Figure 4.17c: Printout of a profile assessment: NWCTA profile assessment scheme

Profiling for vocational preparation

City and Guilds profiles
The next scheme to be described has proved itself one of the most enduring and influential, in this respect, pioneering the use of external accreditation in profiling, capable of continual development and adaptation as the need arises. Partly for this reason and partly because of their status in relation to a national examining board, varieties of City and Guilds profiles have now been incorporated into a great variety of courses and qualifications associated with both schooling and training situations. More than any other scheme, the history of the various City and Guilds profiles reflects the profiling movement as a whole. Entering the field at an early stage, the CGLI took up and developed the 'grid' approach pioneered in the SCRE profile referred to earlier. With the rapidly growing interest in profiling in the further education world which followed the 1979 publication 'A Basis for Choice' which outlined new approaches to curriculum provision, CGLI have played a key role in the development of the profiling movement as a whole.

Indeed, course-based profiling which is externally accredited in the same way that public examinations are has made by far the greatest progress in the more vocational and training-oriented qualifications which were, until recently, largely the preserve of further education. While the public examination still dominates most school subject teaching, the much more wide-ranging and skill-based goals of vocationally-oriented studies make them an obvious candidate for profiling. The greatly increased number of such courses in recent years – in part through the activities of the Manpower Services Commission – has been a major factor in the growth of interest in profiles.

However, early versions of the City and Guilds profile for their 365 Vocational Preparation Course were extensively criticised for their use of an assessment grid. These criticisms included:
1 the use of *vague descriptors* capable of considerable variations in interpretation such as 'is aware of own personality . . . ' as level 4 of 'social awareness', and 'can appreciate the moral consequences of actions, cope sensibly with moral dilemmas', and
2 the identification of *giant steps* from levels 1–4 in the grid, for example, the basic level 4 'can climb a ladder' becomes at top level 1 'can assemble micro-circuits using a microscope', or in *communication*, level 4 'can write simple messages' becomes 'can communicate both information and argument in written form suiting style to audience and content'.

The existence of only four steps between 'Brooke Bond' (making tea) and 'James Bond' (wiring a microcircuit) made it relatively easy to distinguish between the categories for assessment purposes. It aroused considerable disquiet, however, that students could so readily be summed up in a series of boxes in which frequently it was difficult to distinguish between:
- typical versus 'one-off' performances;
- norm and criterion-based assessments;
- skills and attitudes.

3 The existence of such very general categories made it difficult for students to progress between them so reducing the potential of the profile as a diagnostic, and curriculum-related procedure which would help to encourage students' motivation and be positive for all learners.

It was recognised that the grid model is essentially outward looking and is designed to serve the user, not the student.

In its favour, however, is that it is:
1 easy to fill in
2 compact
3 covers a wide area of skills
4 seems to be more informative

(C. S. Frith and H. G. Macintosh, *A Teacher's Guide to Assessment*, Stanley Thornes, 1984)

As SCRE had before them, the City and Guilds rapidly came to realise that more emphasis should be given to:
1 involving students themselves in the process of formative assessment;
2 providing for collaboration and dialogue between student and tutor;
3 distinguishing between formative and summative purposes in profiling.

As Figure 4.18 shows, both the global, student-centred profiles and the more narrow, course-based profiles which CGLI have developed now incorporate student recording and teacher–student review as well as some kind of check-list.

The current version of the City and Guilds *student-centred profile* now contains information on achievements, experience and interests involving both a formative and a summative stage as Figure 4.19 shows.

There is a strong consensus on which skills contribute to 'maturity' and 'employability', and the following skill areas have continued to feature on City and Guilds profiles through several years of development
- communication
- social (work-context)
- practical
- numerical
- decision making.

These have been sub-divided to give between 12 and 18 profile categories. Experience is taken care of by providing brief descriptions of any work, community or residential experience. Students can bias the reporting of the examples cited within each profile category, thereby reflecting their own interests.

Progress profiles are updated at regular intervals by identifying the steps reached and entering the specific examples that act as evidence. Except in the case of the City and Guilds 365 (in scheme 365, a single profile grid and up to five sets of examples representing vocational options are retained in a

Progress Profile

Name of Centre and Course..

Period covered by this Review From.................... To....................

Signed.................... Signed....................
(Trainee/Student) (Supervisor/Tutor)

Main Activities	ABILITIES	EXAMPLES OF ABILITIES		PROGRESS IN ABILITIES	
COMMUNICATION	TALKING AND LISTENING	Can make sensible replies when spoken to	Can hold conversations and can take messages	Can communicate effectively with a range of people in a variety of situations	Can present a logical and effective argument. Can analyse others arguments
	READING	Can read words and short phrases	Can read straightforward messages	Can understand a variety of forms of written materials	Can select and judge written materials to support an argument
	WRITING	Can write words and short phrases	Can write straightforward messages	Can write reports describing work done	Can write a critical analysis using a variety of sources
PRACTICAL & NUMERICAL	USING EQUIPMENT	Can use equipment safely to perform simple tasks under guidance	Can use equipment safely to perform a sequence of tasks after demonstration	Can set up and use equipment to produce work to standard	Can identify and remedy common faults in equipment
	NUMERACY (1)	Can count and match objects, can recognise numbers	Can add and subtract whole numbers to solve problems	Can add, subtract and convert decimals and simple fractions	Can multiply and divide decimals and simple fractions
SOCIAL	WORKING IN A GROUP	Can cooperate with others when asked	Can work with other members of the group to achieve common aims	Can be an active and decisive member of a group	Can adopt a variety of roles in a group
	ACCEPTING RESPONSIBILITY	Can follow instructions for simple tasks and carry them out under guidance	Can follow instructions for simple tasks and carry them out independently	Can perform a variety of tasks effectively given minimal guidance	Can assume responsibility for delegated tasks and take initiative
DECISION-MAKING	PLANNING	Can identify the sequence of steps in everyday tasks, with prompting	Can describe the sequence of steps in a routine task, after demonstration	Can choose from given alternatives the best way of tackling a task	Can create new plans/routines from scratch
	COPING	Can cope with everyday activities	Can cope with everyday problems. Seeks help if needed	Can cope with changes in familiar routines	Can cope with unexpected or unusual situations
	OBTAINING INFORMATION	Can ask for needed information	Can find needed information with guidance	Can use standard sources of information	Can extract and assemble information from several given sources

| | | | | | | Can help others to solve problems |
| | | | | | | Can show initiative in seeking and gathering information from a wide variety of sources |

Main Activities	ABILITIES	EXAMPLES OF ABILITIES		PROGRESS IN ABILITIES	
ADDITIONAL	WORKING WITH CLIENTS	Can help someone to carry out clients requests	Can carry out clients requests under supervision	Can carry out clients requests without supervision	Can anticipate and fulfil clients needs from existing resources
	USING SIGNS AND DIAGRAMS	Can recognise everyday signs and symbols	Can make use of simple drawings, maps, timetables	Can make use of basic graphs, charts, codes, technical drawings with help	Can interpret and use basic graphs, charts and technical drawings unaided
	NUMERACY (2)	Can estimate answers to tasks involving whole numbers, decimals and simple fractions	Can calculate percentages and averages	Can solve problems involving simple ratios and proportions	Can express a problem in terms of a simple formula and solve it
	SAFETY	Can remember safety instructions	Can explain the need for safety rules	Can spot safety hazards	Can apply safe working practices independently
	COMPUTER APPRECIATION	Can recognise everyday uses of computers	Can use keyboard to gain access to data	Can enter data into the systems using existing programs	Can identify potential applications for computers

| | | | | | | Can suggest realistic improvements to services for clients |
| | | | | | | Can construct graphs and extract information to support conclusions |

Source: City and Guilds of London Institute, 1984

Figure 4.18: *CGLI progress profile*

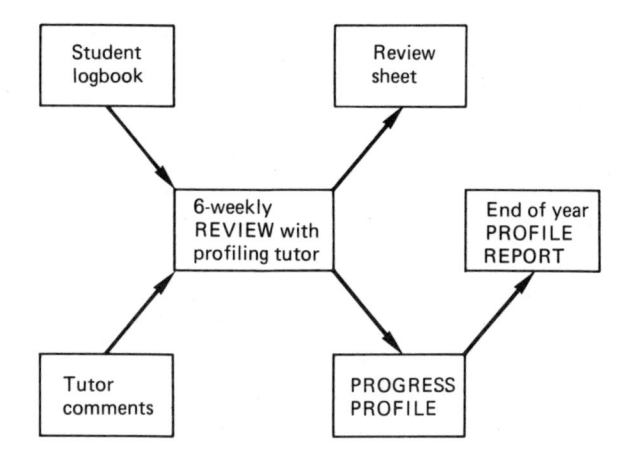

```
┌──────────┐          ┌──────────┐
│ Student  │          │  Review  │
│ logbook  │          │  sheet   │
└────┬─────┘          └────▲─────┘
     │                     │
     ▼                     │
  ┌─────────────────┐   ┌──────────┐
  │    6-weekly     │   │End of year│
  │  REVIEW with    │──▶│  PROFILE │
  │ profiling tutor │   │  REPORT  │
  └────▲────────────┘   └──────────┘
       │           │         ▲
       │           ▼         │
  ┌──────────┐  ┌──────────┐
  │  Tutor   │  │ PROGRESS │
  │ comments │  │ PROFILE  │
  └──────────┘  └──────────┘
```

Source: N. Stratton, *Profiling Systems*, CGLI, 1985

Figure 4.19: CGLI reviewing and profiling system

folder [i.e. no selection is made]), selections are made at the last review for transfer to the profile report. This section is on the basis of 'best, consistent performance'. The trend is towards eliminating the grid 'scaffolding'. This has the effect of placing greater weight on the examples, which then serve to interpret the general 'can do x' statements.

The particular format chosen for the profile report depends in large degree on the logistics of its production. Once student and tutor have made their selections, and these have been proof-read (and spot-checked) by a visiting assessor, the report may be produced either
a) centrally by City and Guilds – typified by YTS profiles.
b) locally (by the centre) – typified by scheme 365 and the current schools pilot.
c) part centrally ('can do x' statements) and part locally (examples and experience) – typified by CPVE and some YTS schemes.

The reporting principles can be stated as follows:
a) positive achievement only is reported.
b) the 'can do x' statements are to be understood by reference to the specific examples that follow.
c) hence the report is not to an absolute standard, but rather relative. When interpreting the 'can do x' statements, individual users are treated as self-consistent, but not necessarily in agreement with others elsewhere.
d) redundant and possibly misleading information is eliminated.
e) the report is highly structured (reflecting the progress profiles) so that pertinent information can be located quickly.
f) context is provided by listing courses or a programme of work, and also describing any work experience, etc.
g) reliability (and hence credibility) is maintained via the systematic reviewing and profiling system.
h) student, tutor and assessor are all party to the report.

i) the report is produced to a high standard, so enhancing its status.

'*Method of compilation* The pupils are issued with a small four ring A5 size log book.

In the *first* part (blue) of the log book pupils are invited to keep a RECORD of their progress (say twice a week), both in school and out of school. They are asked to relate their entries to the eighteen CGLI categories and, where an entry fits, to place a tick against the relevant heading. If they believe their progress merits recognition as one of the five stages of the progress profile, they may enter also the appropriate letter (A, B, C or D or E where D or E represents the most demanding performance in each category). In this they may be assisted by their tutor.

The 18 Categories are these:

Talking and Listening	Safety
Writing	Numeracy I
Reading	Numeracy II
Signs and Diagrams	Working with Clients
Computers	Responsibility
Equipment	Planning
Creating	Information
Classifying	Assessing Results
Coping	Working in Groups

The *second* part of the log book (pink) is the Comment Section where the pupil's reactions to courses, any personal difficulties, interests or hopes may be recorded.

The *third* part of the book (green) deals with the results of the REVIEW, where acting together the pupil and tutor identify and cite evidence
(a) the degree of progress made in each of the categories.
(b) relative strengths and weaknesses, to guide future work.

Each category is regarded as a discrete area with four or five statements of increasingly demanding performance; there is no longer an overall grid.

The *final* section of the log book deals with the Profile Report which will carry 12 of the pupil's best main activities taken from the Progress Profile, a statement of best consistent performance, together with an example for each category, plus details of the courses taken and other information, such as work experience or awards gains.' (NPN)

At regular intervals, reviews are held between student and tutor at which progress under the various profile headings is plotted. At a final review, the student and tutor agree on the information to be transferred to the Profile Report, and both parties sign the document.

City and Guilds appoints a Visiting Assessor, who visits the school or college to check that the profiling and reviewing system is operating smoothly. The Assessor also countersigns the Profile Reports on behalf of City and Guilds and conducts spot-checks on their accuracy.

CITY AND GUILDS PROFILE REPORT (student name)
HASLINGDEN HIGH SCHOOL

      (student)
      (tutor)   (C & G Monitor)

COURSES

English	C.S.E.
Arithmetic	"
Social Studies	"
Urban Studies	"
Religious Education	"
Human Biology	"

MAIN ACTIVITIES
   'Keep fit' (at home)
   Working part-time at garage video shop
   Household duties
   Hospital visits

***

PROFILE OF ACHIEVEMENT

TALKING AND LISTENING

Can communicate effectively with a range of people in a variety of circumstances e.g. takes messages over phone at garage and talks with elderly patients on hospital visits.

WRITING

Can write straight forward instructions and explanations e.g. C.S.E. project work and writes down messages taken over phone at video centre.

READING

Can follow straight forward written instructions and explanations e.g. follows directions in cookery books and written instructions/procedures left for her at a garage where she has a part-time job.

USING SIGNS AND DIAGRAMS

Can make use of simple drawings, maps and diagrams e.g. uses diagrams in Biology practical lessons and maps in Urban Studies.

COMPUTER APPRECIATION

Can recognise everyday uses of computers e.g. has read basic instructions and used computer for 'games'.

USING EQUIPMENT

Can use equipment safely to perform a sequence of tasks after demonstration e.g. helped to set up and use trampoline in P.E. lessons and used cash desk at garage.

SAFETY

Can spot hazards e.g. fire precautions at garage and safety procedures on hospital wards at hospital.

NUMERACY (1)

Can add and subtract whole numbers to solve problems e.g. handles money when serving at garage.

CREATING

Can copy others ideas/work with help e.g. bakes at home and is starting to learn how to play the organ.

CLASSIFYING

Can identify objects using classifying manuals e.g. uses recipe books for cooking and stock lists at video centre.

WORKING IN A GROUP

Can work with other members of a group to achieve common aims e.g. work with other staff at garage and helps nurses on hospital visits.

WORKING WITH CLIENTS

Can anticipate and fulfil clients needs from existing resources e.g. helps to feed and wash patients at hospital and is left unsupervised at video centre.

ACCEPTING RESPONSIBILITY

Can follow a series of instructions and carry them out independently e.g. practical work in Biology lessons, has also 'taken stock' and served at garage.

PLANNING

Can describe the sequence of steps in a routine task after demonstrating e.g. makes beds and feeds patients at hospital.

OBTAINING INFORMATION

Can use standard sources of information e.g. library books for project work and price/stock lists at garage.

ASSESSING OWN RESULTS

Can assess own results with guidance e.g. checks with manageress at garage on best ways to carry out tasks.

COPING

Can cope with unexpected or unusual situations e.g. had to deal with shoplifter at garage and had to cope when her grandad fell from ladder, injuring his leg and suffering from shock.

Source: Guidance to Employers for City and Guilds Profile Report
Figure 4.20: CGLI Profile Report

Figure 4.20 shows what the final report might look like in practice.

CGLI Course-Based Profiles
City and Guilds course-based profiles are somewhat similar in approach, if more precisely focussed in their objectives. The CGLI outlines a basic framework and suggests a number of objectives, which ought to be achieved on a Vocational Preparation course. The term Voc. Prep. is understood in terms of students, who are not yet committed to a particular career direction, and so is in the nature of an exploratory experience. Learning is intended to be experience-based and practical, and the theme is learning by doing. The scheme has three component parts.

I The Common Core
    1) Communications. 2) Numeracy. 3) Economic, Social and Environmental Studies. 4) Extension Studies. 5) Guidance Education.
II Vocational Studies – studying at least three distinct vocational areas.
III An integrated approach to I and II.

The individual school or college works out a potential scheme of work, which could be a suitable base for negotiation with students, and then submits it to CGLI for approval.

Having followed the course the students are assessed:

a) By external examination in Literacy and Numeracy at two distinct levels.

b) By 'profiling' on a grid system.
c) By external moderation of coursework.

In a typical school operating this scheme, each student keeps a daily log book recording experiences and activities, and reflections upon them. The tutors regularly discuss students' progress with them, and negotiate the next stage of development. Every half term or so the team of Voc. Prep. tutors will meet to discuss the individual student's progress in the 4 areas.

1) Communication 2) Practical and Numerical
3) Social 4) Decision Making.
Each category is further sub-divided.

During the meeting tutors will discuss which level of competence the student has reached in each of these sub-divisions. They present their evidence to their colleagues, and the agreed level of competence is shaded in on the grid. The evidence is then marked on Sheet One. One of the Core Tutors discusses the teachers' estimates of standards reached with the individual students. By the end of the course the student will have had five assessments made on their work, and the final assessment will be the final summative assessment for the student. The student will leave the course with:

1 A Certificate stating that the course has been pursued.
2 A Profile which states competencies in basic abilities.
3 A Profile on Economic, Social and Environmental Studies.
4 A Folder of Assignments, and Records of Experience.

(Stratton, 1985)

CGLI in practice Comment by a teacher involved in the scheme

Having used the GGLI Grid system I would wish to make the following comments. The Grid system does not cover traditional subject headings, and makes no pretences in this direction. The official publicity leaflet says: 'The programme will enable the student to develop a range of skills to a significant level' (CGLI, 1984).

What is contained in the Grid is in fact a range of skills, and the Grid Profile makes a number of 'CAN' statements. (What the student can do.) In that some of these skills are related to the individual as an individual and as a member of a group (e.g. the two categories SOCIAL and DECISION MAKING) the profile reports on Personal Qualities. The Profile however does not comment on personal interests – this is in fact recorded in a separate folder by the student in our school, and this folder contains a record of personal achievements in any area in which the student wishes to acquire data.

It is easy to say what the Profile contains, but much more difficult to say whether or not the picture obtained is a fair one. Certainly we have experienced a number of problems in trying to operate this Grid system. Each sub-skill is divided into five levels of competence. The first problem encountered was: what do the 'CAN' statements actually mean? When a group of tutors came to discuss the assessment the problem of meaning became acute, and I am tempted to ask, 'did we always all understand the same thing by the statements?' Different tutors who taught different aspects of the course often found it difficult to come to common agreement on which level of competence in a skill a student had reached. For example, three tutors might think that a student had reached level 4 in a particular skill, two tutors might think that a student had only reached level 2. How then do you decide which area of the chart to shade in? Is it the highest level thought to be reached, or the lowest level, or do you take a majority verdict? Would a majority verdict be an accurate reflection of what had been achieved or might there in fact be genuine differences between aspects.

The next problem encountered was partly a structural one (but not entirely so). When the Grid is turned on its side and the relevant areas shaded in, it has the appearance of a bar/column graph, and to the unwary this might suggest that level three, for example, along the whole range of skills was a similar kind of measurement, or comparable level of skill. E.g. 'Can hold conversations and take messages' is somehow to be equated with 'Can use equipment safely' or 'Can describe the sequences of steps in a routine task'. In fact these skill achievements cannot really be compared with each other. How can they be compared? Yet a bar chart gives the impression that they are comparable.

Connected with this structural problem is also the suggestion (implied) that each skill can be readily broken down into 5 levels of equal proportions, but when we look at the 5 levels of Computer Appreciation, for example, we find:
1. Can recognise the everyday uses of computers
2. Can use keyboard to gain access to system
3. Can enter data into the system using existing programs
4. Can identify potential applications for computers
5. Can construct error free programs.

Are these five steps of increasing difficulty? Might it not be possible for students to master skills 2, 3 and 5, before having a grasp of levels 1 and 4? Is there a confusion of 'skill' and 'appreciation'? Do we not have unequal steps here? Putting statements on a grid, and giving an equal number of levels to each skill creates problems for grid users, let alone grid designers. We experienced this kind of problem with a number of different skill areas on this particular grid.

When we stopped to ask questions about levels of competence reached we met the problem of subjectivity – 'Do I think that the student can do this?' and 'What is the status of my opinion?'

Even when we had a piece of work at hand, it sometimes became difficult to infer a level reached, from a task completed. Was the inference made necessarily a correct one?

If we look at the levels of competence for 'Obtaining Information', we see another problem. The levels described are:
1. Can ask for needed information.
2. Can find needed information with guidance.
3. Can use standard sources of information.
4. Can extract and assemble information from several given sources.
5. Can show initiative in seeking and gathering information from a wide variety of sources.

On the surface these descriptors seem to be very reasonable, but what do they actually mean? Could they not equally be used to mean the standards reached by a CSE candidate and a postgraduate student. What I am suggesting is that these seemingly straightforward statements have to be interpreted, and interpreted in a context. If an outsider looks at a Profile, does he not have to read context into the document, or is he left wondering what the statement really does mean? Are the descriptors useful descriptions, or are they too vague to be meaningful?

The Grid Profile does in fact attempt to give more information than a traditional certificate on completion of a course. (CSE Grade 4 or 'O' level Grade C are significantly lacking in real information.) The profile does really try to give information about what a student can actually do, and yet, as I have tried to indicate, a number of practical problems are experienced when we try to give a more detailed account. Whether the problems are merely due to profiling being a comparatively new approach, or whether they are fundamental and inherent to the system will remain to be seen.

(R. C. Sims, *The Strengths and Weaknesses of Profiles*, 1985)

The problem identified here by Sims is one that is indeed central to profiling. At the present time, many schemes are working on ways of refining the 'grid' approach to develop, for example, 'sentences' or other varieties of empirically explicit, behavioural descriptors which will not be ambiguous in this way. The problem arises, however, that any such descriptors will have to be so narrow as to make it likely that the goal of *broadening* the assessment process which is at the heart of profiling will be forfeited.

One way of getting round this problem is to make a compromise between the ready comparability that the grid structure provides and the greater flexibility and acceptability of the more traditional approach of teachers' comments. But where more open-ended comments are used, great care will have to be taken to avoid the more common pitfalls as set out below.

Categories of Comments to Avoid
Global judgements
- outstanding and highly intelligent
- completely lacking manual skills
- uncooperative and rude
- inarticulate and confused
- quiet, shy and always pleasant

Confusing
- a satisfactory effort yet needs to concentrate more
- a very decided improvement but has slipped back in some areas
- excellent work that has resulted in limited success
- a high degree of mastery of fundamentals
- generally cooperative but tends to work in isolation

Shallow
- capable of better work
- would do better if tried harder
- making satisfactory progress
- if more interest were shown, attainment would be higher

Jargon
- restricted by poor language acquisition
- slight dyslexia is impeding comprehension, lacks coordination in motor skills
- has difficulty in moving from the concrete to the abstract

Gender stereotypes
- a pleasant and cooperative girl
- she presents her work neatly and attractively
- she is a quiet and unobtrusive student
- he is energetic and enterprising
- he is boisterous yet talented
- he is decisive
- she is flighty

Source: D. Suggett, *Guidelines for Descriptive Assessment*, VIJE, Australia, 1985

Partnership profiling initiatives

As we have seen, the early years of profiling were mainly characterised by the development of two or three highly influential prototypes, notably Don Stansbury's RPA, the SCRE Profile and slightly later the Evesham PAR. This was followed by an explosion of development work in individual schools anxious to institute their own profile so that whereas in her 1981 Survey for the Schools Council, Jan Balogh could only find some nine schemes which properly fulfilled her criteria of a profile, in 1986 the National Profiling Network has over 200 individual schemes registered with it.

Meanwhile, following the lead of the further education examination boards – notably, as we have seen, the City and Guilds of London Institute and the Royal Society of Arts – examination boards and local authorities began to get interested in developing profiles with a wider and more official currency. The intention was to bring profiling firmly within the umbrella of the examinations boards and thus give it an unprecedented degree of kudos and selection currency. Since that time, more and more of the new schemes that are now developing have involved liaison with an examination board as the putative validator of the scheme. Now, most of the examination groups are involved in profile development in some way, a trend that, as we have already seen, has been encouraged by a series of government curriculum and training initiatives such as the Technical and Vocational Education Initiative (TVEI), the Certificate of Pre-Vocational Education (CPVE) and the Youth Training Scheme (YTS), all of which are sufficiently different from conventional academic courses in their approach to make profiling a much more suitable form of assessment.

Other contemporaneous developments in the assessment field including graded-tests, credit accumulation schemes and modular courses as well as the major reform of 16+ examining represented in GCSE, have helped to foster a climate of radical change in assessment procedures and to allow new principles of certification at the end of compulsory schooling to become dominant. It remains to be seen how far the government's commitment to instituting records of achievement for all school-leavers by the end of the decade and the pilot schemes it has initiated to this end will link up with the other changes in 16+ examinations scheduled to take place at the same time to bring about national guidelines for records of achievement as an active reality.

Meanwhile it is certain that several of the profiling schemes currently being developed will have a wide take-up. One of these is OCEA. In November 1982, the Oxford Delegacy of Local Examinations, the Oxford University Department of Educational Studies and four LEAs – Coventry, Leicestershire, Somerset and Oxfordshire – joined together to develop a new certificate – The Oxford Certificate of Educational Achievement – due to be launched nationally in September 1987. The rationale for this new initiative was described in March 1984 as follows:

THE PRINCIPLES UNDERLYING THE OXFORD CERTIFICATE OF EDUCATIONAL ACHIEVEMENT

The Intention
The Oxford Certificate of Educational Achievement is designed to offer a wide-ranging response to the whole spectrum of achievement and experience at school. It will be a means of expressing more of the complete person rather than focussing on narrow and isolated abilities.

The Means
OCEA will have three components.
1 There will be a description of the student's experiences, attainments, interests and skills. This will be the P-component.

   The P-component will help the student identify, assess the value of, articulate and record experiences. This process is formative in itself because it leads to enhanced self-awareness in the student. It does not set goals or imply mastery. There is no predetermined hierarchy of experiences against which the student is measured.

2 There will be an explicit record of achievements within the curriculum. Initially, these will be in mathematics, English, science and modern languages but both the range of subjects and their definition may change. This will be the G-component.

   The G-component will help the student to see the extent of a curriculum area and to progress within it. The student's achievements are identified within the whole framework of potential achievement in the area so defined; the potential achievements are predetermined and defined by explicit criteria. The student is measured against the subject since the assessments are criterion-referenced. The achievements may be attained throughout the student's educational experience. This component will recognise and celebrate success rather than indicate failure.

3 There will be a record of all external examination results achieved by the student throughout a school career. This will be the E-component.

   The E-component provides the opportunity to record achievements in existing externally-set examinations such as GCE, CSE, RSA, CGLI and BTEC. Such examinations give the students the chance to relate individual attainments to externally-set standards and to the performance of others. Assessments within such examinations are often aggregated for the purpose of comparing one student with another.

The Certificate
OCEA will offer students frequent and positive recognition of achievement, a positive response to their individual activities and enthusiasms, the identification of goals for further progress and a stimulus to achieve them. In this way, it will enable students to take an active part in the assessment and description of their own development. The assessment process will draw on the student's complete secondary career.

It will also offer schools a coherent and systematic internal monitoring procedure, an informative document for student transfer and a valuable stimulus for curriculum and in-service education. Other users of the certificate, such as employers and further and higher education, will have a full record of the student's achievements, activities and enthusiasms to help them select individuals for jobs and courses.

OCEA is a complete certificate. Each student is seen not as a bundle of parts but as a whole. Within the constituent parts of OCEA, all important talents, skills and attitudes will find balanced representation. The three components of OCEA, no one of which predominates, are designed to give detailed expression to the development of all students in a school throughout their secondary careers. OCEA is an initiative in which, for the first time, assessment procedures are designed to encourage necessary and appropriate curriculum development. The introduction of OCEA will provide schools and colleges with the opportunity for the development of curriculum and organisation of timetables.

(OCEA, 1984. Reproduced by permission of University of Oxford)

The procedure is currently being piloted in schools in each of the four LEAs and in schools that have no local authority support for OCEA, including one independent school and one overseas. Each individual school will have to apply for accreditation as an OCEA centre (see Chapter 7). Individual certificates will not be moderated by the Oxford Delegacy. Rather, following the model currently being aspired to by most such large-scale record of achievement schemes, it is the school, rather than the pupils' work, which will be subject to scrutiny with a view to accreditation, an approach widely used by the City and Guilds Profiling Scheme already described. It will therefore require a major commitment on the part of schools to organisation as well as curriculum.

Modular profiling systems

One of the most recent development areas in the field of profiling which has been encouraged by the advent of examination board involvement discussed in the previous section, is that of modular accreditation. Very much on the lines of the Scottish 'Action Plan' mentioned earlier in this chapter, a number of initiatives are now emerging in which a course has been divided up into a series of modules or units, each with its own objectives and assessment criteria, from which the student makes a selection to construct his or her own curriculum. The student's path through the course is typically supported by the keeping of a personal diary in which the student records progress achieved and by regular review meetings between student and tutor. The final 'record of achievement' awarded is likely to contain several elements – units completed and information on personal and work experience. The significance of this profiling approach is its association with a quite novel curriculum design. In this case, profiling is no longer simply a record of assessments made, it becomes also the curriculum and the scheme of work. To clarify these points, I have included three currently very influential examples – the Certificate of Pre-Vocational Education; the Two Year Youth Training Scheme Certificate; and the Northern Partnership for Records of Achievement.

The Certificate of Pre-Vocational Education (CPVE)
A new one-year full-time pre-vocational course, the CPVE was set up following the publication of '17+: A New Qualification' by the DES in 1982. Run by a Joint Board of BTEC and City and Guilds representatives, it is now in its pilot phase. In the following extract R. C. Sims describes the new qualification from a teacher's point of view.

Profiling is expected to form some part of the assessment, both in the formative process and in the summative certification. During the pilot stage schools may use any existing profiling scheme. The conditions for certification require 'a system of formative assessment, review and profiling based on core and vocational studies to provide evidence for the summative national profile'.

It is anticipated that information received from centres in the form of statements on each of TEN Core areas (made up from a bank of general descriptors which are being developed by the Joint Board) will be moderated and published centrally as part of the Certificate.

The CORE areas are these:
Communications
Numeracy
Science and Technology
Industrial, Social and Environmental Studies
Information Technology
Personal and Career Development
Problem Solving
Practical Skills
Social Skills
Creative Development
Note In addition to the compulsory CORE, studies will be delivered against a vocational base, which will be one or more of these five *vocational* studies:
Business and Administrative Services
Technical Support Services
Production
Distribution
Services to People'

(NPN, February 1985)

Students have to follow at least four modules and are offered a choice of occupational categories. There are three different levels of module.
1) Introductory 2) Exploratory 3) Preparatory
The student may choose his four from one level or from different levels. Some of this work, at least 20 per cent of it, has to be integrated into the Core Area.

In addition, there are extension studies which can be defined in any way the school or student chooses, but must take up no more than 25 per cent of student time. The Joint Board has produced a detailed two volume guide in the form of advice and objectives, and invited institutions to submit schemes based on this document for approval (similar to 365).

At the end of the course the student will receive:
1 a Certificate;
2 a Profile;
3 a Record of Activities undertaken.
The Profile is to be based on the 10 Core areas. It is intended that profiling be a formative activity, which eventually leads to a summative statement. The Board's suggestions are shown in Figure 4.21.

```
                Student and Tutor Review
    AGENDA                          TASK SHEET
    Discussion of work              Description of
    Work experience                 tasks
    General activities
    Hopes, aspirations,
       fears and weaknesses
```

```
    BANK OF STATEMENTS FOR ACHIEVED OBJECTIVES
```

```
    STUDENT PORTFOLIO           SUMMARY OF EXPERIENCE
    Summary of task sheets      Details of work
    for selected pieces of      experience, community
    work with an index          service, service to
                                the school
```

```
              SUMMATIVE PROFILE
```

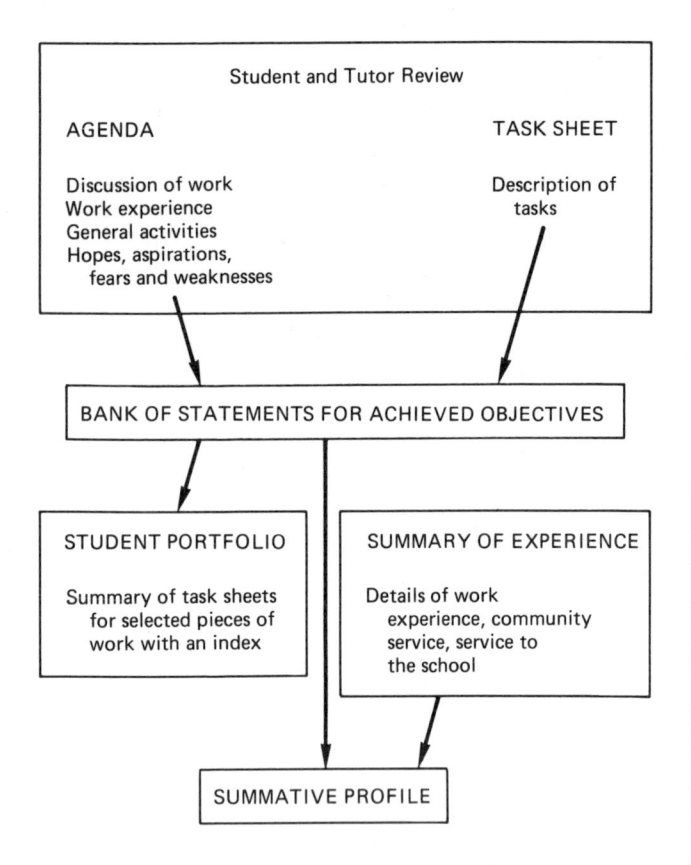

Figure 4.21: Essential features of a formative profiling system in CPVE

The Draft Profile offers a Bank of Statements from which relevant statements may be drawn. The relevant statements will then be printed on a summative profile. The idea of a grid system has been abandoned.

The Bank of Statements relate the 10 Core Areas of the scheme, and each core area is broken down into a number of factors, viz.,

Personal and Social Development	2
Industrial, Social and Environmental	6
Communications	9
Social Skills	5
Numeracy	9
Science and Technology	4
Information Technology	5
Creative Development	4
Practical Skills	5
Problem Solving	5
TOTAL	54

i.e. students will have 54 statements on the profile.

In the Bank of Statements for a given factor the number of descriptors varies from one to six. Performance within some factors is described by a single statement indicating that only one level of performance is considered to be relevant to CPVE. Where more than one statement is given, the statements are meant to be hierarchical. In this case the statement which goes on the final profile will be the one that indicates final level of achievement.

There is no attempt here to divide artificially each factor into a set number of different skill levels. The individual levels of performance within a factor are distinguished by features such as:
1 increasing autonomy of the student in the skill e.g. factor 04;
2 increasing complexity of application of the skills e.g. factor 51.

The final profile will look very similar to the RSA Voc. Prep. Profile. Figure 4.22c shows a draft proforma. The RSA profile, however, is based on a set number of objectives, and for each objective achieved a student will receive one descriptor. The CPVE profile shows no similar equation. The CPVE Handbook (1985) includes so many objectives that it is considered impossible to give separate descriptors for each objective. The Joint Board have therefore made one descriptor fit a number of objectives.

A perusal of the draft profile will show that it contains no reference to traditional subject labels. The new CPVE has been based on the idea of a Core Curriculum, pioneered in the FEU's 1979 publication 'A Basis for Choice', rather than the 1977 Keohane Report's single subject ideas. The Bank of Statements covers skills, and levels of achievement in those skills.

In so far as personal qualities are linked up with skills they will be documented, but generally personal qualities and interests will not come out on the profile. These are much more likely to come out in the summary of experience.

(R. C. Sims, *The Strengths and Weaknesses of Profiling*, 1985)

Reports of student attainment in the core competences will be made on the student summative profile.

The regulations for CPVE require that all students have the opportunity to address all core aims, and it is therefore likely that all students will have at least one core competence statement under each aim. It is not mandatory for students to have statements under all factors.

At the end of the course the centres will draw up a list of the core competence statements achieved by each student. This will be monitored by the Joint Board's moderator who may wish to refer to the student's portfolio for evidence of attainment.

Once approved by the moderator the list for each student must be forwarded to the Joint Board on the form provided for this purpose. The list will then be printed on the student's summative profile.

(CPVE Handbook, 1986)

The CPVE incorporates one of the most far-reaching and novel profiling schemes so far developed. It will certainly be apparent to readers that the profiling schemes now being developed are considerably more *complex* than the early examples described. This is probably inevitable when the cardinal principle of assessment breadth which characterises all such schemes becomes linked with efforts to standardise and

City and Guilds of London Institute   **Business & Technician Education Council**

JOINT BOARD FOR PRE-VOCATIONAL EDUCATION
46 Britannia Street, London WC1X 9RG   Telephone 01-278 2468

```
                  CERTIFICATE OF PRE-VOCATIONAL EDUCATION

                            SUMMARY OF EXPERIENCE


    NAME: _____


    CENTRE: _____



    Period covered by this summary (dates): Start _____ End _____


    This Summary of Experience should be read in conjunction with the
    CPVE Profile which it supplements. The experiences described below
    and the selected items of work listed overleaf are given in greater
    detail within the Portfolio of students' work

            Note: within this space should be provided a student's
            eye view of the course which might embrace core and
            vocational studies of particular interest as well as
            special experiences which are seen to have been valuable
            to the students' development and progress on the course.
            Mention should always be made to the work experience
            element of the course.











            Signed (Student) _____    Date _____


            Signed (Tutor) _____     Date _____
```

Figure 4.22a: CGLI/BTEC first draft CPVE: summary of experience sheet

SELECTED ITEMS OF WORK

The following items of work have been picked from the Student's portfolio to illustrate the core statements made on the profile and to reflect the student's interests.

TASK DESCRIPTION	MOST RELEVANT CORE AREAS

Source: CPVE Handbook

Figure 4.22b: CGLI/BTEC first draft CPVE: selected items of work sheet

NUMERACY CAN carry out calculations involving decimals, fractions and percentages. CAN carry out simple mental calculations. CAN make sensible use of calculator. CAN use imperial and metric units. CAN select and use an appropriate instrument to make a measurement. CAN make reasonable estimates of size and quantity. CAN use simple statistical and graphical techniques to analyse data. CAN construct and interpret charts diagrams and drawings. CAN apply simple geometric techniques to solve problems.

PROBLEM SOLVING CAN distinguish between problems which can be solved personally, and those which should be referred. CAN identify and describe alternative approaches to solving a problem. CAN show initiative in seeking and gathering information from a wide variety of sources. CAN evaluate alternative solutions to a given problem and select the most appropriate. CAN apply problem solving techniques to new situations. CAN produce realistic plan for future development.

PRACTICAL SKILLS CAN recognise own potential and preference, having sampled a range of practical activities. CAN select and use suitable equipment and materials to complete a task to an appropriate standard. CAN perform tasks requiring a high degree of accuracy and manual dexterity to a given standard. CAN adapt practical skills to new situations.

SCIENCE & TECHNOLOGY CAN describe the relationship between science technology and society. CAN suggest appropriate solutions to technical or scientific problems. CAN set up, carry out and record experiments systematically and accurately. CAN recognise the scientific facts, laws, principles and generalisations underlying investigations and problems.

SOCIAL SKILLS CAN play an effective leading role in the work of a group. CAN operate effectively in a range of group situations. CAN recognise the validity of other peoples opinions. CAN recognise the influence of differing roles on behaviour. CAN assess the effects of categorising people and respond appropriately.

PERSONAL & CAREER DEVELOPMENT CAN adapt quickly to new situations taking advantage of personal capabilities. CAN take responsibility in setting personal goals and can make a realistic assessment of personal achievements. CAN recognise the need for personal and career guidance.

CREATIVE DEVELOPMENT CAN justify opinions on a range of product designs and creative activities. CAN identify opportunities for creative activity in a variety of situations. CAN apply own creative and expressive skills. CAN respond to a range of cultural activities drawn from own and other cultures.

INDUSTRIAL SOCIAL & ENVIRONMENTAL STUDIES CAN cope with own financial and legal responsibilities. CAN deal with appropriate financial legal and social institutions to achieve an aim. CAN describe the functions and operation of management and unions. CAN state how individuals participate and progress in an organisation. CAN describe how an individual can influence or participate in local, national and international affairs.

INFORMATION TECHNOLOGY CAN give examples of the developing impact of IT on individuals organisation and society. CAN identify, set up and use an appropriate IT system for a given purpose. CAN use IT equipment in controlling a simple mechanical device. CAN write, debug and run a simple computer programme based on a given specification

COMMUNICATION CAN select, interpret and respond to information relevant to a particular purpose. CAN speak effectively, maintaining the confidence of the listener in a variety of situations. CAN make requests and give instructions when appropriate. CAN initiate and sustain conversations for social occupational purposes. CAN read and understand straightforward instructions and messages. CAN select and use an appropriate style of writing to maintain the confidence of the user. CAN originate and organise written information in a variety of styles suitable for a range of purposes. CAN recognise unsupported and unambiguous statements not justified by evidence. CAN appreciate the relationship between cultural background and communication including the use of a second language or dialect. CAN recognise success or failure in communication and take appropriate action.

Source: CPVE Handbook

Figure 4.22c: CGLI/BTEC first draft CPVE: examples of CPVE summative profile statements

externally validate. In addition, there is a growing conviction that profiles must contain both formative and summative elements and involve a number of different *types* of record appropriate to a range of activities and qualities. This further complicates both process and product. Some quite novel problems are beginning to emerge. These are discussed in detail in Part III of this manual which raises questions about the use of profiles in practice.

Profiling within the Youth Training Scheme (YTS)
Some of the elements of CPVE are also present in the YTS Record of Achievement.

> *Part 1* (Figure 4.23a) of the new Two Year YTS Certificate:
> provides a summary of achievement in respect of objectives achieved or modules and other qualifications. This part of the certificate will form the basis of the new qualifications being created and will be endorsed by a designated validating body.
> *Part 2* (Figure 4.23b) of the Certificate provides details of the trainee, the training programme and the YTS programme in which the qualifications/achievement were awarded.
> *Part 3* (Figure 4.23c) of the certification provides a summary of progress and achievement in respect of the four outcomes (shown in Figure 4.24 on page 59) compiled from progress records and review sheets.
>
> (*Guidance Notes on Compiling the Record of Achievement and the YTS Certificate*, MSC)

> At the start of 2 Year YTS, most managing agents will have to devise their own competence objectives, with some help from the illustrative schemes that have been published. Within the next year or two centrally agreed competence objectives and modules will become available for all the major occupational areas. These will be circulated to managing agents, as soon as possible, in order that they can build them into their schemes.
> THE YOUTH CERTIFICATION BOARD
> MSC is also entering into a partnership with the major validating bodies (City and Guilds, BTEC, RSA and SCOTVEC) which are coming together to form the Youth Certification Board. YTS certification will gradually be taken over by the YCB and the qualifications will be issued by the validating bodies and not by MSC. The new competence-based qualifications will be complementary to, and integrated with, the existing range of qualifications issued by these national bodies.
>
> (G. Jessup, *Assessment, Certification and Qualifications in 2 Year YTS*, MSC, 1986)

The Northern Partnership for Records of Achievement
Based on over 30 Northern LEAs and the Northern Examining Association,

> the long term aim of the Northern Partnership is to develop and to provide for schools and colleges a range of methods of assessing, observing and recording students' achievements in the academic, practical and personal fields. It is envisaged that schools, colleges and LEAs will make use of those elements of the overall provision which best meet their needs and the needs of individual students.

The LEAs wished to see developed a system for validating and accrediting units of work produced in schools. Two possible approaches to assessment and certification were considered.

(a) A unit or student-focussed approach broadly similar to the Boards' current school-based (Mode 3) GCE and CSE schemes.
(b) A centre-focussed approach whereby a school would have to meet and follow specified criteria and procedures.

The view was taken that the second approach, accrediting schools, was more likely to provide the flexible framework necessary for the operation of a scheme on a large scale. For such an approach to command the confidence of the Boards, the LEAs and the wider public, it was considered necessary to define clearly the criteria which a school would have to meet for its units and assessments to be acceptable. These might include assurances on the staffing and resources of a school, agreed procedures for the design of units and record-keeping and appropriate in-service training for staff involved in the scheme. Some of these criteria and procedures would be common to both unit and centre-focussed approaches.

Although the desirability of the centre-focussed approach as the long-term objective was accepted, it was felt that the experience of the Boards and the schools themselves lent itself more naturally in the first instance to the unit-centred approach.

The procedures for the NPRA Interim Scheme of Unit Accreditation may be summarised as follows.
(a) Units of work are devised by schools, or schools and their LEA, to meet NPRA criteria for validation. The criteria relate to matters such as learning objectives and outcomes, the evidence of attainment to be retained for inspection, resources and record keeping systems.
(b) The units are 'pre-validated' by an LEA panel to ensure the criteria are met.
(c) The units are submitted by the LEA to a Regional Validating Committee, consisting of representatives of the NEA Boards and the LEAs.
(d) If the unit is validated it is taught by the school(s). Assessment takes place and appropriate records are kept and evidence of students' achievements is retained.
(e) The school recommends to the NEA that a student be regarded as having successfully completed a unit.
(f) The school is visited by an NEA-appointed assessor who inspects evidence of students' attainments, record keeping etc.
(g) When the student has successfully completed a unit the NEA informs the LEA and the LEA issues to the student a statement of achievement which lists the outcomes which have been achieved.
(h) At the end of the course the NEA issues to each student a letter of credit giving the titles of the successfully completed units.

(NPRA Information Sheet, December 1985)

YTS

CERTIFICATE

PART 1

THIS IS TO CERTIFY THAT

..................JOHN SMITH..................

HAS ACHIEVED THE FOLLOWING

OCCUPATIONAL COMPETENCE – *Summary of Competence Objectives (or modules) Achieved*

```
Taking reservations                    Servicing and clearing plated
Consolidating reservations                                    service
Handling enquiries                     Billing and taking payment
Personal Presentation and Personal Hygiene
Safe working methods
Hygiene Practices
Working in the industry
Setting up kitchen tools and equipment
Costing and menu planning
Organising Kitchen Work
Cleaning (tools/equipment)
Preparing re-constituted and convenience food
Preparing cold food and beverages
Boiling
Grilling
Frying
Preparing for plated service
Taking orders for plated service
Micro-computer applications relevant to  1. Front of House operations
                                         2. Organisation and Administration of
                                            Food and Beverage Service
```

QUALIFICATIONS OBTAINED

```
City and Guilds 700/1 Call Order Cooks
                700/3 Food Service Assistants

First Aid Certificate (St John Ambulance)
```

Chairman's Signature

..........*A. Jones*.......... ....*Boyden Mulholley*..........
Managing Agent's Signature   *Manpower Services Commission*

MSC Manpower Services Commission

TFS 94

Source: Manpower Services Commission

Figure 4.23a: Part 1 of the new two year YTS Certificate

YTS

CERTIFICATE

PART 2

PROGRAMME DETAILS

Surname   SMITH

First Names   JOHN

Date of Birth   15 December 1969

Programme Reference Number   123456

Started on   1 April 1986

Finished on   29 March 1988

Name and address of organisation managing the programme

SUMMARY OF TRAINING PROGRAMME

Occupational Areas   Hotel and Catering

Planned work experience placements with:

1. Sunrise International Hotel – Anytown
2. Collingdale Guest House – Anytown

Off-the-job training and/or education with:

Anytown College of Further Education

One day per month in training department, Sunrise International Hotel

.... *A. Jones* ....
Managing Agent's Signature

MSC Manpower Services Commission

TFS 95

Source: Manpower Services Commission

Figure 4.23b: Part 2 of the new two year YTS Certificate

YTS

CERTIFICATE

PART 3

Trainee's Name ....JOHN SMITH.....................

ACHIEVEMENT IN THE FOUR YTS OUTCOMES

1 Competence in a range of Occupational Skills

Skills acquired:

- acquired a range of food preparation and cooking skills
- handled a variety of equipment on reception duties ie telephone, telex, computer facilities
- acquired basic skills of food presentation and serving
- acquired basic skills in cash, cheque, credit card transactions and elementary accounting procedures

2 Competence in a range of Transferable Core Skills

Number:
- measured, weighted, marked out volumes estimated quantities in food preparation
- worked out and checked numerical information in preparation of bills, cheques, credit cards
- compared costs and recognised value in food buying project

Communication:
- interpreted instructions in recipes and hotel procedures
- provided information to clients and colleagues
- noticed the needs of customers and responded accordingly
- worked in a team with colleagues

Computer and Information Technology: carried out procedures for starting up, loading and running a range of programs and closing down the system.

Problem Solving:
- planned routine jobs in kitchen
- planned duty roster with other colleagues
- dealt with unexpected enquiries while on reception
- monitored progress in food preparation

Practical:
- able to identify and locate tools and equipment in food preparation
- able to use a variety of tools and equipment
- able to clean up and replace equipment afterwards
- generally well organised and tidy

3 Ability to transfer skills and knowledge to new situations

- settled down rapidly in second work placement and took initiative in finding out about methods and procedures used
- applied food preparation skills acquired in college to preparing dishes in hotel kitchen.
- social and communication skills improved and transferred to new situations throughout the programme
- applied word processing skills and knowledge to the operation of a standalone and a general purpose micro-computer

4 Personal Effectiveness

- showed initiative in suggesting new menus, new working methods
- worked reliably without supervision in kitchen and in reception
- by the end of scheme dealt confidently with customers, supervisors and colleagues
- generally mature and responsible for an 18 year old

........*A. Jones*..........
Managing Agent's Signature

MSC Manpower Services Commission

TFS 96

Source: Manpower Services Commission

Figure 4.23c: Part 3 of the new two year YTS Certificate

YTS OUTCOMES

1. Competence in a range of OCCUPATIONAL SKILLS.

    These are the basic skills specific to the occupational area in which the training is being provided.

2. Competence in a range of transferable CORE SKILLS.

    These are the number, communication, problem solving and practical skills which are common to almost all jobs, plus computer literacy and information technology which is becoming increasingly important.

3. ABILITY TO TRANSFER skills and knowledge to new situations.

    This refers to the methods and procedures people use to redeploy their occupational and core skills to new jobs, tasks and situations.

4. PERSONAL EFFECTIVENESS.

    This is the ability to get results. It includes having confidence, initiative and being able to work with other people

OCCUPATIONAL COMPETENCE

Source: Manpower Services Commission

Figure 4.24: Designated outcomes for two year YTS

Currently, pilot schemes are underway to study how centres might be accredited, what criteria would have to be met and how such a scheme might be implemented in order to allow the NPRA certificate to encompass the full range of academic and personal achievements.

Figure 4.25a shows an example of a course unit, devised by teachers and validated by the NEA. Students will be issued with a statement of achievement for each unit successfully completed (Figure 4.25b) and a letter of credit detailing the total number of units completed (Figure 4.25c).

A different approach?

We conclude with an example of a rather different profiling approach, taken from the State of Victoria in Australia. Although it incorporates many of the ideas currently informing some of the schemes we have reviewed, the 'descriptive assessment' mode in the Victorian Higher School Certificate offers some novel pointers for the future. In Victoria, there is a long history of school-level discussions about assessment and reporting and of the desirability of non-graded assessment. Many teachers have begun 'to shape a

---

UNIT ACCREDITATION
SUBMISSION UNIT PROFORMA

CODE: NEA/UA/LS/047
DATE: 12.12.85

SCHOOL: ALLERTON HIGH   LEA: Leeds

UNIT TITLE: The Use of Electrical Appliances in The Kitchen

CURRICULAR AREA: Home Economics

UNIT DESCRIPTION
To introduce students through practical experience to the safe and full use of some of the electrical appliances available today. The student will examine the limitations of the appliances and be aware of cleaning procedures.

OUTCOMES TO BE ASSESSED

In successfully completing this unit the student will have demonstrated the ability to
1. use and clean a microwave cooker
2. use and clean a food processor
3. use and clean a deep fat fryer
4. use and clean a multi cooker
5. use and clean a hand mixer and blender

shown knowledge of
6. the specific features of each appliance eg. ease of use, ease of cleaning, accessories available.
7. British Electrotechnical Approvals Board Mark

EVIDENCE TO BE OFFERED

Student's records of work (1–6) signed by teacher after completion

Worksheet completed by individual student (7)

PROCEDURES FOR MAKING AND RECORDING ASSESSMENT

Teachers will record, date and sign each completed piece of work offered as evidence of the outcomes.

Copyright Leeds Education Authority

Source: Northern Examining Association

Figure 4.25a: An example of an NEA-validated course unit

STATEMENT OF ACHIEVEMENT
Scheme of Unit Accreditation
LEEDS LOCAL EDUCATION AUTHORITY

This unit of work was devised by the Leeds Education Authority and validated by the Northern Examining Association. The title of this unit will appear on a final letter of credit to be issued to the student by the NEA

Elementary Word Processing

R.J. Smithson 21st April 1970 of NORTHERN HIGH SCHOOL

In completing this unit the student has:

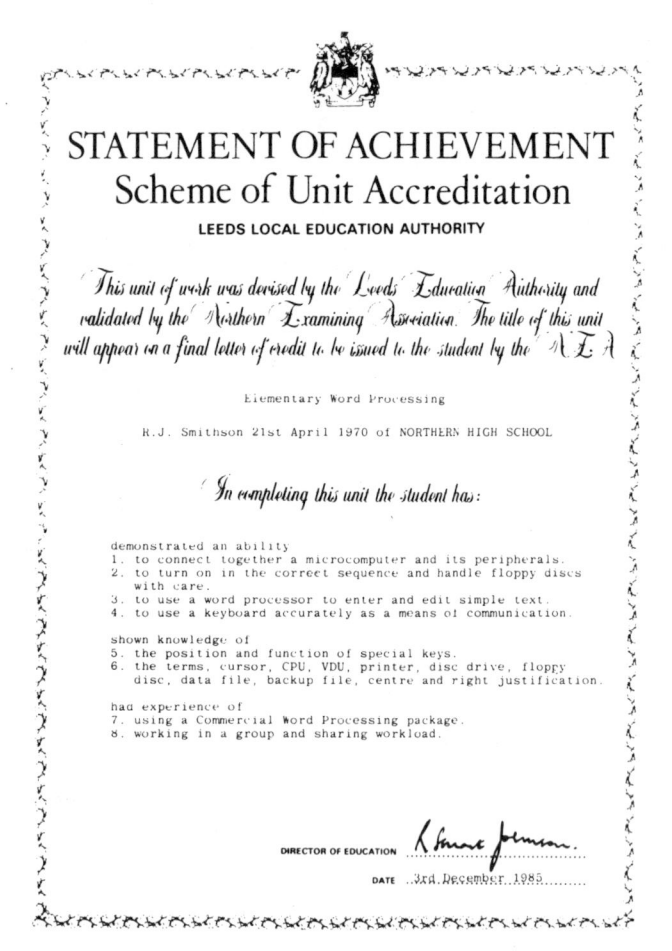

demonstrated an ability
1. to connect together a microcomputer and its peripherals.
2. to turn on in the correct sequence and handle floppy discs with care.
3. to use a word processor to enter and edit simple text.
4. to use a keyboard accurately as a means of communication.

shown knowledge of
5. the position and function of special keys.
6. the terms, cursor, CPU, VDU, printer, disc drive, floppy disc, data file, backup file, centre and right justification.

had experience of
7. using a Commercial Word Processing package.
8. working in a group and sharing workload.

DIRECTOR OF EDUCATION
DATE 3rd December 1985

Source: Northern Examining Association, copyright Leeds Education Authority

Figure 4.25b: An example of the 'statement of achievement' issued for each unit successfully completed

LETTER OF CREDIT

R.J. Smithson
Northern High School

has completed successfully the following units of work; a total of

NINE

In support of this letter of credit, as each unit is completed, a statement of achievement is issued to the student by the

LOCAL EDUCATION AUTHORITY

The statement gives details of the requirements for the successful completion of the unit. Where appropriate the statement lists any further achievements which have been validated by the Local Education Authority.

Units Completed

Science at work: pollution
Elementary word processing
Workshop skills: safety and first aid
An introduction to child care
Library skills
Creative writing: short stories
Managing personal income and expenditure
Conservation in an urban area
Control technology: pneumatics

Chairman, Northern Examining Association

Joint Secretaries,
Northern Examining Association

Figure 4.25c: An example of a 'letter of credit' detailing the total number of units completed

clearer theoretical position on assessment in the curriculum and to develop more defensible classroom techniques and school assessment policies that take account of the fundamental functions of assessment in a democratic curriculum . . . ' (D. Suggett, *Guidelines for descriptive Assessment*, VISE, Australia, 1985)

This is the keynote of the move to promote profiling and records of achievement in the United Kingdom. How to set about working towards such a goal is the theme of this volume for in England we are still a long way from incorporating profiles into the equivalent of the Victorian HSC, namely the GCE Advanced Level. Thus this final example provides the link between the review of existing concerns and attempts to meet them presented in Part I and the detailed strategies which are the subject of Part II.

The extract starts with the formulation of some general principles for course-based 'descriptive assessment' and then provides some specific examples of how these principles should operate in practice.

In practice, such 'profiles' tend to conform to one of three main approaches as described below.

Firstly, there are '*open-ended*' profiles. These profiles start 'with a blank sheet to be filled in by the teacher (and sometimes the student) in whatever way he/she chooses to best describe the student's achievements. The length is determined by the size of the form: the format and content is in the hands of the teacher and is usually written in prose.'

Figures 4.26 and 4.27 illustrate a good and bad version of such reporting.

Secondly, there are '*work-based*' or '*goal-based*' profiles which are structured 'so that student achievements are described in terms of the work set for the course and the work done by the student. A work-based descriptive assessment report is therefore written in a structured and predetermined way and is not so much a "story" about the learning but a clear-cut account of the student's achievements'.

Figures 4.28 and 4.29 illustrate what such a profile might look like for both a good and a weak performance.

Thirdly, there are '*grid-style*' profiles, where 'teachers indicate performance by ticking the descriptor that most clearly reflects a student's achievements. Additional provision is often made for brief written comments'.

This approach is illustrated in Figure 4.30.

Fourthly, there are profiles where 'teachers write brief statements about students' performances in nominated discrete areas, such as skills attained, progress and attitude, or subject-specific competencies' as shown in Figure 4.31.

Finally, there are '*course-based*' profiles where the student work and behaviour required for the course also forms the structure for the profile. This type of profile is illustrated in Figure 4.32.

Guidelines for using descriptive assessment during the school year

Assessment must be integrated with the teaching/learning process. It should match good teaching/learning activities and foster further learning.

Explicit work

The student work (assessment tasks) that comprise a course should be explicit. The student should know clearly what is expected of her/him, see it as fair and be reassured by a clear definition of what each task is, how difficult it is, the sequence of steps to complete the task and when it is to be completed.

Students should also know what other general or umbrella requirements there are in a course, such as those governing attendance, behaviour and homework.

Explicit assessment criteria

Assessment criteria should also be explicit. The requirements for satisfactorily completing each piece of work and the course as a whole should be made clear to the student before, during and after each assessment. That is, the student should know on what basis a piece of work will be assessed; what particular qualities are being looked for, whether the student is being judged against her/his own previous work or against other students, and whether it is expected that all students can do the task.

Similarly the student should know on what basis success in a course will be determined. This may entail requirements such as regular attendance, co-operative behaviour, completion of set work and homework.

Satisfactory completion of the task, unit or course should therefore be attainable; students who do the work in the agreed way should be assessed as having satisfactorily completed the task, unit or course.

Student participation

Many teachers involve students in a co-operative endeavour for making decisions about the work that is to comprise a course, strategies for doing the work, and the criteria by which work is to be assessed. Student-teacher 'negotiation' of course work or course goals does not mean each student designs an individual program nor that the teacher abdicates a teaching role. Rather, the co-operation of teacher and students in determining the work that comprises a course is a key way to ensure the course is relevant and properly understood, and that success is possible for all involved.

Variety of work

Student work for assessment should be varied. It should employ a variety of **forms** (eg written, oral, multi-media), a variety of **types** (eg descriptive, expressive, analytic, reflective), a variety of **lengths**, a variety in the **focus** or audience for the work and there should be variety in the **organisation** or grouping of students to do the work (eg individual, small groups).

Different assessment tasks bring out different qualities in students and these should be valued. Assessment of student work should take into account the difficulty of the assessment task and the student's preparedness for that task.

Variety of regular reports

There should be variety in the method of reporting assessments. For example, written teacher comments, student self-assessment, student/teacher interviews, student checklists or diaries of work activities, student files and peer assessments. Different methods of reporting student achievements promote consideration of the effectiveness of the course as well as consideration of the qualities of student achievements.

(For further reading in this area see HYDE, M. and BRENNAN, M. – 'Real evaluation', in *Study of society*, Vol. 10, No. 2, 1979 pages 11-14; BLACHFORD, K. – 'Assessment' in *Study of society*, Vol. 14, No. 1, 1983, pages 12-13.)

Variety of records

Portfolios of each student's work should be accumulated during the year, containing samples of class work, assessed work, teachers' assessments and students' own assessments. These portfolios may form the basis for summative descriptive assessments at the end of the year and may provide a basis for teacher-student-parent discussions.

Natural not contrived

Descriptive assessment should allow for the emergence of unexpected qualities, so the student can be given credit for what has actually been achieved as well as whether she/he achieved what was intended. In this sense, assessment should be 'naturalistic', concentrating on process and products pursued for their own educational sakes; assessments should not be artificial exercises standing outside the teaching/learning process.

Feedback builds on achievement

Assessment during the year should provide feedback which helps students to identify their strengths and weaknesses. Suggestions should be provided to help students to overcome deficiencies and improve their work. Students should have opportunities to discuss all their assessed work with teachers. Where practicable, teachers may want to include opportunities for negotiating assessments. Teacher-student negotiation in the preparation of descriptive assessments provides a means for making criteria explicit and a way for students to understand the process of assessment as being part of the stream of teaching and learning activities.

Continuity

It is especially important that descriptive assessment be guided by a principle of continuity. The student should be able to see each assessment in relation to previous assessments, and be in a position to form realistic expectations about assessments still to come. There is something wrong with an assessment system where students succeed throughout the year but suddenly find themselves failing towards the end.

Not dogmatic

Teachers should accept that others may firmly hold quite different opinions about a student's work. At the very least, this should counter tendencies to dogmatism about what is desirable in students' work; in some cases, it may encourage us to seek 'second opinions' from other teachers or students. Nevertheless, teachers should resist the temptation to use only those routine methods of assessment which produce results less likely to lead to disagreement.

These guidelines are incorporated into a series of flow-charts:

Stages of a work-based and descriptive assessment approach: a summary table

COURSE INTENTIONS

- WHAT DO I EXPECT STUDENTS TO LEARN FROM DOING THIS UNIT?
    - The aims of the unit

    > eg: — examine how technological change can alter people's lives by a study of Australia in the 1920s
    > or
    > — design and construct a sturdy piece of household furniture

⬇

SATISFACTORY COMPLETION

- WHAT DO STUDENTS HAVE TO DO TO COMPLETE THE UNIT SATISFACTORILY?
    - A straightforward list of 'umbrella' requirements (non-negotiable)

    > eg: — complete all set work
    > — regularly attend classes
    > — take part in agreed class activities

⬇

STUDENT INPUT/NEGOTIATION

- WHAT PROVISION IS MADE FOR STUDENT INPUT OR STUDENT-TEACHER 'NEGOTIATION'?
    - Procedures for involving students need to be adopted

    > eg: — special planning session to determine goals
    > — student-teacher decisions and agreements written down
    > — progress monitored on a regular basis
    > — student self-monitoring encouraged
    > — goals renegotiated if appropriate
    > — sessions for group evaluation of unit

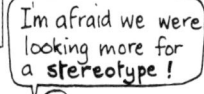

⬇

WORK OR GOALS FOR THE COURSE

- ARE THE WORK GOALS EXPLICIT AND 'DO-ABLE' BY CLEARLY CONVEYING TO STUDENTS:

    WHAT TO DO?

    - A list of work requirements for a unit (eg history)

    > eg: — folder of neat notes from class lessons and library work
    > — two written assignments of at least three pages each
    > — one group project — written and visual
    > — a class talk

    HOW TO COMPLETE THE TASK?

    - A list of processes to follow. The written assignment task might require students to:

    > eg: — select a topic from suggestions
    > — write planning questions ⎫ discuss with
    > — check resources ⎭ teacher
    > — complete a first draft — show teacher
    > — redraft assignment in light of comments
    > — submit assignment for response

    WHEN TO DO THE WORK?

    - A timeline to be followed

    > eg: — an indication of when to start
    > — suggested time to be taken for various tasks
    > — an indication of deadlines for completion of work

    - Such a list of work goals for the student to complete should be:

    > eg: — achievable
    > — related to work which is worthwhile
    > — framed in terms of work to be done, and the behaviour to be expected
    > — stated in a way that allows the student and teacher to see whether the work meets requirements
    > — simply expressed and usually written down
    >
    > Refer to 'Ideas for in-service activities: Developing Goals'

INVOLVING STUDENTS IN ASSESSMENT

- WHAT PROVISIONS HAVE YOU MADE FOR INVOLVING STUDENTS IN THEIR ASSESSMENTS?

  - It is necessary to have a structure to facilitate assessment

    > eg: — timetabled assessment sessions
    >   — files compiled by students during a course containing:
    >   - work goals
    >   - self assessments
    >   - teacher assessments
    >   - class or peer assessments
    >   - significant pieces of work
    >   — teacher/student/parent meetings that use such files to focus discussions about what the course aims to do, what work the student has done, and the like

  - If the work to be done in a course is clearly explained to students beforehand and particularly if the students contributed to the formulation of work goals, then student self assessment not only makes sense, but is easy and worthwhile.

  - Assessment and report-writing become significant and legitimate co-operative classroom activities when work goals are clear.

ASSESSMENT OF STUDENT WORK

- WERE THE REQUIREMENTS FOR SATISFACTORY COMPLETION OF THE COURSE MET?

  - A checking of student achievements against work goals
    > — yes/no

- HOW CAN WORK BE IMPROVED NEXT TIME?

  - Recommendations for ways to enhance achievement
    > eg. — spend more time on rough notes
    >   — build up a new word list
    >   — keep folder in order

Source: D. Suggett, *Guidelines for Descriptive Assessment*, VISE, Australia, 1985

An inappropriate report for a satisfactory performance

ENGLISH (1 UNIT)					MARILYN

an unnecessarily negative beginning to an account of a term's work	Marilyn's written expression continues to reveal weaknesses. Her film review was disjointed and unstructured, failing to elaborate a central idea into a coherent whole. She used awkward syntax and failed totally to support any of her judgements with detail from the film. She has not really grasped the techniques of analysis or criticism.***	an analysis of work done is clearly relevant for the student to improve but expressions like 'fails totally' and 'has not really grasped' are extreme statements that discourage rather than encourage improvement
why not say 'she contributed to class discussion although . . .'	Her descriptive pieces lacked structure and depth, although they exhibit fewer grammatical or spelling errors. In place of her autobiography, she completed a short story which, although based rather closely on one we had read in class, nevertheless showed care and effort. Her contribution in class discussion remained fairly sporadic, although it is plain that she listened carefully, her comprehension of finer details and subtle differences is lacking.***	
dangerous speculation		
this would be a more positive beginning to the report	Her attitude, attendance and completion of her contracts for the term earned her the second unit in English.*** End of statement	

- An unsympathetic report of a student's work. It concentrates on the weaknesses rather than the strengths of the work completed.
- A reader might be surprised that the student's work in the unit was satisfactory after reading the details of the report.
- A more detailed elaboration of the criteria for success and the work completed are essential.
- This report is clearly unstructured and not written to a predetermined plan and so speculation and random evaluations dominate the report.
- Claims could be made that the level of criticism and the form it takes are gender-stereotyped, namely, females are criticised for lack of clarity, lack of depth and shallow analysis but praised for careful listening, careful preparation and effort.

Source: D. Suggett, *Guidelines for Descriptive Assessment*, VISE, Australia, 1985

Figure 4.26: *An example of a VHSC* open-ended descriptive assessment*

* VHSC Victoria Higher School Certificate

An appropriate report for satisfactory performance

PHYSICS PRACTICAL (1 UNIT)				DOMINIC

vague generalisations successfully avoided	Throughout the year Dominic carried out the research directions outlined in the lab guide in a methodical way. As the year progressed he came to rely less heavily on step-by-step instructions. A developing involvement in experimental construction was accompanied by a greater independence and experimental honesty. He reported directly where experiments did not meet expectations. His experiments on motion exemplify this: after seeking guidance as to the type of equipment required for investigation related to the removal of friction from consideration, he designed and implemented his experiments on momentum exchange.***	shows improvement
comments on the person, specific to observable behaviour		
	His ability to establish links between theory and practice varied from topic to topic. In the experiment on magnetic fields surrounding a single wire he was unable to abstract or visualise results in more complex situations, such as with parallel wires. In 'light', however, he was able to apply the formulae developed from the models of wave behaviour directly to the ripple tank experiments on single and double slit interference patterns.***	careful analysis of levels of achievement
supporting evidence	Dominic was often more interested in description than in precise measurement. In 'magnetism', his observations were concise and lucid. However in the experiment on the effect of a magnetic field on the path of a beam of electron, he made no attempt at calculation of magnetic strength from the path observed.***	assessment here is specific to a major course objective
acknowledgement of emergence of unexpected qualities	This preference for description and interest in the role of science produced perhaps Dominic's best work in his project on laser technology, where he was as concerned with issues of social impact as he was with the operation of laser technology itself.*** End of statement	

- This style of report is difficult to write well and is time consuming.
- It is a 'story' of how the student worked and, although there is specific mention of work requirements and assessment criteria, the report is not structured around specific goals of work. The report could quite easily be 'end-on' to the course rather than a direct representation of the structure and values of the course.
- Some teachers and students value this style of reporting because it conveys more information and subtle perceptions about student work than does a tightly structured, work-based descriptive assessment report.
- Most, however, feel that there are numerous pitfalls in attempting to make fine qualitative judgement about a student's work and that it is often wiser to modify the 'open-endedness'.

Source: D. Suggett, *Guidelines for Descriptive Assessment*, VISE, Australia, 1985

Figure 4.27: *An example of a VHSC open-ended descriptive assessment*

67

An appropriate report for a satisfactory performance

MATHEMATICS (3 UNITS)   MARIA

course details relevant for selection purposes → Maria has satisfactorily completed three units of mathematics. Maria worked independently and completed the work promptly. She negotiated a course which would give her a background for a career in primary school teaching.*** ← *a context for the student's work*

'technical' details included for specific reasons → Maria has demonstrated arithmetical skills and is able to apply them to consumer problems. She is also competent at algebra, being able to factorise polynomials and solve equations. She is able to transfer matrix algebra skills to business problems, though she experienced difficulty with 3x3 matrices. Her ability to think logically has improved with practice in solving problems using a variety of strategies, especially Venn diagrams and matrix elimination.***

Her research into the teaching of mathematics was well organised and presented, but part of the report on course outlines lacked detail. She arranged a work experience at a primary school (grade 2) and visited others. She attended an inservice for primary school principals and was a support teacher in a year 7 class for three lessons. Her observations of teaching strategies, use of equipment and student attitudes were well documented. She showed an improvement in being able to critically analyse ← *development and improvement*
teaching methods and became more aware of factors which influence student motivation. She prepared evaluation worksheets for a grade 6 class, indicating a need for clearer instructions and an alternative organisation of questions for mathematics lessons. Her preparation for year 7 classes involved learning geometrical concepts, for example transformations, and discovering tesselations.*** ← *variety of student work*

A culmination of her research was an outline of a suitable workshop for years 10 and 11 students.***   End of statement

- This report is respectful of a student's work. It does not employ assessment cliches, but carefully accounts for the work done.
- While this report is a clear account of a variety of student achievements in a mathematics course, it is also a verification that the course was relevant to the student's needs and interests. It is thus an informative report.
- The report gives technical detail on achievements in mathematics. The teacher in this case judged that these details would assist the student, whereas on other occasions technical details might impede general understanding of a report.

Source: D. Suggett, *Guidelines for Descriptive Assessment*, VISE, Australia, 1985

Figure 4.28: *An example of a VHSC work-based descriptive assessment report*

An appropriate report for a satisfactory/unsatisfactory performance

MATHEMATICS (3 UNITS)   TOM

Tom successfully completed two units in Mathematics and did not complete one unit. He completed the required work for two units, attended the required number of classes during term 1 and term 2, took a very active part in the course decision-making process and contributed confidently and logically to class discussions. Tom learnt to use an Apple II computer and simple BASIC programming skills. He wrote programs to manipulate whole ← *account of work completed*
numbers, for example, to find the area of a rectangle. Tom worked with a small group of students on data collection, presentation and simple

clear account of the observable context in which work was not completed → analysis. Tom worked with the class on the investment area and was able to use the formulae and make the calculations necessary to solve problems on depreciation, interest and annuities.***

However he did not seek help from his teacher on the more complex areas of correlation, measures of speed and variation and was not able to understand and complete this section. The setting out of problems was not
straightforward comment → detailed and his numerical answers were not adequately explained. His attendance for term 3 was not satisfactory and two contracted pieces of work were not completed.***

The work Tom did submit showed improvement during the year in detail and clarity of setting out. He was able to understand the requirements of written material and make correct numerical calculations.*** ← *concentration on student's strengths*
End of statement

- A straightforward account of work completed and work not completed.
- The report is positive so that what the student **did** in the course is the focus for a reader rather than an account of the student's failure and speculation on ability deficiencies.

Source: D. Suggett, *Guidelines for Descriptive Assessment*, VISE, Australia, 1985

Figure 4.29: *An example of a VHSC work-based descriptive assessment report*

SUBJECT: Business Mathematics			DATE: August
NAME: Fred Kelly			GROUP: 10D

	TICK WHERE APPROPRIATE	COMMENT IF NECESSARY
DESIRE TO WORK		
Continuous desire to work		
Generally positive and effective	✓	Pleasant and co-operative student.
Inconsistent worker		
Requires constant supervision		
SKILLS		
Has achieved the skills required		
Has achieved most of the skills		
Has achieved some of the skills	✓	Not quite up to standard but a good effort.
PROGRESS		
Excellent		
Progressed very well	✓	Improvement over the year.
Has shown improvement		
Little progress		

GENERAL COMMENT

Fred still has a way to go if he is to have a successful year. He tries very hard but needs to ask more questions when work is difficult. He gets along well with other class members and is well behaved.

TEACHER C.C. James

- This style of grid profile is easy and quick to complete and tends to be popular for those reasons.
- The increase in performance from the lowest through to the highest level given by the descriptors may be unrealistic (eg a 'continuous desire to work' to 'requires constant supervision').
- This style of report does not give clear direction to the student as to how improvement can occur. The arbitrary separation of attitude, skill acquisition and rate of improvement is a distortion of the learning process. The elements of learning are better described in relationship to particular pieces of work or groups of tasks.
- The reader does not know what work comprised the business mathematics course or how the judgements of performance were reached.

Source: D. Suggett, *Guidelines for Descriptive Assessment*, VISE, Australia, 1985

Figure 4.30: A grid style VHSC profile

| NAME Michelle White | Mathematics | TERM II | YEAR 9 |

MASTERY OF TOPICS

	Previously Mastered	Mastered	Partially Mastered	Yet to Master
FLOW CHARTS				
writing flow charts		✓		
using flow charts		✓		
FRACTIONS DECIMALS PERCENTAGES				
Equivalent fractions		✓		
+ − × ÷ of fractions		✓		
× + decimal by powers of 10			✓	
Multiples, common multiples, lowest common multiples				✓
Conversion of decimals to fractions and vice-versa			✓	
Conversion to and from percentages				✓
USE OF CALCULATOR				
Use of +/− key and of memory				
Standard form – use and interpretation				
Approximations				
Estimations				

WORK DONE IN CLASS

	Satisfactory	Unsatisfactory
CLASSWORK		
Logical and neat bookwork	✓	
Corrections of work done	✓	
Follow-up of incorrect work	✓	
Amount of work completed	✓	
HOMEWORK		
Regularity and punctual submission	✓	
Logical and neat book-work	✓	
Correction of work done	✓	
Follow-up of incorrect work	✓	
PARTICIPATION		
Application to work in class	✓	
Asking questions when requiring help	✓	
Helping other students when able	✓	

- The profile is a judgement of the mastery of the content components of the course along with a judgement of the way the work was done.
- The information is not based on work completed in the subject but on the demonstration of mastery of the nominated topics that comprise the course. (This mode of assessment may well be more appropriate for mathematics than for other subjects.)
- The profile contains useful and detailed information on the specific content of the subject. The long list of items and ticks for student performance may, however, be confusing to some parents and students.
- The profile could be improved through the following modifications:
  — indicate in an introduction how mastery of a topic is ascertained
  — reduce the number of categories and ticks required
  — introduce brief written comments for attitude and behaviour
  — provide a category for recommendations for improvement.

Source: D. Suggett, *Guidelines for Descriptive Assessment*, VISE, Australia, 1985

Figure 4.31: VHSC profile – competencies

SUBJECT Study of Society: Women in Australia	NAME Shar Banette
WORK REQUIREMENTS FOR SATISFACTORY COMPLETION	YEAR II TERM 2

MAINTAIN A SUBJECT FOLDER	• present notes and complete set exercises • select newspaper clippings • keep records of group and personal goals
PARTICIPATE IN A COMMUNITY ACTIVITY	• organise an activity of one week in an organisation directly concerned with the lives of women • prepare a seminar that evaluates the role of the organisation
CONDUCT A RESEARCH PROJECT	• identify a clearly defined problem appropriate to the theme • collect relevant material according to the suggested techniques • interpret the material in response to the problem • present the project in approximately 800–1000 words.
PARTICIPATE IN DISCUSSION AND CLASS ACTIVITIES	• listen to others' point of view and be willing to contribute. • be willing to participate in class seminars and any agreed activities

WORK COMPLETED

MAINTAIN A SUBJECT FOLDER

Shar's folder was well-organised and comprehensive by the end of Term. A checklist of all required work was included. Newspaper clippings were well selected and a useful resource. Early in the term some class exercises were not completed in the required way and on time. However, Shar followed directions to re-do them and included them in her folder.

PARTICIPATE IN A COMMUNITY ACTIVITY

Shar and a male student arranged work experience in a day-care centre. Their report and seminar gave an account of the views of child care and suggested improvements particularly in relation to child care provision at the place of employment. Their seminar promoted lively discussion. Shar appeared to experience difficulty with the independent nature of this activity earlier in the year but seemed confident with the task this term.

CONDUCT A RESEARCH ACTIVITY

The topic was defined as sex and difference and the problem concerned the effects of schools on how children devlop identity. Shar arranged interviews and observations and selected references. She collected extensive material but interpretation was difficult. The project was well presented in clear language although some material could have been in an appendix so as to allow the argument to flow. Shar was prepared to redraft the conclusion of her project and her work improved accordingly. Her conclusions were relevant to the problem and insightful.

PARTICIPATE IN DISCUSSION AND CLASSROOM ACTIVITIES

Shar appears to enjoy discussion is a small group. She has participated in all class activities and took responsibility for arranging the visit of a speaker for the class.

SUMMARY COMMENT AND RECOMMENDATIONS

Shar was enthusiastic about the theme and thought deeply about the issues. Her written work communicated information and ideas in simply constructed accounts. Shar should however regularly complete all class work and homework to build up the skills for enquiry and commentary. She should therefore work at home for at least 1 hour on two nights of the week for this subject.

TEACHER Ursula Crisp

- The structure of the profile is based on the work required of students during the progress of a term
- The work requirements are a combination of 'processes' to be followed and 'products' to be completed.
- The details entered by the teacher describe the work completed by the student and comment on the way the work was done. The description of the student's achievements is consistent with the guidelines in Section 4.
- However, the profile does not attempt to record all observable features apparent in the student's work, attitude and behaviour; the student is not under constant observation for the purposes of assessment. Rather, the student should be well-informed as to what work, attitude and behaviour is required for satisfactory completion of the subject and should be assessed on the attainment of the set goals.
- The profile is intended as part of the learning program; it is not constructed so as to enable a reader to make fine discrimination among students in the class group nor to determine a rank order for performance.

Source: D. Suggett, *Guidelines for Descriptive Assessment*, VISE, Australia, 1985

Figure 4.32: VHSC profile: work-based

Summary

These examples, together with their accompanying comments, provide a clear and comprehensive summary of the issues that have been raised in this chapter. They illustrate the advantages and disadvantages of more or less structured 'profiles'; the potential that each approach has for being either negative or positive in its effect depending on how it is *used* as well as how it is *designed* and they show that even an officially-validated scheme can be designed to provide individual centres with the possibility of considerable flexibility in their choice of approach.

Part II
The attack

Chapter 5
Establishing a profiling scheme

Introduction

In its Policy Statement of June 1984, the government made a commitment to providing all school-leavers with a record of achievement before the end of the decade. One effect of this policy is likely to be that virtually all secondary school teachers – and many primary and special school ones as well – will, before very long, find themselves involved in profiling. Despite the massive growth in both interest and involvement in recent years, there are still many teachers who feel they know little about 'profiles' and even less about how to use them.

The first part of this manual, which reviewed the range of past and current practice, has been designed to help meet the first of these needs. In this section of the manual, we turn to the second, more practical issue of how to design, implement and use profiles to meet the needs of a particular school or classroom.

The section is structured in terms of a number of key issues and is designed so that individuals, groups or whole institutions can work through the issues and identify their own profiling priorities. In so doing, we shall be adopting the same approach to implementation as this manual advocates for assessment, which is depicted in Figure 5.1.

The circular process represented in Figure 5.1 underlines the *dynamic* nature of any successful profiling scheme. The intentions of the scheme, its working and its effects, must be subject to a continuous process of review and change, if it is to continue to meet the needs identified at the outset. Thus, while there are obviously some questions which only apply at the initial planning stages of such a scheme, most of the questions in this section need to be returned to repeatedly and discussed even in the context of long-established schemes.

The first section is entitled 'design issues' and discusses a number of issues relating to how the actual design of the profiling approach adopted may be arrived at, including:
- general priorities for change
- formative–summative balance
- content – skills; subject-attainment;
  personal qualities;
  experience
- assessment techniques
- reporting style

The discussion that follows is divided into two parts. The second section is entitled 'framework for innovation' and discusses a range of context issues relating to the implementation of a profiling scheme, including:
- origins of interest
- management
- coordination
- consultation
- priorities
- compatibility, curriculum implications
- resources
- in-service training

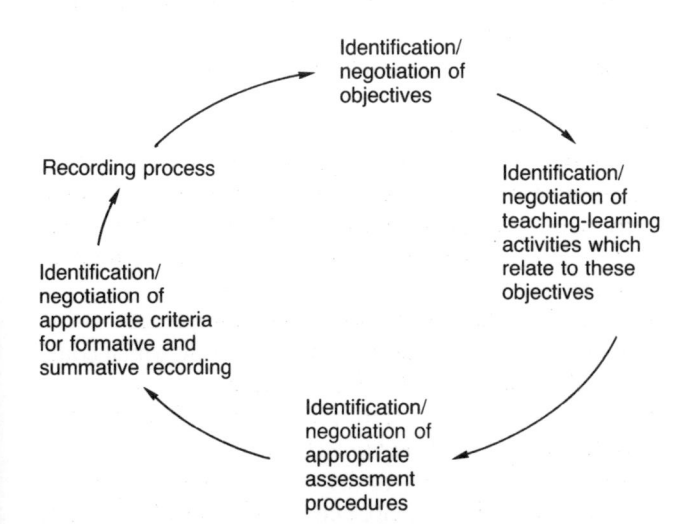

Figure 5.1: Stages in the development of a profiling scheme

Design issues

Choosing an approach

Changes within the profiling movement as a whole make it more and more likely that many of the schools and colleges keen to introduce such a scheme will not have a free choice. As Chapter 1 set out, we have now reached a stage where profiles are rapidly becoming 'big business', with examination boards and local authorities in particular keen to introduce county or regional schemes. This is because, despite the continuing success of many individual schools in pioneering profiles, it has become increasingly apparent that summative profiles need to have a wider currency if they are to make the maximum impact on consumers. Ideally, this means getting the imprimatur of an examination board and the considerable public credibility it embodies. Thus most local authorities now have their own schemes. Some of these, typically based on consortia of LEAs, are likely to become nationally available in due course. The increasing scale of many profiling schemes is also one of the reasons way the government is proposing to introduce *national* guidelines for records of achievement by the end of the decade.

Meanwhile many other profiles, such as City and Guilds and RSA, are already national in character, as we saw in Chapter 4. In an increasing number of situations, such as the new CPVE, profiling is a *requirement* of the course and teachers will have no choice but to be involved in it.

It is therefore less and less likely to be the case that schools and colleges will find themselves starting from scratch in their development work. But although the status of the initiative will significantly affect the freedom of the institution to design and operate its own model, it will still be necessary for schools to go through a process of defining their own priorities even if in the end this becomes simply the basis for deciding whether or not to opt into a pre-existing scheme, rather than providing the foundations for the development of a new scheme.

Identifying objectives

The first stage in such a process, as the model at the beginning of this chapter suggests, is to get clear the objectives that the scheme is designed to fulfil. A steering group, or the staff as a whole, will need to address the following questions before they can proceed to the choice of a profiling scheme:

1   What are the most important reasons for introducing profiling?
    - To help diagnose pupils' strengths and weaknesses in a subject?
    - To improve record keeping/assessment in a particular subject?
    - To improve record keeping/assessment in the school as a whole?
    - To guide pupils in their choice of courses?
    - To promote the professional development of teachers?
    - To promote the school?
    - To improve communication with parents?
    - To provide information for employers, trainers and tertiary education?
    - To involve pupils in their assessment?
    - To provide feedback for staff on their teaching?
    - To extend the range of attributes assessed?
    - To provide the 'public' with better measures of the outcomes of education?
    - To improve guidance and advice to pupils relevant to post 16 decisions?
    - To promote curriculum development?
    - Others (please specify)

(A more elaborate version of these questions devised by June McNaughton for the Essex LEA pilot scheme is given in Figure 5.2.)

Assessment and record keeping in school should:	As part of formative process	As part of summative portrayal	As part of whole process formative and summative	Not important
be an intrinsic part of the learning process				
involve learners as partners in determining course activities				
motivate students				
emphasise pupils' strengths				
point out deficiencies or weaknesses				
inform parents				
provide information for employers				
provide information for F.E. establishments				
describe, but not judge				
begin at the age of 11 years				
develop students' self image				
describe personal/social qualities as well as academic skills				
give feedback on performance				
be linked to curriculum objectives				
diagnose learning problems				
facilitate curriculum change				
build up students' self confidence				
be based on negotiation between student and teacher				
increase dialogue between student and teacher				
produce a policy for marking				
be linked to staff development				
improve documentation for benefit of leavers				
be criterion, not norm. referenced				
include some norm. referenced items				
offer opportunities for student self assessment				
offer opportunities for peer assessment				
help pupils measure their own capabilities				
give students a chance to make decisions				
particularly meet the needs of non-examination pupils				
help pupils to produce evidence about personal qualities				
assess cross-curricular skills				

Source: J. McNaughton, Essex LEA Pilot Scheme, 1985

Figure 5.2: Intentions and principles: a check-list of priorities

2   What kind of profiling scheme do we want?
    - e.g. A profile for a particular course or subject?
    - A personal-recording scheme?
    - A comprehensive, whole school profiling scheme?
    - Formative and/or summative?

3   *Profile priorities*

Formative and summative profiles are likely to have different users. Is it likely that a single format could fully serve the needs of both? How will these uses differ? (e.g. student 'use'; institutional 'use'; employer 'use'.)

For whom is the profile principally intended?

Is it possible to produce a formative profile which could form the basis of a summative profile?

Given a choice between formative and summative profiles what would be your choice?

(You may like to refer to the 'aide-memoire' below for a summary of the principal characteristics of each type of profile.)

'Aide-Memoire'
A typical summative profile:
- takes account of vocational needs;
- gives a rounded portrayal;
- emphasises positive achievements;
- uses a variety of sources of evidence;
- maximises utility to consumer.

A typical formative profile:
- is integrated within the curriculum;
- supports curriculum development;
- involves student in dialogue;
- is a frequent and continuous record;
- is constructive;
- may contain negative information.

Timetabling
What would be the best time allocation for profile recording:
- in timetabled periods?
- during existing courses on the timetable?
- within the pastoral system?

4   *The content of profiles*
   How important is it that the following are included in profiling?
   - Traditional subject attainment
   - Skills and qualities such as basic mathematics and language skills
   - Cross curriculum skills such as listening and problem solving
   - Practical skills such as the ability to use tools and equipment correctly
   - Personal qualities such as punctuality and initiative
   - Norm-referenced assessments, e.g. standardised tests
   - Criterion-referenced assessments where both the pupil and the profile user are aware of the criteria used
   - Ipsative assessments – where a pupil's present performance is compared with his own past performance
   - Others (please specify)

Ownership issues

Ownership of the profile is related to the control of both its content and access to it, and raises a number of important issues. Given that schools no longer have the right to keep secret files on pupils, all the information on a profile may be accessed by pupils and their parents. This will tend to deter teachers from writing negative, unsubstantiated comments or damaging information even where that information is known to be true. In fact it is quite alien to the spirit of most profiling schemes to seek to keep any of the record secret from the pupil it concerns. The priority given to the formative potential of such records in helping youngsters come to terms with their strengths and weaknesses would be quite contradicted by any element of secrecy. Rather both pupil and teacher will learn some of the many shortcomings of more traditional reporting in coming to realise how important it is to be specific, constructive and provide evidence to substantiate a comment. To be *formative*, records and reports should inform, motivate, encourage and build on previous statements. In the past, quite the opposite has often been the case where:

> remarks are often no more than a series of repetitive cliches. Common ones are 'satisfactory', 'works well', 'could do better', 'steady progress', 'makes little effort'. Such comments generally give little advice or information. Grades too are of course open to all sorts of misinterpretation by student, teacher and parent alike. (The Bosworth Papers.)

The result has been reports which:
- are often irrelevant to the pupil's own concerns;
- are de-motivating;
- give little advice about how to improve;
- may have little relationship between comment and grade;
- result in a steady erosion of self-esteem leading to a number of anti-social forms of behaviour;

Source: D. Suggett, *Guidelines for Descriptive Assessment*, VISE, Australia, 1985

Figure 5.3

- do not help the pupil to become self-evaluative;
- often contain misleading or inadequate information because a teacher has not had the time or opportunity to get to know a pupil sufficiently well;
- reflect teachers' own biases and values rather than the pupil's.

It is partly because of all the many shortcomings of traditional reports that profiling has embraced the principles of openness and dialogue so strongly. While there will probably always be a need for confidential reports and references, in certain circumstances, we are more and more moving towards a position that:

- information recorded about a person should be shared *with* that person if it is to be *educational* in its effects;
- pupils themselves should control their own formative records;
- they should control how that information is used for summative purposes;
- the pupil should decide whether a copy of that record stays on the school's files; and
- they should have the power of veto over confidential references being sent out.

Those already involved in profiling will be quick to point out that the relationship of mutual respect and trust between tutor and student that successful profiling involves makes these injunctions a lot less radical in practice than they sound in theory. Nevertheless, the issue of ownership is a vital one and is another area that requires very careful consideration before profiling can be introduced.

Most practitioners have already taken the stance that a profile belongs to the pupil, and the DES Statement of July 1984 affirms this principle quite clearly. However, the issue is not quite as straightforward as this implies. There still remain problems associated with who physically keeps the profile during its compilation. To what extent should the material recorded in the profile be available to the school for possible future use in references? Is the school entitled to retain copies of the profiles for its own internal records, and to what extent does the pupil control the copyright of material within the profile?

Teachers will want to consider their priorities in relation to the list of objectives outlined above. They

"Well, well, well, well, well! Man, have they got *your* number!"

Source: Sunday Express, 1 March 1970

Figure 5.4

will then be in a position to consider if such a profile is already available, for example:
- within the LEA itself?
- within an LEA-examination board consortium?
- on a national basis?
- as developed in another school?

or will the school individually or in consultation with other schools have to design their own scheme if their needs are to be fully met?

Thus a school still has a great many decisions to make in relation to *whether and how to implement a profiling scheme*, even where the characteristics of the scheme itself are largely pre-determined.

Compatibility of initiatives

One of the most important of these decisions is the need to consider a profiling scheme in relation to other forms of assessment, reporting and certification in which the school or college is currently involved. Schemes such as OCEA, described in Chapter 4, provide for three components in the eventual certificate – the 'E' component which records 'any national/publicly recognised qualification'; the 'G' component which records progress in relation to OCEA-devised criteria in mathematics, English, science and modern languages; and the 'P' component which is a personal progress record negotiated jointly by teacher and pupil. It is desirable that an institution wishing to become part of OCEA be willing to take on all three components of the recording procedure, and be accredited to do so by the OCEA Accreditation Board. Thus a decision to apply to join such a scheme is likely to have implications for very many different aspects of institutional life and the implications thereof will have to be very carefully considered.

Many schools at the present time find themselves caught up in a whole variety of assessment developments concerned with, for example, graded tests and assessments, modular courses, GCSE, and new curricular initiatives such as TVEI. Some of these initiatives involve examination boards, some do not. The attempt to introduce profiling may or may not be linked to such developments but in either case, the implications of the combined impact of these various schemes will need to be carefully reviewed. Resources such as time and training are clearly crucial in this respect, but perhaps even more fundamental is the need for coherence in the educational philosophy on which the various schemes are based so that the school's efforts to build an overall curriculum and assessment policy in relation to its agreed goals are concerted rather than fragmented. At the present time, there are considerable contradictions between the various assessment initiatives which schools are trying to introduce. Not least is the difference between a still very traditional subject-based examination which has little or no formative component and a two year lead-in, and the emphasis within profiling and modular accreditation schemes on short-term feedback, curriculum diversity, skills and work experience. The very different curricular and pedagogic implications of these two approaches to certification are unlikely to be able to coexist indefinitely in schools.

Profiling within a school assessment policy

Where the profiling initiative proposed is on a more modest scale – perhaps in one subject department or mainly in pastoral work – it is still important that teachers are not faced with contradictory assessment procedures. At best, the continued existence of, for example, old and new procedures, norm and criterion referenced assessment, school reports and profiles, is likely to result in confusion, assessment overload and resentment. At worst it will mean that none of the procedures is done properly. It is therefore vital that an institution develop an *overall policy* for integrating all the various curriculum, communication and accountability aspects of assessment which it desires to fulfil. Such a policy is likely to include:

- diagnostic assessment – in day to day classroom teaching
  – of pupils with special needs
- pupil self-assessment – of curricular and personal progress
- periodic assessments – at the end of a unit of work
- periodic reporting to parents – in discussion and written form
- assessment and recording – for curriculum guidance and subject choice
  – for careers service and other external agencies, references, etc.
- school-leaving certificates
- provision for institutional self-review and external communication

At the present time, many teachers find themselves duplicating effort in communicating the same information in a variety of forms to meet the needs of different agencies. This represents wastage of a valuable and scarce resource – teacher time. Increasingly, therefore, the advent of a whole range of new assessment ideas and possibilities has led schools to develop such a policy and to consider their assessment, recording and reporting needs across the board. Given that the making of a comprehensive record of a wide range of skills and achievements and qualities is a defining characteristic of profiling, it is very difficult to introduce such a scheme without making it part of a larger policy commitment. This has thus been an unanticipated benefit of many schemes.

A simple model of how such a policy might be formulated is set out in Figure 5.5. This is followed by a brief example of how one school has formulated a whole school approach to assessment.

Whether emanating from regional or county consortia, an individual LEA, school or subject department, profiles are typically concerned to promote:
- greater clarity on the part of both teacher and pupil about learning goals;

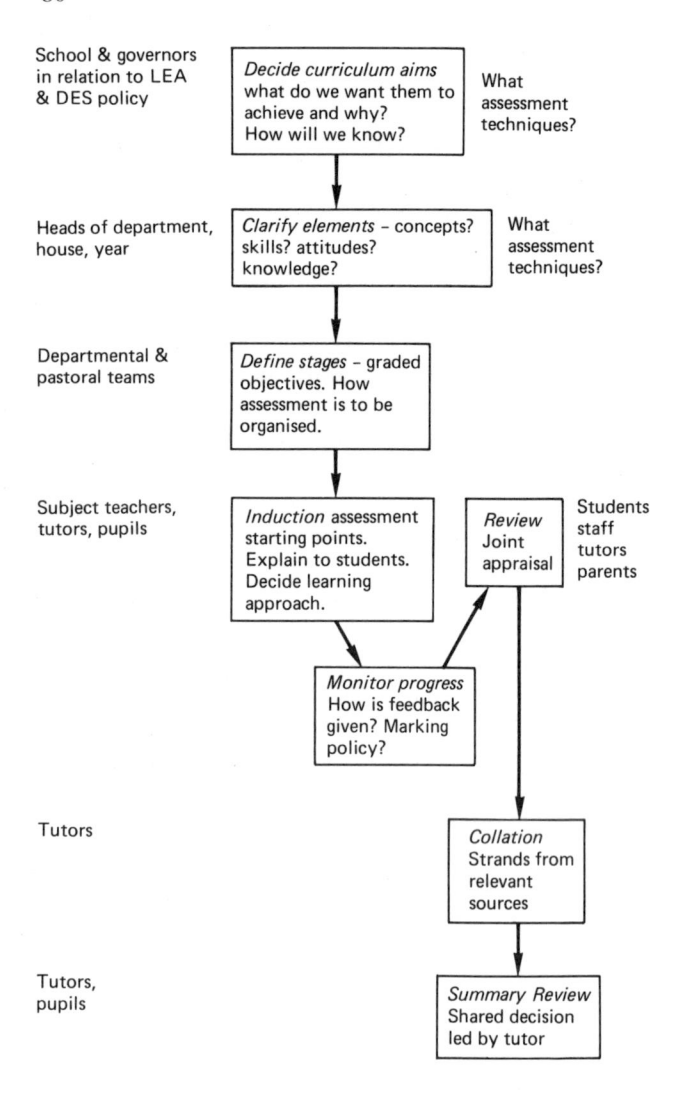

```
School & governors      ┌─────────────────────┐
in relation to LEA      │ Decide curriculum   │   What
& DES policy            │ aims what do we     │   assessment
                        │ want them to achieve│   techniques?
                        │ and why?            │
                        │ How will we know?   │
                        └──────────┬──────────┘
                                   ▼
Heads of department,    ┌─────────────────────┐
house, year             │ Clarify elements –  │   What
                        │ concepts? skills?   │   assessment
                        │ attitudes?          │   techniques?
                        │ knowledge?          │
                        └──────────┬──────────┘
                                   ▼
Departmental &          ┌─────────────────────┐
pastoral teams          │ Define stages –     │
                        │ graded objectives.  │
                        │ How assessment is   │
                        │ to be organised.    │
                        └──────────┬──────────┘
                                   ▼
Subject teachers,       ┌─────────────────────┐    ┌──────────┐  Students
tutors, pupils          │ Induction assessment│    │ Review   │  staff
                        │ starting points.    │    │ Joint    │  tutors
                        │ Explain to students.│    │ appraisal│  parents
                        │ Decide learning     │    └──────────┘
                        │ approach.           │
                        └──────────┬──────────┘
                                   ▼
                        ┌─────────────────────┐
                        │ Monitor progress    │
                        │ How is feedback     │
                        │ given? Marking      │
                        │ policy?             │
                        └──────────┬──────────┘
                                   ▼
Tutors                  ┌─────────────────────┐
                        │ Collation           │
                        │ Strands from        │
                        │ relevant sources    │
                        └──────────┬──────────┘
                                   ▼
Tutors,                 ┌─────────────────────┐
pupils                  │ Summary Review      │
                        │ Shared decision     │
                        │ led by tutor        │
                        └─────────────────────┘
```

Source: J. McNaughton, Essex LEA Pilot Scheme

Figure 5.5: A possible model of the assessment process

- greater teacher–pupil dialogue about both curriculum and assessment;
- more effective monitoring of progress;
- more useful and constructive reporting.

Southway School, Devon, asks its teachers to go through a very similar process of reflection and evaluation as set out in Figure 5.6.

Having appointed a coordinator for assessment to oversee developments in all aspects of evaluation, recording and reporting within the school, Southway's starting point is to ask all teachers:

A i)   What is your intent?
   ii) How will you carry out your intent?
   iii) Does the teaching intention match the pupil's ability?
   iv) What should the expectation be for the individual?
   v)   What evidence will there be to prove your intentions have been realised?
   vi) Can the actual outcome of your teaching intent inform your future teaching action?
B i)   To what extent can pupils be 'let into' the process?
   ii) Do they know clearly what your intention is?
   iii) What expectation is there for the pupil?
   iv) Can pupils be involved in feeding back some measure of personal assessment – an expression of the effective curriculum?

The twin elements of diagnostic assessment and pupil involvement in assessment represented by A and B respectively in these instructions to teachers are built into the day to day assessment policy of the school. Starting with an initial assessment procedure as set out in Figure 5.6, all pupils are monitored every six weeks by all teachers to alert staff to problems and to allow pupils to review their own progress and to allow all to judge whether learning is going well. Supported by a coordinated tutorial programme of non course-based, personal recording and social education, assessment policy throughout the school is based on clearly specified objectives which can begin to identify cross-curricular skills, attitudes, concepts and understanding and produce much more comprehensive records. All the assessments made involve the students and school practice is subjected to a sustained process of review and rigorous analysis of its effectiveness in meeting the goals it has identified for itself. (Southway School, Devon, 1985.)

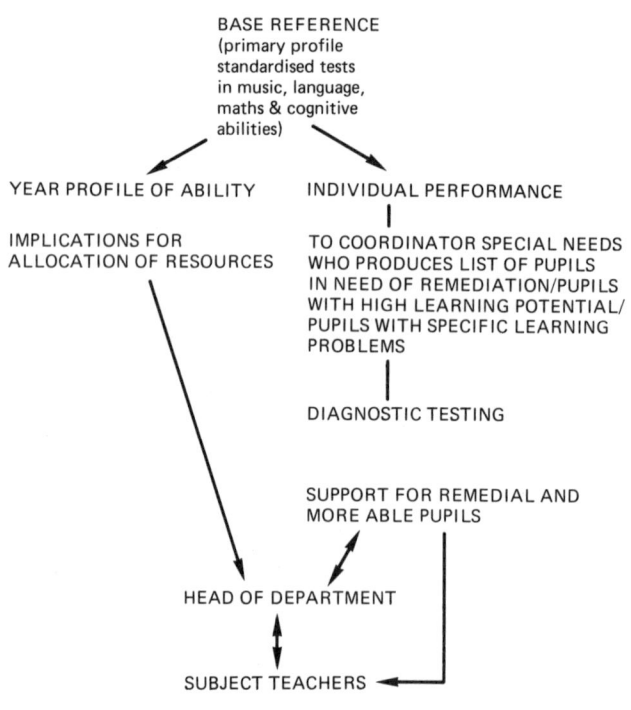

```
                    BASE REFERENCE
                    (primary profile
                    standardised tests
                    in music, language,
                    maths & cognitive
                    abilities)
                   ╱              ╲
                  ▼                ▼
    YEAR PROFILE OF ABILITY    INDIVIDUAL PERFORMANCE
              │                        │
    IMPLICATIONS FOR          TO COORDINATOR SPECIAL NEEDS
    ALLOCATION OF RESOURCES   WHO PRODUCES LIST OF PUPILS
                              IN NEED OF REMEDIATION/PUPILS
                              WITH HIGH LEARNING POTENTIAL/
                              PUPILS WITH SPECIFIC LEARNING
                              PROBLEMS
                                       │
                              DIAGNOSTIC TESTING
                                       │
                              SUPPORT FOR REMEDIAL AND
                              MORE ABLE PUPILS
                   ╲              ╱
                    ▼            ▼
                  HEAD OF DEPARTMENT
                         ↕
                  SUBJECT TEACHERS ◄──
```

Source: Adapted from Southway School Presentation, E. Goddard and C. Harris

Figure 5.6: 'A first snap shot'

The importance of incorporating a profiling initiative into the larger work of the school underlines the need for careful management of the innovation and this is the subject to which we now turn.

A framework for innovation

Identifying a coordinator

Drawing up a school assessment policy is frequently made much easier by the identification of a member of the management team with this particular responsibility. It is a short step from establishing a decision-making framework for assessment policy as a whole to formulating the arrangements for setting up a more specific profiling initiative. Thus most schools have found it useful to nominate a coordinator for the scheme who will be in charge of its initial piloting and subsequent running. In many cases the coordinator's work is supported – even directed – by a school working party or other such group of interested staff entrusted with the task of thrashing out the issues and proposing a scheme.

The need for consultation

Just as important as the need for the design of a new scheme to be integrated into the school's work as a whole, is the way in which this design is arrived at. Where the desire to introduce a profiling scheme first originates is likely to prove significant to its eventual success. Experience suggests that where an LEA or a senior management team seeks to *impose* a scheme on an institution, this is likely to evoke considerable resentment. By contrast, where there is a groundswell of support for the initiative, and an opportunity for each staff member to contribute to the process of innovation, there is a much greater chance of a successful outcome as the following extract sets out:

> One of the first criteria for successful profiling is that the decision should be endorsed by the staff who will be expected to operate the system. This does not mean that 100% of staff have to record their positive support for profiles – it would be difficult to find any initiative within a school which could command such universal approval. It *does* mean, however, that the steps taken towards profiling should involve teachers in consultation, and in full discussion. There should be ample opportunity for teachers to advance suggestions, to air disquiet, and to incorporate the development of profiles within any curriculum development procedures which may exist within the school. Profiling which emerges as a result of an integrated curriculum and assessment policy is much more likely to be viewed by the whole staff as both viable and useful. Where profiling results from an imposed, top-down model, the chances are that the infant will be sickly and weak.
>
> In addition to consultation covering the curriculum and the principles governing policy, consultation with staff could, and probably should include factors such as how the timetable might be rearranged in order to accommodate profiling, what is to be included in any prospective profile, what is to be assessed, by whom and how frequently. Consideration of the ways in which the curriculum will need to be enriched and broadened in order to provide opportunity for development of the skills and qualities to be assessed also forms an important part of the consultative process.
>
> (G. Hitchcock in P. Broadfoot, 1986)

It goes almost without saying that those in a managerial role cannot hope to impose such a scheme on other staff without first establishing a groundswell of support for it.

Most successfully implemented schemes have also invested considerable time and effort in liaising with parents, pupils, local employers, school governors, education officials and any other interested party likely to be affected by the scheme. Where the main weight of the scheme is formative, this falls more centrally within what tends to be regarded as the preserve of the professional and the need for external consultation is likely to be less acute. The need for internal consultation is likely to be even greater since there is likely to be a larger commitment to the time-consuming processes of reviewing and discussion. Where there is a major concern with producing summative profiles, it would be foolhardy indeed to ignore the views of the potential consumer. Indeed many successful schemes have involved local employers and parents in the initial design stages of the scheme and their support has been of major importance in making the scheme work. Even where an 'off the peg' scheme is involved, local consultation is still likely to be vital if the scheme is to take root and grow to its full potential.

Such consultation is also likely to be of considerable importance in helping the school to clarify its original reasons for wanting to institute such a scheme. Figure 5.7, taken from Williams and Johns (1986), gives a diagrammatic representation of the various external elements involved in the design of one such scheme. Note how the more general currents of the profiling movement resulting from the work of bodies such as the Further Education Unit and the Schools Council are combined with the internally-defined aims and objectives of the particular school. These various ideas are then incorporated into a prototype approach by the Deputy Head which is then in turn offered back to individual departments for further development. (See Figure 5.8)

Apart from its essential role in generating a firm basis of support for the new scheme, such consultation will also help teachers and outsiders to articulate their worries about the proposed innovation.

Common concerns

Those outside the school or college are most likely to need reassurance that standards will be maintained and will want clarification on the relationship between profiling and, for example, public examinations. At a time when the number of new assessment and certification procedures being introduced is probably greater and more far-reaching in its effects than ever before, the potential for confusion has also never been greater. It is therefore important to bear in mind the old adage that 'a confused mind says no'.

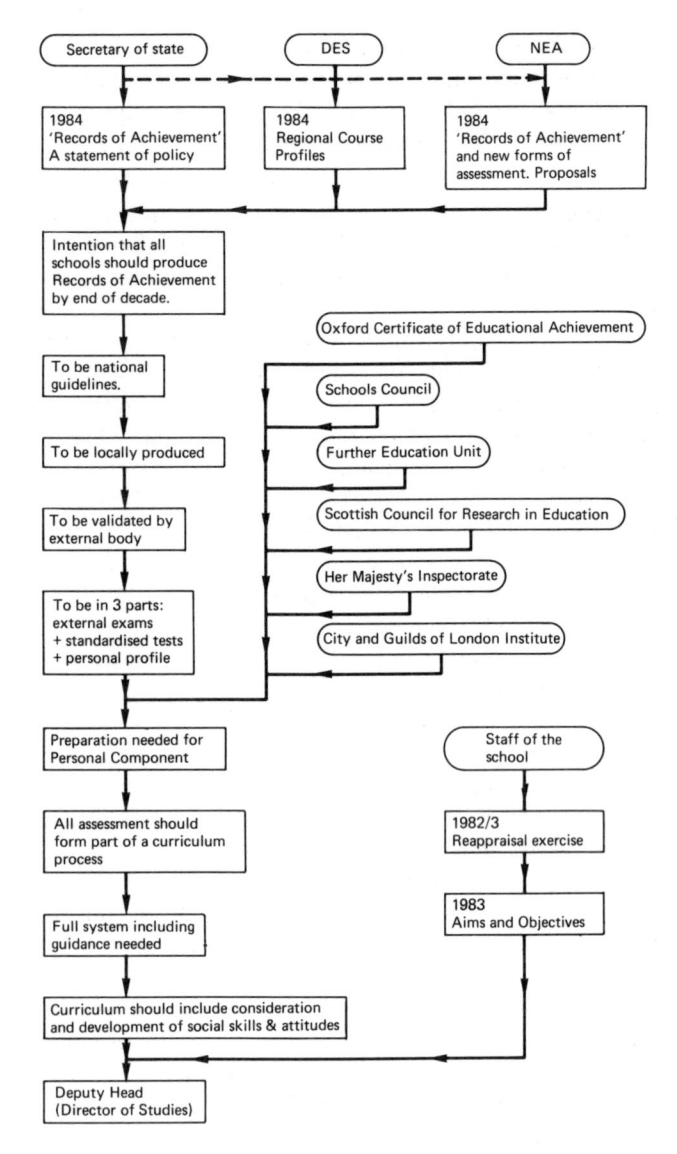

Source: quoted by M. Williams and D. Johns, 1985

Figure 5.7: The impulse

The tide of modular courses, graded assessments, records of achievement and profiles also brings with it a new 16+ examination and AS levels – a deluge quite sufficient to swamp the most sanguine watcher on the shore. Given that there are plenty of selling points in such new schemes, a commitment to investing time in consultation and collaboration with the other partners in the educational enterprise is likely to repay handsome dividends in terms of outside support and go a long way towards overcoming some of these fears.

The worries of those on whom the load of implementing a profiling scheme will actually fall are much harder to alleviate. Existing experience suggests that these worries are principally:

1. time – to do the recording
2. space – to engage in dialogue with pupils
3. skill – in making the assessments
4. fear – of the new style of teaching and learning relationship often required.

The one word that includes all these concerns is *resources*. With sufficient funding, time, facilities, equipment and in-service training can all be provided.

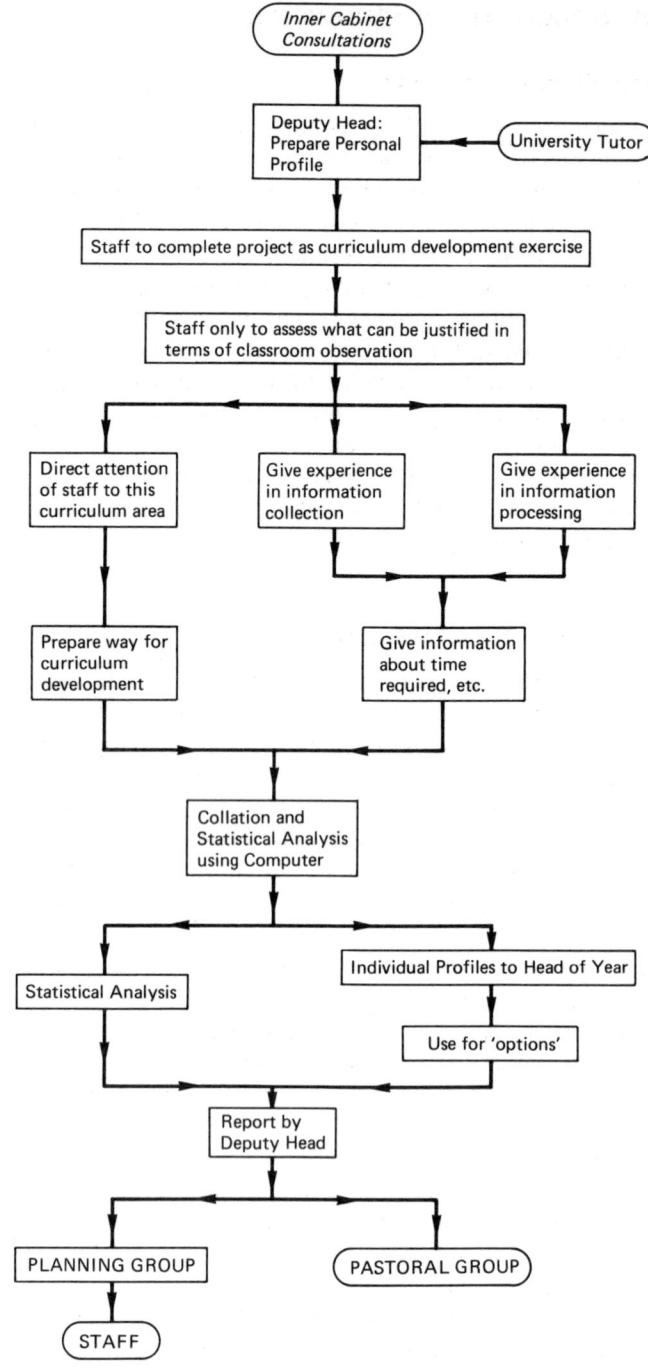

Source: quoted by M. Williams and D. Johns, 1985

Figure 5.8: Initial action

Without it, it may only be the exceptionally well-organised, talented, hard-working and committed teachers who can make profiling work. The question of *resources* is undoubtedly one of the most important issues facing profiling schemes at the present time, as the following comment on Figures 5.9 and 5.10 demonstrates:

> The Senior Teacher showed much concern over the time the process of profiling had taken (as documented in Figures 5.9 and 5.10). As she stated
> '... it is a lot of time, and especially if there's no

recognition, as is happening at the moment when everyone's telling teachers how bad they are . . . What I have now asked for is teacher time. I have sent a report to the Education Committee . . . I honestly couldn't see us going on with it without teachers having time . . . There is a point where you say, "Well, I can do so much and I can't do anything else, not properly, not professionally . . . "'.

Total number of pupils in fourth year = 151

	Hours spent on Pupils' Records		
Subject	Departmental meetings	Compiling comment banks	Writing profiles
English	4	7	27
Mathematics	3	10	23
Languages	2	4	18
Design	3	3	13
Home Economics/ Needlework	2	8	9
Office Practice/ Typing	0	20	24
Religious Education	0	0	27
Science	1½	8	22¼
Humanities	2	10	19½
Outdoor Pursuits	0	4	3
Expressive Arts	0	12	3
Rural Studies	0	4	1
Physical Education	0	4	21
TOTALS	17½	94	210¾

Figure 5.9: Time spent on fourth year pupils' records of achievement 1984–1985

Number of pupils in each form	Time spent by form tutors
17	4
16	3
29	10
30	12
30	3
29	3
TOTAL 151 pupils	35 hours

Figure 5.10: Time spent by form tutors collating subject profiles for fourth year pupils 1984–1985

What is evident in these tables is that developing and implementing profiling are activities which do not fall equally on departments and form tutors. It is evident that, even in a year in which teachers' innovatory work has been severely disrupted by industrial action in schools, profiling has taken a great deal of teachers' time. The figures quoted are only for part of the school year, principally Winter and Spring terms. Because of union action some profile reports were unfinished and therefore, in normal circumstances, hours spent would have been much greater. Although the participating teachers had studied the comment banks and other information from Clwyd LEA, they did not replicate this material but sought to adjust it to their own circumstances. It is this lack of transferability which is one reason why profiling is so expensive in staff time.

(Quoted by M. Williams and D. Johns, 1985)

It is still too early to say how crucial the issue of resources will prove to be. Meanwhile, the existence of many different schemes – some supported and some not supported by additional resources – suggests that there are ways of overcoming this problem even without additional resources. These include:

● *a change in teaching method* to include more resource-based teaching, individualised learning and group work, thereby freeing teachers for more one to one interaction with pupils;
● *the replacement of some or all existing reporting schemes* by a profiling procedure where the more comprehensive and systematic approach can cut down on repetition and clerical chores;
● *the replacement of some or all existing in-school examinations and tests* with continuous assessment criteria built into the curriculum;
● *giving pupils more responsibility in the assessment* so that they become increasingly self-evaluative;
● *extending timetabled tutorial and pastoral time*;
● *using microcomputers for processing and printing the profiles* – in some cases pupils themselves have been made responsible for managing their own records in this way.

Whether or not any of the above suggestions can help in the critical problem of providing time for teachers to do profiling, this is certainly an issue that any department or school will have to consider most carefully if

Source: Adapted from D. Suggett, *Guidelines for Descriptive Assessment*, VISE, Australia, 1985

Figure 5.11

profiling is to be a successful innovation. The very act of showing serious consideration to the problem is likely to be helpful in alleviating staff worries on this score. Fundamentally, the resolution of the problem requires a new approach to teaching and assessment in which the latter is seen as an integral and vital part of the curriculum, and so justifies the time spent on it. While teachers who have given such a key curriculum role to assessment readily perceive its benefits, this requires a range of skills that have not been part of the professional training of many teachers. There is thus a crucial role for in-service training to play in this respect – a point which reinforces once again the resources question. In each case it is vital that the school as a whole:
1 establishes the direction in which it wishes to proceed;
2 identifies its priorities within this general direction;
3 initiates the organisational changes that such priorities require;
4 provides appropriate in-service training.

In-service training

... No profiling schemes can be implemented without adequate in-service education and training. The extent of available LEA support in terms of in-service days, increased staffing ratios which accommodate regular teacher involvement in INSET, or supply cover for occasional INSET activities, varies considerably. This factor will have implications for schools considering profiling. It may be that less fortunate schools will need to find time for in-service support largely within their existing provision; in other cases generous supply cover is made available.

Whether provision is generous or meagre, it will still be necessary to embark upon a programme of in-service education if a profiling scheme is to be successful. The quantity and type of such in-service work will vary from institution to institution. Some schools will feel that assessment is a priority, and teachers look for help in assessment techniques related to both subject attainment and cross-curricular skills. Other schools will seek to develop their staff's counselling and negotiation skills, or even the straightforward techniques of reporting. A combination of approaches to INSET is likely to prove the most helpful. This will include the provision of externally provided courses offering information; the opportunity for teachers to draw upon the experience of practitioners from other schools and other areas; school-based in-service activities where the emphasis lies in answering the identified needs of the individual school; and faculty or department based workshops where attention is focussed upon the needs of a particular group of teachers. Many of those now involved in profiling have found that participation in practical exercises and activities has provided the most useful insight and preparation for their new role.

In-service education provides the key to many of the difficulties associated with the introduction of a profiling scheme. It can help to overcome subjectivity by encouraging teachers to look at what they are assessing, and at the factors influencing their judgements; it can help to obviate the dangers of profiles being used as tools for social control by raising awareness of the problem, and at least making teachers conscious of such records' potential for harm. To the extent that it allows untrained staff to be converted into trained staff, in-service education can help the teacher to make more effective use of time spent on profiling . . .

(G. Hitchcock, *Profiles in Action*, FEU, 1983)

Preparing pupils

In the long run, preparing pupils for a rather different role in the assessment process than they are used to is likely to be just as important to the eventual educational success of the scheme as preparing the staff who will operate it. One of the key principles of profiling is that it should enhance pupils' motivation by offering them a more responsible and informed role in the learning process.

Serious consideration will need to be given to:
1 general discussions with pupils about the purposes of profiling and the reasons for the current government policy commitment to providing all pupils with such a record;
2 more specific discussions with pupils about the nature of the particular scheme with which they will be involved; how it works and how it is intended to help them;
3 continuing opportunity at every stage for pupils to express *their* concerns and be listened to;
4 training in the techniques involved. Some pupils will respond more naturally to the opportunities profiling provides than others. As Chapter 4 set out, the teacher–pupil dialogue at the heart of profiling is the most potentially exciting but also the most dangerous aspect of the process. If *all* pupils are to benefit from it, they must be carefully prepared and receive training equivalent to that being provided for teachers.

One illustration of how this might be done is provided by the East Midlands Record of Achievement Consortium. Pupils being trained to operate a diary system progress through the following stages from simple factual records to more perceptive accounts:
1 Initial Concrete Recording
 (Things I/we did or had)
2 Preferences
 (I enjoyed . . . or I don't like . . .)
3 Differentiation
 (I enjoy this/that aspect more than . . .)
4 Reflection
 (I enjoy this because . . . 'my qualities')
5 Perception of self-development
 (I used to . . . now I . . . have developed/changed)

6 Sharing/communicating
   (A first stage dialogue with others to increase perceptions)
7 Analysis
   (I think I work well with Mavis because . . .)
8 Portraying/communicating
   (I would like you to understand me better through . . .)
9 Synthesis/target setting
   (In future I hope to . . . I will try to be . . .)

(EMRAP Newsletter 1, 1986.)

We know very little, as yet, about the impact of profiling on pupils but it is a theme that needs to be very much to the fore in the design, implementation and subsequent monitoring of a scheme.

Priorities and constraints

The preceding section has set out some of the issues that need to be considered in any new initiative to introduce profiling. The penalties for not so doing are graphically described in Goacher (1983) in which several schools were forced to abandon their attempt to introduce profiling because they had not prepared the ground sufficiently thoroughly.

The circumstances surrounding every individual initiative are a unique blend of factors. Thus the points to bear in mind which have been raised in this chapter can only be identified in very general terms. The aim has been rather to stress the importance of addressing questions such as:

1 What are the priorities we want profiling to achieve in our school, department, college?
2 Who is to be involved in choosing the scheme – school management team, school working party, profiling coordinator, staff as a whole, pupils, parents, governors, employers, LEA . . . ?
3 Is the profile to be a 'ready-made' or 'home-made' scheme – or a combination?
4 How will it be validated – by the school alone, by an external agency (e.g. examination board), by the LEA?
5 Whose support and encouragement inside and outside the institution is essential if profiling is to be a success?
6 What provision for consultation needs to be made?
7 How are staff as a whole to be involved in the scheme? What points are most crucial?
8 How will its importance be projected in the local community amongst e.g. employers, parents?
9 What activities and tasks are essential to bringing about the development and in what order? e.g. parents' meetings, staff meetings, pupil discussions, production of materials . . .
10 What supports will be needed as work progresses? e.g. finance, time, equipment . . .
11 What existing constraints need to be taken into account?
12 What in-service training needs can be identified?

The FEU have provided a useful diagram to represent the kind of questions that will need to be asked when designing a scheme. This is shown in Figure 5.12.

Evaluation

Of course, this need for discussion, reflection and consultation does not finish once a profiling scheme has been launched. It will be necessary to subject the scheme's operation and impact to a continuous process of review and evaluation. Given the importance of this aspect and the rather different issues involved, it is reserved for a separate chapter.

Summary

Many of the points made here about introducing a profiling scheme are echoed in the chapter that follows which describes the experience that one county coordinator for profiling has built up in working with a number of schools to introduce a profiling scheme.

The importance of these questions and how they may be applied is best demonstrated in relation to some actual examples of profiling innovations which are described here in some detail. As you read, try to apply the twelve questions listed above and the three global questions given below.

- What has been successful?
- What has been unsuccessful?
- What might have been done differently?

Try to analyse your own reaction to each of the schemes described in terms of:

- its goals;
- the clarity of criteria identified;
- the preparation of interested parties;
- the involvement of the school as a whole;
- management approaches;
- profile design and likely outcomes;
- potential for abuse and safeguards;
- resources.

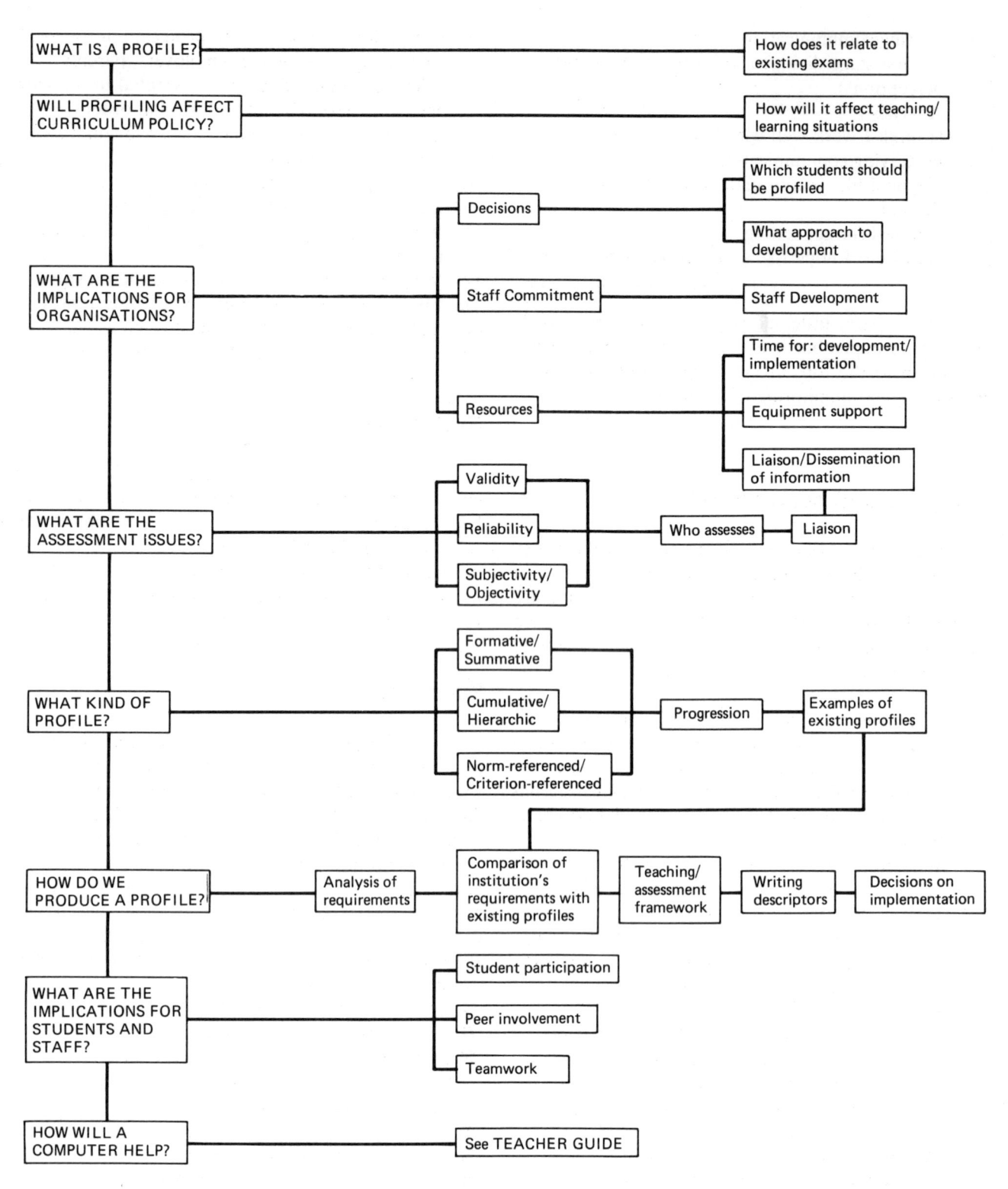

```
WHAT IS A PROFILE? ─────────────────────────────── How does it relate to
                                                    existing exams

WILL PROFILING AFFECT ───────────────────────────── How will it affect teaching/
CURRICULUM POLICY?                                  learning situations

                                                    ┌── Which students should
                                       Decisions ───┤   be profiled
                                                    └── What approach to
                                                        development

WHAT ARE THE ──────────────────── Staff Commitment ──── Staff Development
IMPLICATIONS FOR
ORGANISATIONS?
                                                    ┌── Time for: development/
                                                    │   implementation
                                       Resources ───┼── Equipment support
                                                    └── Liaison/Dissemination
                                                        of information

                                   Validity
WHAT ARE THE ──────────────────── Reliability ──── Who assesses ──── Liaison
ASSESSMENT ISSUES?
                                   Subjectivity/
                                   Objectivity

                                   Formative/
                                   Summative
WHAT KIND OF ──────────────────── Cumulative/ ──── Progression ──── Examples of
PROFILE?                           Hierarchic                        existing profiles
                                   Norm-referenced/
                                   Criterion-referenced

HOW DO WE ──── Analysis of ──── Comparison of ──── Teaching/ ──── Writing ──── Decisions on
PRODUCE A PROFILE? requirements institution's     assessment      descriptors  implementation
                                requirements with  framework
                                existing profiles

WHAT ARE THE ──────── Student participation
IMPLICATIONS FOR
STUDENTS AND ──────── Peer involvement
STAFF?
                ──────── Teamwork

HOW WILL A ──────── See TEACHER GUIDE
COMPUTER HELP?
```

Source: FEU, 1977

Figure 5.12: Profiling: a sequence of questions

Chapter 6
Case studies of school-based innovation

Developing a school-based profiling scheme: case study 1
(By Michael Williams and Donald Johns, University of Manchester Department of Education)

Introduction

The school selected for this study is located in a metropolitan borough in the North of England. It is a split site comprehensive school and one part of the school is in new purpose-built buildings. The school is currently involved in developing profiles for pupils both within subject departments and across the curriculum.

The initiative for profiling

Profiling began to be talked about in the school some time in 1982 at which time a number of staff were dissatisfied with their own current mode of reporting. As the Senior Teacher commented, 'The old-fashioned report books were not doing what we really wanted them to do'. The production of some kind of profile to improve the situation was discussed by the senior management of the school. The major external influences on the development were Manchester's Assessment Development Unit and the Local Authority Working Party on Profiling. The research by B. Goacher (*Recording Achievement at 16+*, Longman, 1983) and the Clwyd LEA Scheme had also helped to formulate ideas.

Organisational aspects

The responsibility for profiling in the school was not totally that of a Senior Teacher. A Deputy Head was responsible for the organisation and administration of the curriculum of the school and pupil assessment was part of this. A Senior Teacher had been given the title of Research Officer with responsibility for the receptiveness of the school to innovation. There was also a senior management committee in the school, consisting of the Head Teacher, three Deputy Head Teachers and four Senior Teachers, of whom one was the Research Officer, with whom changes needed to be discussed.

There had been LEA coordination of the work in local schools through the activities of the Working Party on Profiling which was to issue guidelines for all local schools. These would be about the 'How' and 'Why' of profiling and not about the 'That'. An in-service group was to be set up as a reference point for schools. Any financial help had been through MSC funding.

At the time of our study two profiling systems were being developed in the school. One was for pupils in the Lower School and the other for fourth and fifth year pupils.

Most of the teachers in the school had been involved in the development of the Lower School Profile. The work had been carried out through a series of stages: first, by identifying the weaknesses in the current system and realising the need for change. The question of what had to be done resulted in subject departments examining their aims and objectives in order to determine what to assess and hence to produce an assessment document. Further stages were envisaged involving discussion with pupils about, first, the pupils' progress and then what ought to go into the profile.

The Fourth/Fifth Year Profile was structured by three members of staff: the teacher in charge, the Head of Upper School and the Head of Fifth Year. This had a 'mixed reception' due to infrequent meetings and misunderstandings 'about what it was trying to do and how it would operate'. The Senior Teacher had attended a CRAC Course at Nottingham and he reported that he had 'one or two ideas I would like to incorporate into what we are doing so that it would be a case of meeting the staff and floating those ideas and producing a sort of democratically agreed document, which is the way we have worked lower down the school, and is the way really. Unless you involve all the staff from the beginning it is very unfair to, sort of, impose an idea'. Parents had been informed at a parents' evening so that they understood the procedure and they were encouraged to use the feedback section of the report. Some senior staff had visited local employers and obtained feedback from them.

The question as to whether the school should retain a copy of the summative report seemed to be one which had not been completely resolved. The pupil was given the profile and was free to use it as he/she thought fit. The formative reports (Lower School) were returned by parents and kept by the school.

Documentation of profiling

At the present stage of development the Lower School and Fourth/Fifth Year Profiles were not seen as final documents but as a stage in an evolutionary process. The system being developed was regarded as replacing the old system and not as an addition to it.

(a) The Fourth/Fifth Year Profile

The Fourth/Fifth Year Profile was initially conceived as an in-school development which was not subject-based but identified cross-curricular skills. This was not particularly successful so it was abandoned and the one piloted in 1984/85 was produced using the DES (*Draft Policy Statement: Records of Achievement for School Leavers*, 1983) document on profiling.

As can be seen in Figure 6.1, the Fifth Year Report is composed of three pages. The first page comprises a list of twenty-five subjects arranged alphabetically with columns placed alongside to indicate the level (O, 16+, CSE and Non-exam.) to which the subject was studied by the pupil. The second page (Figure 6.2), titled 'Individual Pupil Reference', provides space for information on the pupil's attendance, punctuality and appearance and the bulk of the profile is arranged to permit subject specialist teachers to comment on the pupils' achievements in communication, numeracy, creative talents, physical ability and practical skills. There is a final space for recording any other comments. This page is signed by the form tutor and the Head of Year/Upper School.

The final page (Figure 6.3), titled 'Individual Pupil Personal Assessment', is designed for completion by pupil and teacher together. Spaces are available for comments on the pupil's extra-curricular school activities, hobbies and interests, voluntary work, college courses attended and work experience placements.

(b) The Lower School Profile

The Lower School Profile was subject based and varied in content and format with each subject but included cross-curricular personal and social skills and qualities which were reported on an A4 sheet. Teachers had been provided with guidelines for reporting personal and social qualities and these are indicated in Figure 6.4, including a list of qualities that might be included and advice to include positive statements only.

For July 1985 second year pupils received an end of year report comprising profiles for ten subjects (Humanities, Music, Art/Design, Physical Education, Dance/Drama, Mathematics, Science, English, Modern Languages and Home Economics). Each of these comprised a single page of A4 but the design and content of each page varied markedly from subject to subject. In addition, there was a page for recording the pattern of progress in personal and social education and this took account of up to six modules studied by the pupils. These modules included Health Education, Social Education, Religious Education and Active Tutorial Work. A page was set aside for a form teacher's assessment and this included a record of merits awarded, absences and punctuality with room for comments on each, plus information on extra-curricular activities and tutor's comments. Parents were invited to sign and write comments at the foot of some, though not all, of the subject profiles and a whole page was available at the end for parents' comments.

HIGH SCHOOL

5th YEAR REPORT SUMMER 1985

PUPIL'S NAME _____

FORM _____

Subject taken	O level	16+	CSE	Non-exam
Art				
Biology				
Careers				
C.D.T.				
Chemistry				
Computer studies				
Drama				
English				
French				
General science				
Geography				
History				
Home economics				
Mathematics				
Metalwork				
Model engineering				
Music				
Needlework				
Office practice				
Physical education				
Physics				
Social studies				
Technical graphics				
Typewriting				
Woodwork				

Figure 6.1: Existing fifth year report

```
┌─────────────────────────────────────┐
│                      NAME _____  │
│                      FORM _____  │
│  ATTENDANCE  _____   │
│  PUNCTUALITY _____   │
│  APPEARANCE  _____   │
├─────────────────────────────────────┤
│  Communication                      │
│                                     │
├─────────────────────────────────────┤
│  Numeracy                           │
│                                     │
├─────────────────────────────────────┤
│  Creative Talents                   │
│                                     │
├─────────────────────────────────────┤
│  Physical Ability                   │
│                                     │
├─────────────────────────────────────┤
│  Practical Skills                   │
│                                     │
├─────────────────────────────────────┤
│  Any other comments                 │
│                                     │
├─────────────────────────────────────┤
│  Signed Tutor _____   │
│  Head of Year/Upper School _____   │
└─────────────────────────────────────┘
```

Figure 6.2: Individual pupil reference

```
┌─────────────────────────────────────┐
│                      NAME _____  │
│                      FORM _____  │
│  DETAILS OF:                        │
├─────────────────────────────────────┤
│  EXTRA CURRICULAR SCHOOL ACTIVITIES │
│                                     │
├─────────────────────────────────────┤
│  HOBBIES AND INTERESTS              │
│                                     │
├─────────────────────────────────────┤
│  VOLUNTARY WORK                     │
│                                     │
├─────────────────────────────────────┤
│  COLLEGE COURSES ATTENDED           │
│                                     │
├─────────────────────────────────────┤
│  WORK EXPERIENCE PLACEMENTS         │
│                                     │
└─────────────────────────────────────┘
```

Figure 6.3: Individual pupil personal assessment

```
┌──────────────────────────────────────────────┐
│ Form teacher's comments on profiles should   │
│ contain only positive statements. These      │
│ statements should relate to the following:   │
│                                              │
│  curiosity            perseverance           │
│  willingness to learn tolerance              │
│  confidence           empathy                │
│  adaptability         consideration for others│
│  autonomy             involvement            │
│  co-operativeness     enjoyment of work      │
│  commitment           self-reliance          │
│  reliability          value-judgements       │
│  self-discipline                             │
└──────────────────────────────────────────────┘
```

Figure 6.4: Guidance to first and second form tutors

```
┌────────────────────────────────────────┐
│   ┌──────────────────────────────────┐ │
│   │ PUPIL NAME .................... │ │
│   │ SUBJECT REPORT ................ │ │
│   └──────────────────────────────────┘ │
├────────────┬────────────┬──────────────┤
│ CONTINUOUS │ ATTAINMENT │   EFFORT     │
│ ASSESSMENT │            │              │
├────────────┼────────────┼──────────────┤
│EXAMINATION │ PERCENTAGE │  POSITION    │
├────────────┴────────────┴──────────────┤
│                                        │
│                      Signed..........  │
└────────────────────────────────────────┘
```

Figure 6.5: Lower school profile

Both Upper and Lower School profiles are targeted on the whole year group. As the Senior Teacher stated, 'At no stage would we tolerate it being a lower ability thing – it has so many implications it would never be considered'.

Resource implications and staff development

The school had arranged for both formal and informal support for the staff. The Senior Teacher saw the role of teacher in charge as being one of consultant; 'I've been available for consultation all the way through in terms of how the documents looked, inherent weaknesses, potential problems in completing it, but

Pupil Name....................................	Date.........................
Details of Activity	
Standard Achieved (if appropriate)	
Signature of Teacher	

Figure 6.6: In-school activities

Pupil Name....................................	Date.........................
Details of Activity	
Standard Achieved (if appropriate)	
Signature of Leader/Organiser	

Figure 6.7: Out-of-school activities

the departments have been given a free hand and then have entered into dialogue with me in many cases'. Only TVEI personnel had attended outside courses, plus a number of senior staff. No real resistance was attendant on the introduction and implementation of the profile but there was resistance at the administrative stage due to the amount of time required to complete the profiles. The problem was partly resolved by giving teachers extra time. Thus time during registration time in the mornings had been made available, also report forms were available for use for most of the year, not just for the last two weeks of term, so they could be filled in during the year. The Senior Teacher pointed out, however, 'In reality it is often less than a year, and with the thing (document) developing all the time it's not possible, nor is it desirable, to have a pack of a thousand produced and just reel off two hundred each year . . . but it takes away the mad rush and the thoughtlessness that went with the old reports'. Further, he thought that as teachers gained more experience with profiling and as teachers and pupils engaged in more discussion, profiling would eventually become more integrated into the teaching.

Conclusion

This study illustrates the developmental work required to establish a system of profiling. The study has focussed on the management and staff development aspects. These aspects are essentially concerned with the mechanics of profile construction and implementation. No attempt has been made to investigate the classroom changes, in curriculum and teacher–pupil relationships which are important underpinnings and consequences of the developmental work.

Developing a school-based profiling scheme: case study 2 (By M. Williams and D. Johns, 1985)

Introduction

The school selected for this study is located within a metropolitan borough in the North of England. It is an 11–18 year old comprehensive school situated in an affluent area where parental support for achievement is strong. The school had recently had a change of Head. The reputation of the school had been built up on academic standards, hence vocational education had a minor role and the school had not been involved in recent developments in that field. Plans were afoot, however, for the development of such courses in the fourth, fifth and sixth forms.

The information presented in this report was obtained principally in an interview with a Deputy Head responsible for school administration and who had overall responsibility for profiling in the school.

The initiative for profiling

Thinking about profiling in a formal way began in October 1983 when the Deputy Head joined the LEA Profile Working Party. He had read articles in the educational press on profiling which interested him: 'It was one of those things one was aware of and, from comments from the DES at that stage, it seemed that it was to be a form of reporting that comprehensive schools were going to be involved in . . . if not in the

1980s, then in the 1990s, and since I was a Deputy Head I had a responsibility to prepare the staff. I arrived here in September 1983 as Deputy Head and I wanted to follow up the ideas so I contacted the Teachers Centre warden and I asked him what was happening. He invited me along to the meetings of the Profile Working Party and that's how we got started here'.

Organisational sequence

The school started in September 1984 by being involved in the LEA Pilot Scheme, using 30 children in the fifth year, 'to see how the system worked and to work out a school system which could cope with the different requirements of profiling, and to sell the idea to the staff who were rather wary that it was going to take up a lot of their time' (Deputy Head). Since this was a trial with just a few pupils, the normal school reporting system continued, i.e. a cheque book system. After the trial a number of difficulties with the scheme, as it existed, were identified. These difficulties were largely due to the fact that the profile had been computerised and the language was rather stilted; 'the personal skills paragraph and the personal qualities paragraph didn't really say what a teacher, who really knew the child, would have written'.

The result of this evaluation was that the staff of the Geography Department began, in January 1984, to develop a profile to meet the particular needs of the school, rather than the LEA Profile. The LEA Pilot Scheme was based upon that developed by the Geography Department in this school, with a certain degree of flexibility possible within individual schools.

This was to be piloted in the schools as soon as possible with the whole of the fourth year. The emphasis was to be on formative evaluation which was to take place each half term: 'It is to make the point with staff that it is not the bit of paper at the end which is so important, but the process through which the children and teachers operate. Because so many are involved, we have had to reinvent the report procedures in the fourth and fifth year, we have done away with the cheque books and invented a grade report system that reflects what has happened throughout the profile and not just assessing their abilities in English, French, Maths, etc. Their grade report gives them a teachers' consensus of opinion of how they are developing in all the skills that are in the profile' (Deputy Head).

The current profile report

The current profile had twenty-four categories to be reported (see Figure 6.8). As can be seen, each category has six statements representing different levels of achievement. These statements comprise a data bank. The categories are:
- *basic skills*, such as listening, reading, writing and numeracy;
- *personal skills*, such as courtesy, helpfulness, accepting responsibility;
- *social qualities*, such as working in a group;
- *work related skills*, including cognitive skills such as data interpretation and evaluating results;
- *practical skills*, such as using equipment;
- *physical skills*, as appropriate to the specialist subject.

The subject teachers, perhaps in discussion with the pupil, produce a profile in that subject for each pupil by choosing an appropriate level of achievement from the data bank and inserting the appropriate number for each category of behaviour on a sheet (see Figure 6.9). A profile for each pupil is then compiled from these reports by the form tutor. An example of such a profile is included as Figure 6.10. This is a summative profile and will be tried out in the school in the near future.

Along with this profile is an uncomplicated document bearing the pupil's name and giving space for him/her to record aspects of his or her experiences in and out of school. Guidance is given in a document titled Pupil's Personal Record (see Figure 6.11). This document encourages the pupil to consider experience in sport, work, hobbies, societies, excursions away from home, service to others and music.

To carry out formative evaluation a Personal Development Disc has been devised (see Figure 6.12). This records the level of achievement for each behaviour category by the filling in of the appropriate segment of the circle with coloured pencil. This might be done by the subject teacher alone or by the teacher in discussion with the pupil. The records from the discs for each pupil are then put into an Interim Profile Report (see Figure 6.13) which is sent out to parents. This is a formative profile. The formative profile is to be the subject of a trial in the school in the near future.

Responsibility for profiling

Profiling is the direct responsibility of two people: one, who was appointed as Assessment Development Officer to have responsibility for the day-to-day running of the profiling scheme; and the other, the Deputy Head in overall charge. 'In the first term we met every Friday to discuss problems, another fifth year teacher helped as well.' Since inevitably the profile report system will replace the original system throughout the school, the Assessment Development Officer will be in charge of all assessment in the school. This teacher had a scale three post but has left for promotion. The school is negotiating for a replacement 'the new Head is supportive of profiling but is wary of allocating the points he has available too quickly'.

Support for profiling

The LEA has given little or no financial help to the school but has provided stationery. Psychological support was provided by support given to the schools through the Working Party which enabled cross fertilisation of ideas and experiences to occur. This proved a very useful means of innovating for participating institutions. Supportive in-service courses and conferences were arranged by both the LEA and the school itself,

		1	2	3	4	5	6
		No comment					
A	COURTESY		He seldom understands the need to be courteous and considerate.	He needs encouragement to maintain an acceptable level of courtesy and consideration.	He maintains an acceptable level of courtesy and consideration, with only occasional lapses.	He behaves in a courteous and considerate manner at all times.	He always shows high standard of courtesy and consideration.
B	HELPFULNESS		He rarely helps those around him.	He does not always recognise when others need help.	He will help others if the task interests him.	He is willing to help others but occasionally lacks necessary confidence.	He helps others spontaneously.
C	ACCEPTING RESPONSIBILITY		He needs encouragement to take responsibility.	He will accept responsibility if the duties are clearly defined.	He will accept responsibility in straightforward situations.	He willingly accepts responsibility in a variety of situations.	He willingly accepts responsibility in all situations and shows sound judgement.
D	WORKING INDEPENDENTLY		He needs constant help and guidance when working on his own.	He can work on his own, when guidance has been given.	He can work independently only when he is interested in the task.	When required to he works independently on most occasions.	He can work independently when required in all situations.
E	WORKING IN A GROUP		He finds difficulty in recognising the need to co-operate with others.	He needs constant guidance in order to work in a group.	He is able to co-operate with other members of a group.	He is a co-operative and effective member of a group.	He is a constructive and decisive member of a group who helps and encourages others to implement decisions.
F	LISTENING		He demonstrates some ability to listen to instructions.	He demonstrates some ability to listen to and to retain spoken information.	He retains spoken information.	He readily retains and interprets spoken information.	He analyses spoken arguments clearly.
G	TALKING		He makes appropriate replies when spoken to.	He converses with others.	He converses fluently with others and is able to convey clearly both description and explanation.	He communicates effectively with a range of people in a variety of oral situations.	He is fluent orally and skilled in negotiation.
H	READING		His reading and understanding is limited to short simple text.	His reading and understanding extend to straightforward passages.	He is able to follow clearly, written instructions and explanations.	He usually understands a variety of forms of written materials.	He shows sophistication in selecting and judging written evidence to support a point of view.
I	WRITING		He is able to write short sentences.	He writes descriptively with clarity.	He writes logically.	He writes logically with appropriate supportive evidence.	In his written work he can express complex arguments and weigh the evidence sustaining them.
J	NUMERACY		He is capable of basic counting.	He has understood the techniques of addition and subtraction in solving problems.	He has understood the techniques of multiplication and division in solving problems.	He is able to calculate ratios, percentages and proportions.	He demonstrates an intelligent use of formulae.
K	FOLLOWING INSTRUCTIONS		He can follow simple verbal instructions.	He can follow simple verbal and written instructions.	He can follow verbal multi-step instructions.	He can follow written and verbal multi-step instructions.	He can follow difficult multi-step instructions with confidence.
L	PROBLEM SOLVING		He accepts situations uncritically.	He is able to assess situations and can proceed with guidance.	He is able to assess basic problems and seeks solutions independently.	He can reason through ideas to solve problems of moderate difficulty.	He is able to assess complex problems and use alternative strategies to seek solutions.
M	PLANNING		He identifies with prompting the sequence of steps in everyday pieces of work.	With help he can describe the sequence of steps in a routine piece of work.	He can choose from given alternatives the best way of tackling a task.	He can modify given plans to meet changed circumstances.	He has originality creating new plans and routines.

(continued)

		1 2 No comment	3	4	5	6
N	PREPAREDNESS	He sometimes arrives prepared for lessons.	He is fairly thorough in preparing for lessons.	He is usually well organised and arrives prepared for the task in hand.	He can be relied upon for sound organisation and preparation for tasks undertaken.	He shows a high level of organisation and preparation for every task undertaken.
O	OBTAINING INFORMATION	He finds information with guidance.	He is willing to ask for information.	He uses standard sources of information to develop his work.	He extracts and assembles information from several given sources.	He shows initiative in seeking and gathering information from a wide variety of sources.
P	DATA INTER-PRETATION	He recognises everyday signs and symbols.	He makes use of maps, simple diagrams and timetables.	With help, he can make use of basic graphs, charts, codes and technical drawings.	He interprets and uses basic graphs, charts and technical drawings unaided.	He constructs graphs and extracts information to support conclusions.
Q	ASSIGNMENTS	His assignments are adequately completed.	He organises assignments with care.	He can plan, organise and prepare assignments.	Assignments are fully completed.	He always develops and completes assignments in a detailed and comprehensive manner.
R	USING EQUIPMENT	With guidance, he can use equipment to perform simple tasks.	After demonstration, he can use equipment to perform the successive stages of a task.	He selects and uses suitable equipment and materials for the job without help.	He accurately sets up and uses equipment to produce work to standard.	He is able to identify and remedy common faults in equipment.
S	SAFETY	He can remember safety instructions.	He is able to recognise risks if given guidance.	He shows a reasonable attitude to safety matters.	He is willing to accept the necessity of safety procedures and co-operates to reduce risks.	He is fully aware of all aspects of safety and would act immediately to reduce risks of accidents.
T	PHYSICAL SKILLS	He has developed basic physical co-ordination.	He can co-ordinate bodily movement and fine manual skills.	He develops manipulative skills quickly.	He is competent and exhibits above average physical and manipulative skills.	Has outstanding ability and awareness in all physical activities.
U	CREATIVE SKILLS	He is occasionally able to express given ideas creatively.	He is usually able to express given ideas creatively.	He is always able to express given ideas creatively.	He shows imagination in creative expression.	He is an outstanding innovator in creative expression.
V	TECHNICAL ACCURACY	He occasionally produces accurate work.	He is capable of producing accurate work.	His work is mostly accurate.	His work shows a high level of accuracy.	It is rare for inaccuracy to be found in his work.
W	PRESENTATION OF WORK	The presentation of his work is occasionally of a reasonable standard.	The presentation of his work is frequently of a reasonable standard.	The presentation of his work is of a reasonable standard.	The presentation of his work is of a high standard.	He always produces meticulously presented work.
X	EVALUATING RESULTS	He relies on others to assess his results.	He assesses his own results, with assistance.	He assesses independently his own results in routine tasks.	He assesses independently his own results in tasks including the non-routine.	He assesses his own performance and identifies possible improvements.

NAME _____

FORM _____

SCHOOL _____

Figure 6.8: Data bank comments

FORM _____

TEACHER _____

NAME OF PUPIL

COMMENT

A
B
C
D
E
F
G
H
I
J
K
L
M
N
O
P
Q
R
S
T
U
V
W
X
Others

Figure 6.9: Subject teachers' compiled sheet (form teacher)

NAME _____ FORM _____

TUTOR _____

SUBJECT AREA

Courtesy	
Helpfulness	
Accepting responsibility	
Working independently	
Working in a group	
Listening	
Talking	
Reading	
Writing	
Numeracy	
Following instructions	
Problem solving	
Planning	
Preparedness	
Attaining information	
Data interpretation	
Assignments	
Using equipment	
Safety	
Physical skills	
Creative skills	
Technical accuracy	
Presentation of work	
Evaluating results	

Figure 6.10: Individual pupil profile

PUPIL'S PERSONAL RECORD

You are invited to write down all those things in which you are actively interested: it is useful to you to record them and interesting to anyone who needs to know about you. It is worth taking some time over this: you don't want to miss anything in justice to yourself nor do you want to put anything in which is not a real interest, for a short discussion would soon show your lack of knowledge. To help you is this list of headings for you to use as you wish. All these headings can be thought of in two equally important ways: (i)   in School
(ii) at Home

SPORTS
INDIVIDUAL SPORTS
TEAMS
POSITION OF RESPONSIBILITY
(e.g. Secretary, Captain)

WORK
ORGANISED BY SCHOOL
PART TIME JOB

HOBBIES
PERSONAL INTEREST
CLUBS
COMPETITIVE
(e.g. Photographic competitions)

SOCIETIES
MEMBER
POSITION OF RESPONSIBILITY

STAYED AWAY FROM HOME
(e.g. Field Trips, Scout Camps)

SERVICE TO OTHERS
COMMUNITY SERVICE
FIRST AID

MUSIC
Playing an instrument or singing
General interest in Music

Figure 6.11: Pupil's Personal Record

NAME:
FORM:
SUBJECT:
FORM TUTOR:

KEY:

A	COURTESY	P	DATA INTERPRETATION
B	HELPFULNESS	Q	ASSIGNMENTS
C	ACCEPTING RESPONSIBILITY	R	USING EQUIPMENT
D	WATCHING INDEPENDENTLY	S	SAFETY
E	WORKING IN A GROUP	T	PHYSICAL SKILLS
F	LISTENING	U	CREATIVE SKILLS
G	TALKING	V	TECHNICAL ACCURACY
H	READING	W	PRESENTATION OF WORK
I	WRITING	X	EVALUATING RESULTS
J	NUMERACY		
K	FOLLOWING INSTRUCTIONS		
L	PROBLEM SOLVING		
M	PLANNING		
N	PREPAREDNESS		
O	OBTAINING INFORMATION		

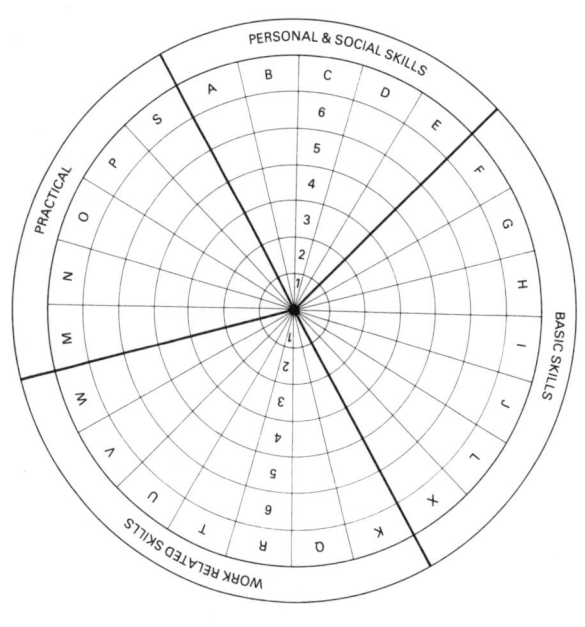

1–6 LEVELS OF ACHIEVEMENT
1   NO COMMENT

Figure 6.12: Personal development disc

with invitations to outside experts to help. Time, however, seems to be the major resource which is required. 'Time has been a problem. We have pointed out to the LEA all along that the teachers' time is not infinite and last term was particularly difficult with the teachers' action . . . then we got through with a good deal of goodwill, with no additional staffing from either the teaching staff point of view nor ancillary staff point of view . . . on the Clwyd experience we should have been given at least half a teacher if not a full teacher, plus a lot of secretarial help. They (the TVEI schools) are the only schools really that have the resources to follow through the formative aspects of profiling'.

Employer and parent involvement

When the first profile was tried out in the school in 1984 'we had a parents' evening and the parents and pupils came in and went through the profiles, giving us valuable feedback about what they thought about the system. We have links with employers through our liaison committee; from October onwards we showed them the profile . . . although it was already started then . . . it was a matter of asking them what they thought about it . . . we did a mock-up of what the final result might be like for an average child and got feedback from them that way'. Employers were involved in the production of the second profile through the LEA Working Party. 'Parents and employers thought there was more in the document than the teachers did. The teachers were a little disappointed', due to the reasons given previously in this report.

Resistance to profiling and management response

A good deal of resistance has been generated by the idea of using the Development Disc in formative eva-luation, the reason generally given being the lack of time for discussion with the pupils, which could be seen as being due to a lack in resourcing the scheme. 'If our school were ideal all the teachers would be doing it in all the faculties, half termly. I think realistically it will take several years to get all the teachers doing it . . . we could just say all teachers have to do it, but that would guarantee that half of them would ruin the system before they have even accepted it in their own minds . . . therefore we are playing that one softly, softly at the moment – there are areas who are using the idea "I haven't got time" to avoid the formative aspects and the Developmental Disc . . .'

Overcoming resistance

One of the ways in which the school is attempting to overcome resistance is the provision of in-service work in terms of the development of the necessary skills. 'We have provided training "in house". I do believe in training on the job as well, and I think by going ahead, even though we were a bit wary about how teachers would cope, has helped. At the beginning the Science Department staff, virtually as a body, were against the system and now a majority of them can see the value of it, but we have still a long way to go but . . . actually using it, as opposed to being told about it, has meant people have had time . . . We try to involve the whole staff in criticism of the system . . . and we started out by pointing out that it was a new system, it wasn't our own scheme . . . they would have the opportunity to influence . . . certainly, what our own school did.'

Difficulties exist in particular areas such as Science, Craft, Physical Education, and Drama which are subjects in which active learning goes on, and in which there would be difficulties in giving the rest of the class something to do while the teacher 'consulted' with one pupil at a time, 'perhaps the answer is to reduce class

| Name _____ | Form _____ | Date of assessment _____ |

Date of parents' evening _____

Attainment of Skills		* 1-5
Personal Qualities	Manners	
	Helpfulness	
	Motivation	
Social Qualities	Working in a group	
	Accepting responsibility	
	Awareness	
Communication	Talking and listening	
	Reading	
	Writing	
Practical and Numerical	Using signs and diagrams	
	Using equipment	
	Numeracy	
Decision making	Planning	
	Obtaining information	
	Coping	
	Evaluating Results	
Presentation	Neatness	
	Technical accuracy	
	Scope	
	Organisation	
Expression	Physical educability	
	Expressive ability	
Safety	Safety	

*Please note:-
(a) that 1 represents basic level and 5 represents high level.
(b) the number represents the overall view recorded by the pupil's subject teachers.

Subjects	Level	Grade	**
Mathematics			
English Language			
English Literature			
POOL 1.			
2.			
3.			
4.			
5.			
P.E.	Effort only:		
General Studies	Effort only:		

**Please note that a tick indicates a subject teacher's request to see parents at the parents' evening.

Tutor comment _____

Parent comment _____

☐ Absence   ☐ Times late

Figure 6.13: Interim profile report

sizes or change teaching styles or use time out of class to remove or reduce these difficulties'. Another strategy is available to overcome resistance, 'by getting teachers to sell it to other teachers . . . It is far easier for teachers at the chalk face to say "my children are responding in this way" . . . and this has already started at our in-service this term; teachers were standing up saying these kinds of things . . . also some teachers made a video . . . and sold our profile to the other teachers. . . . The LEA profile is basically that of our school with some alterations. Once you get people in this frame of mind it is unstoppable as long as we can keep up the momentum . . . that is my role . . . to try to make sure it is resourced'.

Conclusion

This study illustrates an innovation which started through the initiative of a member of the management of the school, was then taken over and developed by members of a particular department. It was then taken out to influence other schools in the area.

The grassroots development and the particular role played by the school management ensures its present viability.

Developing a school-based profiling scheme: case study 3
(By T. Wilkes, *'Pupil Profiling: Demanding Innovation'*, Diploma in Advanced Studies in Education dissertation, University of Bristol, 1985)

The context for this case study is Hreod Parkway School, Wiltshire LEA, a newly reorganised 11–16 comprehensive school in the 'M4 corridor' area. The bitterness and resentment which tend to follow such upheaval were only part of the problems the school faced. The introduction of a faculty-based structure and block timetabling were intended to enable development but proved onerous initiatives in the early stages.

In the first year, the school volunteered to take part in an LEA Careers Service profiling pilot scheme. This is described in Figures 6.14 and 6.15 a–d. Inadequate communication with both the organising group and other schools involved in the scheme meant a great deal of confusion at the start. These problems were further exacerbated by difficulties in gathering the necessary evidence for the profile, finding the time to meet with pupils and with other teachers to discuss progress and standardise criteria. Despite the impetus given to the scheme by the LEA reorganisation which meant that all fifth formers had to make a choice between employment, YTS and sixth form college, the inadequate groundwork and support for the scheme resulted in its being prematurely terminated. A brief history of this 'top down' approach to innovation is given below.

Meanwhile the school itself had been involved in reviewing its internal reporting procedures and there was general agreement that existing procedures were inadequate. Coupled with the developing interest in, and experience of, profiling that some staff had acquired from the LEA pilot scheme, the result was a commitment to improving subject-based, school-wide recording and reporting practices. Some staff referred to this as 'profiling by the backdoor'.

The following proposal was put to a management meeting in May 1984.
- Faculties were to design their own assessment sheet and it was to be faculty, as opposed to subject, based.
- It would use A4 sized paper.
- It must be capable of providing information for tutors on specified year groups.
- The pilot scheme would be based on the fourth year and would initially replace the single sheet pattern for October 1984.
- Faculties were to develop their own criteria for this pilot.
- Discussion or consultation was offered at this stage, rather than presented as obligatory.

At this time, as has already been noted above, no official meetings were taking place due to the industrial dispute and this could have been one major factor determining the disparity between faculties in the development of their sheets. Some faculties were already developing internal methods of assessment and were able to adapt their approaches to suit the agreement. In some cases individual teachers were either already studying for higher awards and keen to include work of this nature, or had a personal interest in such activity. Some faculties consulted widely, whilst others waited until just prior to the deadline before producing a sheet which could be used.

To be fair to individuals and groups it must be noted here that certain faculties were different in size, which created problems. Some contained staff with a more suspicious approach to curriculum development, whilst other faculties had a mixture of experiences and attitudes which created difficulties in reaching a consensus.

Tossell (1984) conducted a similar survey in a school developing self-assessment schemes and raised the following points. Departments can be cruelly affected by change, particularly by a change of Head of Department. Priorities can become confused and the organisation of the teaching will usually take precedence. He quotes Ball (1981) arguing that different cultures exist in Science, Maths and Languages departments who may be more concerned with the pursuit of academic excellence and the acquisition of knowledge than other departments in a school.

Dear

PROFILING PROJECT

During 1984 and 1985, some pupils will be taking part in a small pilot project, which aims to help pupils assess their strengths and weaknesses over a wider range of skills than is usually covered by a normal school report.

These skills are those which have been identified in recent large scale studies about qualities which are particularly important to employers. They include, for example, the ability to listen and talk to groups of people effectively, being able to use equipment properly, the ability to accept responsibility, to obtain information, to appreciate the uses of computers and to be able to work effectively as a member of a small group.

Until the end of the fifth year, your son or daughter will be talking individually with a tutor about his or her strong points and weaker points, as they relate to the adult working world. Together, pupil and tutor will seek to identify the skills which the pupil feels confident about and the ones which will need more attention. With each skill, both pupil and tutor will have to investigate and record the evidence which can prove that a particular skill has been learned or that more experience is necessary. The profile is the document on which progress is recorded. The pupil holds the record and he or she will no doubt bring the profile home to discuss with you, later in the year.

These skills which are important in obtaining employment and making progress at work, can be gained from experiences at home or in leisure time as well as school life. As parents you will have a great deal of evidence about your child's abilities and personality. In helping pupils to see the relevance of experiences and skills which can be gained out of school, your comments on some aspects of the profile will be particuarly important. From time to time, therefore, your son or daughter may bring home a question slip which asks for your comments about a particular type of skill which both pupil and tutor are investigating. Your information will then form part of the pupil's profile. It should be stressed that all the information gained is open to pupil, tutor and parents. It will be regarded as confidential information and will not be passed to any agency outside the school without consulting both pupil and parents.

Looking at pupils' abilities in this way and creating a profile takes a great deal of staff time and therefore only a few pupils are involved at present. They have therefore been selected at random, to include all levels of academic ability. We feel that this approach to analysing skills could be particularly important for pupils' future careers, because it has been developed from employers' views of what makes for success in working life. We hope, therefore, that you will agree to your son or daughter taking part in the project. It will not, of course, change pupils' timetables in any way.

If you would like further information, the tutor involved will be .... Please contact the tutor if you wish and we hope that you will also have the opportunity to talk with the 'profile' tutor at the next Parents Evening.

I should be grateful if you would confirm your receipt of this letter and your agreement to your son or daughter taking part. Would you please send back to school the enclosed reply slip.

Yours sincerely,

(Headteacher)

21 December 1983

Figure 6.14: Draft letter to parents of pupils taking part in the 14–16 profiling project

County Council
Education Department

CONFIDENTIAL

EDUCATION AND TRAINING — 16 PLUS PUPIL PROFILE

SURNAME _____ FIRST NAMES _____

SCHOOL/COLLEGE _____ DATE OF BIRTH _____

HOME ADDRESS _____

_____ HOME TEL. NO. _____

INITIAL JOB IDEAS   1. _____   2. _____

EXAMINATIONS RECORD

Subjects	Exams	Working to ability	5th yr. 'mock' results	Actual Grades
_____	S C O	YES/NO	_____	_____
_____	S C O	YES/NO	_____	_____
_____	S C O	YES/NO	_____	_____
_____	S C O	YES/NO	_____	_____
_____	S C O	YES/NO	_____	_____
_____	S C O	YES/NO	_____	_____
_____	S C O	YES/NO	_____	_____
_____	S C O	YES/NO	_____	_____
_____	S C O	YES/NO	_____	_____
_____	S C O	YES/NO	_____	_____
_____	S C O	YES/NO	_____	_____
_____	S C O	YES/NO	_____	_____
_____	S C O	YES/NO	_____	_____
_____	S C O	YES/NO	_____	_____

OTHER STUDIES

Topic	Test & Grade	Date of 'test'
_____	_____	_____
_____	_____	_____
_____	_____	_____
_____	_____	_____
_____	_____	_____

Figure 6.15a: LEA careers service 16+ profile: Part 1

It is useful to observe, however, that in the development of assessment systems there will be present in any school not only different management problems across the faculties or departments, but also different culture problems and that any straight-jacket imposed school-wide will inevitably meet severe resistance. This does not imply, however, that all pilot assessment sheets should be set in stone nor that work is impossible in developing ideas and approaches across certain areas of the school. What it does imply, is that the focus of the work should not necessarily be directed towards the same goal by everyone.

All of the faculty sheets were generated in time for a pilot scheme to run in October 1984 and extracts of some of these are shown in Figures 6.17 to 6.22. All faculties were given the same deadline for presentation of the assessment information and were asked to pass the collated returns to the Director of Studies. From here the sheets were combined with returns from other faculties and then distributed to the appropriate tutors.

With over 300 in a year group and eight faculties producing information (some of them using self-assessments as well) over 2500 sheets of A4 paper had to be handled at this stage and immediately a few practical points emerged, to be noted and raised at a later review. With the exception of a few 'strays' all assessments were completed and delivered to tutors on time,

OTHER SUBJECTS I WOULD LIKE TO HAVE TAKEN AT SCHOOL _____
_____
_____

BASIC SKILLS PROFILE

SPECIAL ABILITIES	O.K.	ETN	N/O
1. WORKING WITH CLASSMATES	_____	_____	_____
2. WORKING WITH THOSE IN AUTHORITY	_____	_____	_____
3. SELF AWARENESS	_____	_____	_____

COMMUNICATION
4. TALKING AND LISTENING
5. READING AND WRITING
6. VISUAL UNDERSTANDING

PRACTICAL AND NUMERICAL ABILITIES
7. USING EQUIPMENT
8. DEXTERITY AND COORDINATION
9. MEASURING
10. CALCULATING

DECISION MAKING ABILITIES
11. PLANNING
12. INFORMATION SEEKING
13. COPING WITH PROBLEMS
14. EVALUATING RESULTS

HEALTH AND PHYSICAL QUALITIES   A. NO PROBLEM _____ B. MAYBE PROBLEMS _____

N.B. TICKED NOTE BRIEF DETAILS _____
_____

VERBAL REASONING

Figure 6.15b: LEA careers service 16+ profile: basic skills list

3.
ADDITIONAL INFORMATION AND COMMENT   (From tutor, Parents and Student)

INTLS	DATE

Figure 6.15c: LEA careers service 16+ profile: additional information sheet

POST 16 DECISIONS

A. JIIG-CAL SECTIONS   AB   BC   CD   DE   EF   (Circle)

B. JIIG-CAL TYPE | 1 | 2 | 3 | 5 | 6 | (Priorities)

C. JOB TRAINING FAMILIES   PRIORITIES

1. Administrative, clerical and office services   _____
2. Agriculture, horticulture, forestry and fisheries   _____
3. Craft and Design   _____
4. Installation, maintenance and repair   _____
5. Technical and scientific   _____
6. Manufacturing and assembly   _____
7. Processing   _____
8. Food preparation and services   _____
9. Personal Services and sales   _____
10. Community and health services   _____
11. Transport services   _____

D. SPECIFIC JOB CHOICES

1. _____   2. _____

E. AFTER 5TH FORM ACTION _____
_____
_____

F. PREFERRED PLACE OF STUDY OR TRAINING

1. _____
2. _____
_____

Student signature _____ Date _____

Figure 6.15d: LEA careers service 16+ profile: careers information

PILOT SCHEME – 'TOP DOWN' MODEL

Chronological sequence of events:

March 1983	– Issue of document on 16+ Profile from Careers Office	April	– Letter to parents
Summer	– Decisions taken to involve pilot schools, contacts made	May	– Tutors make initial moves to contact pupils
		June	– Pupils assembled for briefing. Note in staff circular announces project
Sept	– New 'comprehensive' opens. Initial contact from Careers Office. Discussions of trials	July	– Set up Junior School liaison exercise for profiling pupils
		July	– Half day INSET for tutors
Oct	– INSET course. Participating schools send representatives	Sept	– Contact from Careers Office urging negotiations of assessments and outlining plan for academic year
Nov	– Meeting to arrange details of materials, target group, training requirements, etc.	Sept	– Bank and Building Society launch – some 'profile' pupils involved
Feb 1984	– Further meeting concerning 'negotiation' with pupils and suggested examples of activity	Oct	– Some tutors use 'can do' slips
		Nov	– Tutors collect information for reference
Feb	– Tutors identified (volunteered)	Dec	– One 'profile' tutor leaves school
March	– Final meeting of group prior to launch. One tutor from case study school attended. Details regarding issue and use of materials	Dec	– P.A.G. group takes over project
		April 1985	– Contacted by above. Decision to 'wind up' project
		June	– Letter from school to parents
March	– Meeting in school. Tutor distributes documents. Pupils identified	July	– Questionnaire for profile tutors to complete

Figure 6.16: Chronology of pilot scheme

together with some covering notes (Figure 6.23). Tutors were then asked to review the information produced, order it logically and prepare for a tutor based parent evening to be held immediately after the Autumn half term.

The parent evening duly went ahead and the fourth year tutors were asked to provide feedback on the system. The following points were made.

The assessment sheets as they stood provided a great deal of information, even where they had only been completed to a 'minimum' standard. Extracting the information, however, had proved to be a major task. The amount of time a tutor had spent prior to the parent evening varied from very little to fifteen hours. Some tutors worked directly from the sheets whilst others extracted information from each one and produced an 'impression document' to work from with parents.

Some tutors had mistakenly assumed the assessments to be 'closed', i.e. parents and pupils were not to see them. The majority though had welcomed an open system and used the assessments as part of tutor period work with pupils and as a basis for discussion. The lack of consistency in the layout of the sheets, however, had proved to be a major problem and also the confusing use of apparently conflicting grade systems. Should 1 mean 'good' and 5 'poor' or the reverse? The criteria covered varied enormously from sheet to sheet and on some assessments an explanation on how to interpret the information was requested. Some sheets were intended as a 'snapshot' whilst others were intended to be progressive.

The physical handling of the sheets was clumsy and standard A4 ring binders or wallet folders failed to provide much help.

From a faculty viewpoint the pilot had been welcomed. The blank sheets were made much more accessible to staff than being placed in a central staff room (as with the 'old' system), but some difficulty had been experienced in checking that all staff had produced the information required and also in finding the time or organisation to place sheets in tutor group order before passing them on. Faculties had not previously encountered this particular organisational problem as it had been handled in the past by the 'pastoral' system. Also, what would happen to the information

3.G. FACULTY

4TH YEAR ASSESSMENT

SUBJECT.. TEACHER..

NAME.. TUTOR GROUP..

	Criteria		Date		
1.	Attendance — Regular — Absence affecting work				
2.	Organisation (equipped for lessons) — Always — Usually — Never				
3.	Behaviour — Very good — Good — Acceptable — Unsatisfactory				
4.	Effort — Very good — Good — Acceptable — Unsatisfactory				
5. Homework — Always attempted and in on time — Rarely attempted or often late Key 1. — Excellent quality 2. — Good quality 3. — Satisfactory quality 4. — Finds difficulty but tries hard — Does not make adequate effort					
6.	Examination (Predicted if present progress maintained - O/RSA — Borderline O/CSE Level — Mid range CSE attained — Low CSE — Non—examination				
7.	Particular strengths				
8.	Particular weaknesses				
9.	Recommendations for improvement				

Figure 6.17: Fourth year assessment: business studies

HUMANITIES
GEOGRAPHY HISTORY
COMMUNITY STUDIES SOCIOLOGY

Date:
Name:
To:
Teacher:

EXTRACTING INFORMATION FROM BOOKS etc	Tends to copy	Easily discouraged by expanse of print	Finds task difficult	Quick grasp of essentials
	Doesn't select, over thorough	Lacks confidence	Works well with a partner	

UNDERSTANDING OF IDEAS	Weak grasp of key ideas	Tends to need individual explanation
	Lacks confidence but usually understands	Quick to grasp concepts

GRAPHICAL/ TABULAR SKILLS	Inadequate understanding of scale	Unable to transfer figures into graphical form	Enjoys task but weak mathematically	Neat and careful	Very competent

MAP SKILLS

	Untidy	Clear grasp	Easily confused	Careless
Grid references				
Contours				
Sketching				
Scale				
Cross sections				
Tracing				
Map drawing				

IMAGINATIVE WRITING	Finds difficulty	Too brief	Relevant	Imaginative, gets involved

MECHANICS OF WRITTEN WORK

	Inadequately understood	Understood but careless	Consistently accurate
Sentence structure			
Basic punctuation			
Spelling			

Handwriting	Illegible	Untidy	Clear and neat

CONTRIBUTION TO DISCUSSION	Disruptive	Lacks confidence	Irrelevant	None	Rare	Thoughtful
	Impulsive	Confident	Relevant	Frequent		Imaginative

APPROACH TO WORK	Individually	Poor	Only under supervision	Purposeful and independent
	In a group	Lacks confidence	Quiet but involved	Contributes well	Takes leading part
		Disruptive			Constructive

HOMEWORK	Sometimes late often late	Only under pressure	Done with little care	Satisfactory	Consistently well done
	Worse than	Same as	Better than	Classwork	

EQUIPPED FOR LESSONS	Never	Seldom	Usually	Always late	Often late	Sometimes late

Figure 6.18· Fourth year assessment: humanities

LANGUAGE FACULTY ASSESSMENT SHEET

SUBJECT: _____ DATE: _____

NAME OF PUPIL: _____ TUTOR GROUP: ____

SUBJECT TEACHER: _____ CLASS/SET: _____

ASSESSMENT USED:

| 1-EXCELLENT | 2-VERY GOOD | 3-GOOD | 4-FAIR | 5-POOR |

STUDY SKILLS		1	2	3	4	5
ORAL/AURAL	EFFORT					
	ATTAINMENT					
WRITTEN	EFFORT					
	ATTAINMENT					
HOMEWORK	EFFORT					
	ATTAINMENT					

TEST RESULT(%) _____   CLASS AVERAGE (%) ___

OTHER REMARKS:

Figure 6.19: Language faculty fourth year assessment sheet

'now', as there was only one copy? Would it return to faculties or go to the pupil file?

Pupils, it seemed, had welcomed the breadth of information provided and the opportunity to discuss with their tutor the overall view supplied. Parents, who in the past had complained that a tutor based evening was lacking in information, seemed to welcome the subject overview passed through the tutor but also found the style and layout of the sheets confusing when actually shown a set of teacher comments. Their main criticism was that they had not received their own copy of the information.

All this was presented to a management group meeting in early December 1984. This pilot was agreed to be enough of a success to extend and a small working group was organised to review the comments made and produce recommendations back to the management group as soon as possible. The meeting also agreed to use the faculty based A4 assessment system for the forthcoming third year options information, and that the working party should have a wide enough brief to encompass all aspects of school based assessment and reporting. This last point followed the strong feeling that, as applied so far, the new assessment system was thorough but time consuming and was being run in addition to the already established booklet style report system – the combination producing an intolerable burden on staff.

TUTOR GROUP

NAME:

SECTION ONE: WRITING Look back at the writing you have done during this half-term. Explain and comment on your work as fully as possible.

DATE:

Drafting. (Writing stories, poems etc.)	
Journal	
Opinion writing (essay)	
Report writing	
Feedback	
Problems (conventions: spelling etc)	

Try to say what you thought of your work and try to say what you thought you gained/learned during the writing

SECTION TWO: READING

a. *Individual Reading* Which books have you read/started to read?	
Write a sentence or two about the most enjoyable thing(s) you have read.	
b. *Reading in a Group* Write down all the books stories you have read this half-term.	
Write a couple of lines about the reading you have done with the class.	
Write about any future plans for your reading activities.	

Figure 6.20: Reading and writing profile: self assessment

BOYS PHYSICAL EDUCATION FACULTY – YEAR 1984/5   Name: _____

Tutor Group: _____

Criteria	ASSESSMENT 1 Date:						ASSESSMENT 2 Date:						ASSESSMENT 3 Date:					
	B	P	A	G	VG	EX	B	P	A	G	VG	EX	B	P	A	G	VG	EX
Participation																		
Motivation																		
Effort																		
Standard of Kit																		
Games Ability. Athletics.																		
School Teams																		
House Sport																		
Extra Curricula Activities																		
Other comments																		

Staff Signature _____

Figure 6.21: Boys physical education faculty assessment sheet

The working group, consisting of the two Directors of Study and three Heads of Faculty, met just before the end of the Autumn Term with the following agenda:

Short term problems
● Who should hold the recently completed fourth year assessments?
● What were the major problems to be resolved over the third year assessments to be started soon after Christmas?

Medium term
● What would/should be the pattern of fourth year assessment up to the end of the year?
● What should be the pattern of third year assessment up to the end of the year?

Long term
● Suggested principles for assessment/ communication for the whole school.
● Suggested pattern of the above across five years.
● Methods of delivery.

In the event, the meeting quickly reached consensus on all of the above points and a report was produced and presented for distribution at the start of the Spring Term.

As a short term measure, however, a guidance sheet for the production of the third year options assessment was produced in an attempt to rationalise the approach of the individual faculties and suggest evidence of good practice. The second faculty based assessment sheets show in general that the suggestions were followed. See, for example, Figures 6.24 and 6.26.

Before the axe of industrial action fell again, early in

SCIENCE   ANNUAL ASSESSMENT SHEET

	Oct	Dec	Feb	Apr	May	July
Understanding (1–4)						
Effort (1–4)						
Practical skills (1–4)						
Oral communication (1–4)						
(1–4)						

Name:..

T.G..

COMMENTS:

Stats.	Topic	A	B	C	D	E	F
	Mark						

Teacher's initials						
Pupil's initials						

Figure 6.22a: Annual assessment sheet: science

SCIENCE PROFILE: Self assessment

Name: ....

Tutor group: ....

Science teacher: ....

Date: ....

Self-assessment is being responsible for your own progress. YOU will be the one to benefit if you develop your abilities.

Read each section carefully. Answer the questions honestly in the space provided. Ticking boxes may be the simplest response but if you need more space add a sheet of paper.

1. UNDERSTANDING

Look back and think of the work you have done.
(1) How easy has it been for you? Do you get all/most/some/none of it?

(2) Explain which work was easy or difficult for you and why.

2. EFFORT

(1) Do you always do your best?

(2) Do you ask for help every time you need it?

(3) Do you use reference books in class, at home or in the library?

(4) Do you avoid hard work if you can get away with it?

(5) What could you do to improve?

(6) How could we help you to improve?

Figure 6.22b: Annual assessment sheet: science pupil self assessment (contd. on p. 107)

3. PRACTICAL SKILLS

(1) What apparatus have you used lately? For example glassware, circuits, balances, machines or microscopes?

(2) How well can you set things up and get them to work? Comment on your successes and failures.

4. ORAL COMMUNICATION (talking and listening)

Type of oral work	How often done?			Are you confident?		
	Often	⟶	Rarely	Very	⟶	Not
Take part in whole class discussion						
Listen to teacher						
Small group discussion (2-4 people)						
Talk with your teacher						
Talk with another adult						

Do you talk to (a) share ideas, (b) solve problems, (c) explain or describe, (d) predict, (e) chat. Underline those you do.

5. WRITTEN COMMUNICATION

Type of writing	How often done?			Are you confident?		
	Often	⟶	Rarely	Very	⟶	Not
Copying from the board, sheet						
Writing own reports						
Drawing						
Graphs						
Tables						
Flowcharts						
Other (Specify)....................................						

Figure 6.22b: Annual assessment sheet: science pupil self assessment (contd)

FOURTH YEAR ASSESSMENTS – Oct/Nov '84 – TUTOR NOTES

Background – All faculties were asked to produce their own assessment schedules because:-
    a) No agreement could be reached over standard layout and therefore assessment areas and style
    b) Much disagreement with staffroom based procedures (folders on a table etc.)
    c) Poor and often meaningless information for tutors and therefore, at times parents, produced by previous systems.

Explanation – Each faculty has produced their own assessment sheet
    CS have two, different sheets, 1 for DCT and AR
                                  1 for HE
    PE have boys and girls sheets
    LS and SI have self assessment sections as part of the process
    MA, LA and HU have room for only one assessment per sheet

This whole process is seen as a pilot in terms of schoolwide assessment and information processes, although it does have implications *within* faculties (some more than others).

Objectives for tutor role – organise sheets into a logical sequence
    a) Use the information provided to clarify pupil 'position', especially with regard to options.
    b) Identify areas where particular praise is due – set against previous pupil standards (ipsative) – could be difficult for new tutors.
    c) Identify particular problems – especially where a 'pattern' emerges.
    d) Use the information, as far as possible in a formative way (in general terms) to encourage/discuss progress.
    e) Prepare information based on assessments for use at 4th tutor-parent evening on Weds Nov 21st. (I intend to plan this on an appointment basis)
    f) Assist in the evaluation of the whole pilot process in preparation for the management meeting of Nov 14th in the following areas:
        i) Design of forms – clarity, content, suggestions for some uniformity?
        ii) Comments on usefulness of information supplied
        iii) Handling in terms of quality, quantity, timing, return – how and who?
        iv) General suggestions for modifications.

SOME SHEETS MAY HAVE BEEN MIS-ROUTED, PLEASE CHECK AND PASS TO CORRECT TUTOR
LET ME KNOW ABOUT ANY LARGE SUBJECT 'GAPS' YOU WANT ME TO CHASE

Figure 6.23: Fourth year assessments: tutor notes

the Spring Term of 1985, the management group were able to have one meeting at which they reviewed the report of the working party on assessment. From this meeting the following proposals were made, accepted and endorsed as school policy.

- That, if practical, all assessments in future would be faculty based on a development of the pattern used in the recent third and fourth year.
- That, if practical, all reports, i.e. formal communication to parents, should also be based on the same system.
- That a coherent and coordinated pattern of assessment and reporting should be established across all five years.
- That all assessments should be open, i.e. to be read by pupil and parent, with the exception, at present, of the fifth year summative reference for colleges, employers, YTS, etc.
- That a suitable method of multiple copies, for these assessments, be produced as soon as possible.
- That a tutor or pastoral based assessment should be devised to match the current faculty based assessments and that an enclosing folder or binder be developed.
- That a more common approach be devised for the individual sheets, taking into account local and national developments.

The general framework for an assessment pattern was accepted and the group were asked to develop a more detailed version, including parent evenings, for further discussion. This was duly done.

A timetable for reporting was developed and agreed (see Figure 6.27).

Conclusion

Fourteen months after the initial ideas for a school based assessment scheme were raised it is possible to draw some conclusions, to raise theories to be tested and to offer opinions and proposals for further action.

The amount of development which can be achieved in a short space of time and with an enthusiastic and committed staff can be almost frightening. From May to October 1984 there were only fifteen working weeks and yet a radically different and relatively successful faculty based assessment pattern was devised and implemented. Within two months the system had been further developed and used with a different year group. By January 1985, just 27 working weeks after the initial idea, the school had decided in principle to completely alter its whole system of schoolwide assessment, to pursue a coherent five year pattern based on the new proposals.

The pace of the development was not fuelled solely by enthusiasm of course. The LEA profile project, the attendance of staff at courses and conferences based around the issue of profiling, the publication of the DES documents (1984 Records of Achievement), and the fact that the school was too new to have developed its own established pattern anyway, all helped to add some urgency to the development. How frustrating then for this to cease in February 1985 as the industrial dispute prevented all but a very few meetings from taking place. It also meant the ceasing of all parent evenings and, most important of all for this development, prevented the writing of any more 'reports', either under the new or old systems.

The two 'runs' of the new assessment system and the use of a faculty based approach to fifth year reference assessments, taught the school a great deal about handling the system. Key areas, however, included checking that faculties had designed, printed and distributed assessment sheets in time for completion by the required date; supplying suitable folders to contain large numbers of the sheets for transporting them around the

CREATIVE STUDIES FACULTY.

THIRD YEAR ASSESSMENT.

NAME: _____

TUTOR GROUP _____

DATE _____

Subject	Home Economics / Needlework		Art / Pottery		CDT / Graphic Communication	
Teacher/s name/s						
	*	Notes	*	Notes	*	Notes
Flair						
Understanding						
Achievement						
Interest shown						
Initiative						
Progress						
Organisation						
Independent work						
Group work						
Practical skill						
Oral contribution						
Homework						
Attitude						
Behaviour						

Key:- * (5) Excellent in this Area.   (4) Doing quite well   (3) Coping
       (2) Some cause for concern   (1) Very weak in this aspect.

Subject	How strongly Recommended for Course (5-1)	Possible Exam	Possible non Entry	Further comment when necessary PTO.	Accepted on Course
Art					
Pottery					
Home Economics					
Needlework					
Child Care					
Graphic Communication					
Modular Technology					
Design Studies					
Technical Studies					
Craft					

Please tick

Figure 6.24: Third year assessment: creative studies

Music Department

3rd Year Music Assessment

Name _____   Tutor Group _____

3rd Year pupils receive one music lesson of 1¼ hours duration each fortnight.

School Music Lessons Assessment	(Pupil in Black/Tutor in Red)				
	A	B	C	D	E
Singing (Effort and Participation)					
Theory and Rudiments. (Recall)					
Listening and Appreciation. (Attitude to varied styles)					
Aural effort. (Response to questioning)					
Written Work. (Presentation)					
General attentiveness and conduct.					

Musical Instruments learned at school: _____

Last Examination passed: _____

Musical Instruments learned privately: _____

Last Examination passed: _____

Any other musical activity either at school
or privately including singing: _____

Other comments:

Staff Signature   Date

Figure 6.25: Third year music assessment

school site; allowing ready access and keeping them secure and safe, before returning them to their ultimate destination.

The feedback from the faculties suggested that although they were happier with their own sheet design than with a schoolwide, imposed assessment sheet and would prefer to use something similar to it instead of the booklet style report, they were not yet happy enough, in most cases, to risk a high quantity, high cost run on, say, NCR paper, which would allow copies to go home. How could we get the quality and quantity of input required to both improve individual sheets and also to develop a more standard approach across the faculties?

The developments so far had been almost entirely restricted to the subject areas and, as can be seen from the sheets produced, were largely cognitive in target. Little in the way of cross-curricular assessment had so far been attempted and little in the way of affective assessments. How was this area to be opened up?

The information supplied in most cases was a 'snapshot' assessment. Even those faculties which had originally hoped to use a progressive and therefore I would suggest, a potentially more formative approach, had been restricted by the system itself, again by the industrial action and also by a lack of understanding on the part of their colleagues. The pupils in the third and fourth years had seen the assessments and in most cases had discussed them with their tutors (and in some cases with their teachers), and actions had resulted from this – e.g. option choices or 'remedial' help over behaviour, attendance, quality of work, etc. The full formative value, however, had hardly been explored because, although the whole system had affected the area of communication between teacher and tutor and was beginning to affect the area between school and parent, it was having very little effect on the interaction between teacher and pupil and on the assessment methods employed in and around the classroom. How could this area be tackled?

SCIENCE FACULTY.
THIRD YEAR ASSESSMENT.
SCIENCE.

PUPIL NAME _____
TUTOR GROUP _____
DATE _____
TEACHER _____

	4	3	2	1
Understanding				
Effort				
Practical Skills				
Oral Communication				
Written Communication				

(Tick appropriate box).

Understanding 4 — Appreciates reasons and purposes. Quickly detects patterns.
       3 —
       2 —
       1 — Follows instructions mechanically and uncritically.

Effort   4 — A consistent trier – very persevering
       3 —
       2 —
       1 — Quickly gives up without constant help.

Practical Skills   4 — Chooses correct tool technique or procedure. Observes many details.
       3 —
       2 —
       1 — Unable to select and manipulate apparatus successfully. A poor observer.

Oral Communication: 4 — Can express ideas coherently in different contexts, including publicly.
       3 —
       2 —
       1 — Doesn't respond much even in a one-to-one situation.

Written Communication: 4 — Explanations, thoughts and ideas are clearly expressed.
       3 —
       2 —
       1 — Disjointed language making little sense.

Recommendation for Option Choice.

	Recommendation	Exam Potential	Comment
Double Science			
Single Science			
Plants and animals			

Figure 6.26: Third year science assessment

If the profile is to be of a formative nature, then it is desirable that the profile should provide the cornerstone of the system of recording and reporting. (Garforth, 1983.)

With the minimal use of self-assessment it was possible for at least two faculties to draw information and ideas, but even with these faculties the impact was very variable. How could this area be developed in those faculties who had yet to recognise self-assessment as a useful learning tool?

Some teachers clearly feel threatened by the involvement of students in the area of assessment, since it often includes adverse criticism of teaching methods. (Tossell, 1984.)

Problems of a practical, tactical and theoretical nature seemed to surround the development by the close of the Summer Term of 1985 and, with no apparent end in sight to the industrial dispute, the development seemed doomed to its transitory state. Some areas of the school were already talking openly of returning to previous practice (although even that meant very different things to different people!).

The release of major funding through the TRIST proposals, brought to the LEA the possibility of a new initiative in the area of profiling. A three year project was launched. The school was to be included in the first year of activity (1985/86). This would mean the release of one senior member of staff for one day per week, plus the use of extra INSET time; a group of people from various schools sharing ideas; a project coordinator to assist developments; research work on areas of the curriculum and assistance with funding. Development work has begun once again. . . .

Summary

The events of this second cycle of development work are summarised below. As it now enters its third phase

	YEAR 1	YEAR 2	YEAR 3	YEAR 4	YEAR 5
1 September					
2					
3					
4					
5 October					
6					
7					
8	Tutor Pa. Ev.			Assessment	
HALF TERM-NOV					
9		Assessment		Tutor Pa. Ev.	
10					Mock
11					Exams
12					
13 December					Assessment
14					Report
15					
CHRISTMAS					
"					
1 January	Tests		Assessment		Subject Parent
2			Report		Evening
3			(Options)		
4					Mock Exams
5 February	Assessment				
6	Report		Subject Pa. Ev.		
HALF TERM					
7					
8 March		Tests			
9				Subject Pa. Ev.	
10	Subject Pa. Ev.				EXTERNAL
EASTER-April					
"					
1		Assessment	Tests		
2		Report			
3 May					
4					
5					Examinations
6					
7					
HALF TERM					
8 June		Subject Pa. Ev.			
9				Exams	
10				Exams	
11	Primary Ind.			Assessment	
12 July				Report	
13					
14					

Please note — a) The frame ▭ around assessments, indicates the length of time allocated to complete them. The final line of the frame shows the week in which they have to be passed to the recipient e.g. – tutor or parent.

b) Testing can, of course, take place at any suitable time for years 1–3, however the weeks indicated are to be left clear of any other activity e.g. – trips etc.

Figure 6.27: Assessment pattern 1985/86

A NEW SCHEME EMERGES

Chronological sequence of events:

Sept 1983	– New school opens.
	– Assessments based on system developed in old school.
Jan 1984	– Options assessment, single sheet.
April	– Notes from Director of Study to Academic Deputy outlines 'new' approach.
Summer Term	– Some faculties produce draft framework for new pattern.
Oct	– Fourth Year faculty based assessments piloted.
	– Fourth Year tutor parent evening.
Nov	– Constructive criticism gathered.
Dec	– Working party meets to evaluate and propose.
Jan 1985	– Proposals of working party distributed.
Jan/Feb	– Third Year (options) faculty based assessment piloted.
	– Proposals for second Fourth Year assessment raised.
	– Management meeting agreed new system to replace booklet style reporting.
	– Working party meet, review and propose five year pattern.

ACTION RESTRICTS ALL DEVELOPMENT – NO MEETINGS POSSIBLE, NO MORE REPORTS

March/April	– Proposals for personal assistance record.
April	– Launched to staff and pupils with minimal consultation.
	– Review of pastoral assessment.
May	– Comments gathered on five year assessment pattern.
June	– Five year assessment pattern accepted as basis for school calendar.
July	– Costing for A4 assessment sheet duplication.
	– Inauguration of the TRIST funding – discussions begin on one year development programme.

Figure 6.28: Chronology of the emerging new scheme

of profile development, the school which is the subject of this particular case study provides a very clear reflection of the changing character of the movement as a whole. In particular it shows the movement from school based initiatives without extra resources towards much larger scale projects, substantially funded and with a measure of external accreditation. The implications of this change in the impetus for profiling developments are considered at length in other parts of this book.

Postscript

It should now be clear that the stages of identifying profiling priorities, designing or choosing a scheme and subsequently implementing it, is a delicate and probably lengthy process. Any attempt to skimp on the processes of consultation, reflection and preparation described in this chapter is likely to result in a scheme which does not achieve its goals either because it is faulty in its design or because it does not enjoy the support of all members of staff. Profiling is a high-risk strategy. Enthusiasm and commitment are vital to its success because fundamentally it is about changing the nature of pupil–teacher relationships.

For most people, the recording side is of secondary importance, its principal role being to provide a basis and an incentive for this dialogue to take place. Indeed, one of the principal dangers associated with the very success of the profiling movement is the increasing likelihood that uncommitted teachers will find themselves coerced into cooperation with a scheme with which they are not in sympathy. Up to now it has been individual teachers' determination to 'make it work' and their freedom to devise a scheme to meet their idiosyncratic needs which has been crucial in the successful implementation of profiling. The more institutional support and direction becomes available and indeed, imposed on a large scale, the more likely it is that this 'grass-roots' enthusiasm will be lost. Even without the declining morale among teachers that is all too prevalent at the present time, it is likely to be even more vital in the future that careful planning and sensitive management accompany any innovation attempt. Given the current industrial climate it is amazing that so much is still being achieved. Great care will need to be taken by people at every level of the system not to extinguish this enthusiasm.

Part III
De-briefing

Chapter 7
How well are we achieving our goals?

The need to evaluate the success of any attempt at innovation may seem dull in comparison with the down to earth concerns discussed so far. Nevertheless, the issues which this chapter addresses are likely to prove the most fundamental of all in the long term to determine whether profiles maintain the important place they have captured in the educational imagination. Unless schemes are flexible enough to respond to changing needs and circumstances; unless they can win public acceptability and unless they can form a coherent whole with other developments in assessment and certification, the enthusiasm on which profiling depends will rapidly succumb to the erosion of time and disillusion.

In this section, therefore, we shall start by considering some of the questions which schools themselves will need to keep in mind as they consider the progress of a particular scheme. In many cases, it is the answers to these same questions which will form the basis for the offering or withholding of external accreditation and this will be discussed later in this chapter.

In Chapter 2 I identified a number of stages for the profiling movement.
1. 'Initiation' – of the early schemes, mainly pupil recording and profile 'grids'.
2. 'Diversification' – including the rapid development of profiling in vocational initiatives.
3. 'Institutionalisation' – into much larger-scale county and regional schemes often including an examination board.

We are now entering a fourth stage which may be termed '*evaluation*' in which there is a growing interest among individual schemes and national bodies in the collection of detailed evidence about the impact and operation of profiling schemes. Such evaluation work, including the very substantial evaluation of its own pilot schemes funded by the DES, will provide much needed insights into the effects and implications of profiling. It will also provide the basis for the fifth and possibly final stage in the movement – that of '*nationalisation*' in which national guidelines for records of achievement are instituted. It is still too early to predict what form these guidelines will take. Many of those currently involved fear that they will constrain undesirably the spontaneity and flexibility that have been the great strengths of the movement so far. Others welcome the considerable strengthening of the currency of such records that such national status is likely to bring. Still others see 'nationalisation' as an irrelevance to their essentially formative, school-based recording procedures.

Meanwhile, the growing concern with evaluation is likely to be more generally welcomed. Whatever the scale of the initiative, it is essential that certain key questions about its operation and impact are answered.

Evaluation

As the word itself implies, evaluation inevitably involves the formulation of particular criteria or 'values' against which a judgement may be made. Thus any evaluation requires a clear specification of goals and, ideally, an equally clear specification of assessment criteria which will allow a judgement to be made as to whether those goals have been achieved. These requirements may be expressed as three key questions which all schools need to answer, namely:
1. What are our objectives in instituting profiling?
2. How do we know when we have achieved these?
3. If we are not achieving them, what are the reasons?

The detailed specification of goals for any particular profiling system is likely to be unique, and this was discussed in detail in Chapter 6. But, for the purposes of this discussion, we may take those goals identified in the DES Policy Statement, since they are likely to provide a basis for the national criteria which will eventually be formulated by the government, and thus the framework within which most schemes will choose to work.

Purposes of records of achievement

11 The Secretaries of State believe that there are four main purposes which records of achievement and the associated recording systems should serve. These purposes overlap to some extent.

i) Recognition of achievement. Records and recording systems should recognise, acknowledge and give credit for what pupils have achieved and experienced, not just in terms of results in public examinations but in other ways as well. They should do justice to pupils' own efforts and to the efforts of teachers, parents, ratepayers and taxpayers to give them a good education.

ii) Motivation and personal development. They should contribute to pupils' personal development and progress by improving their motivation, providing encouragement and increasing their awareness of strengths, weaknesses and opportunities.

iii) Curriculum and organisation. The recording process should help schools to identify the all round potential of their pupils and to consider how well their curriculum, teaching and organisation enable pupils to develop the general, practical and social skills which are to be recorded.

iv) A document of record. Young people leaving school or college should take with them a short, summary document of record which is recognised and valued by employers and institutions of further and higher education. This should provide a more rounded picture of candidates for jobs or courses than can be provided by a list of examination results, thus helping potential users to decide how candidates could best be employed, or for which jobs, training schemes or courses they are likely to be suitable.

(DES Policy Statement on Records of Achievement, 1984)

Given this kind of general statement of purpose, how can schools evaluate their own schemes in relation to questions 2 and 3 above? The first step must be to break down the very broad objectives of the scheme into a number of key questions such as those which follow:

1 *Operation*
   a) How well does profiling fit into and support the school's other activities?
   b) What have been the principal difficulties in operating the scheme in terms of, for example:
      ● staff preparation and training;
      ● pupil/parent attitudes;
      ● time;
      ● resources;
      ● enthusiasm;
      ● other initiatives?
   c) Are there any technical difficulties with the scheme itself, e.g. grid 'steps' too large to allow for sense of progress, wording incomprehensible to pupils?

2 *Effects*
   a) What effects, if any, does profiling seem to be having on pupils? For example:
      ● Is it positive for all learners?
      ● Is the negotiation still teacher-dominated?
      ● Are pupils more self-aware, more motivated?
      ● Are pupils acquiring new learning skills, attitudes?
   b) What effects, if any, does profiling seem to be having on staff and the work of the school as a whole?
   c) What effects, if any, does profiling seem to be having on relationships with those outside the school, especially parents, local colleges, employers? What is the currency of the profile?

These deceptively simple questions are likely to involve the staff or a sub-group of it in a good deal of heart-searching and discussion. In some cases it may be deemed necessary to solicit views systematically by means of a questionnaire. In other cases, evaluation and 'trouble-shooting' may be very informal involving a continuous process of review and response. Clearly there can be no standard recipe for success for, even if all schemes were aiming at the same set of goals and using the same procedures – which as we have seen is certainly not the case – institutional circumstances dictate an idiosyncratic resolution to problems. However, there are some very general problems and issues that may usefully be discussed and this is the focus for the following case study.

Profiling in CPVE

CPVE is likely to prove one of the most significant 'seed beds' for profiling as it moves out of its pilot phase to become a widely-available alternative 17+ qualification. Whilst in practice the flexibility built into its design will allow the CPVE course to be operated differently in each institution, there is nevertheless a curriculum and assessment approach which is subject to external moderation. It is for these two reasons that I have chosen the experiences of one CPVE pilot scheme to illustrate some of the key issues any profiling scheme must address. The institution concerned is a sixth-form college in its second year of CPVE work. Staff have identified the following problems.

1 The status of CPVE in this institution is undermined by its location at the bottom of a list of options that includes 'A' and 'O' levels, BTEC general, RSA diplomas etc. This makes it hard to 'sell' the summative value of the resultant qualification to pupils.

2 The CPVE students are a distinct group whose course aims, ways of working and close relationship with staff tend to isolate them from other groups of students. The impact of the CPVE pro-

filing on the larger organisation and curriculum of the college, itself bound by the structural constraints of various traditional examinations, is therefore negligible

3 As larger numbers of staff are involved, some are only doing CPVE work in a small way (two periods a week). Some thus lack understanding of CPVE profiling and time to implement it.

4 Some staff get to know students very well in the course of working on individualised assignments. Many feel a more meaningful and less laborious assessment could be produced by an open-ended, negotiated descriptive report.

5 In a review situation where the form (Figure 7.1) has to be filled in, it is very difficult for staff to work with students they have not taught. Students tend to forget what they have done in previous weeks even though they are supposed to keep their own record. Staff who have taught them are able to remind them and understand the learning objectives involved. In addition, the areas identified under the 'special attention' (c) section of the form are not easily fed back to the teachers concerned for them to take action. When the review tutor is also the teacher concerned, this kind of information is likely to be well-known anyway, and not need this degree of formalisation. To be formative and useful, staff feel reviewing time should be built into the timetable. Having to withdraw students from class is extremely disruptive for all concerned and results in reviews being very infrequent.

6 The profile also presents a number of technical problems. How does one assess:
   'Can appreciate a range of dialects and languages.'
   'Can recognise orders of magnitude in everyday applications.'
   'Can recognise the scientific facts, laws, principles and generalisations underlying investigations into problems.'
And what do these things mean? Does the comment bank contain imprecise descriptors, and if so, will the resultant profile be any more meaningful to outsiders than the more traditional reports and certificates?

Another major problem with this draft profile is in those areas where hierarchical descriptors are supposedly to be found. The CPVE 'Notes for Pilot Schools' (March 1985) (p. 2, notes 11 and 12) say:

Performance within some factors is described by a single statement indicating that only one level of performance is considered to be relevant to CPVE. . . .

Where more than one statement is available for a factor, this indicates that a range of student performances can be expected and recognised within the CPVE population. The most basic level of performance is given first, the highest last. Each higher level subsumes those lower in the factor.

Only one statement from the hierarchy is to be placed on the final profile. When we look at actual examples we find problems. For example:

CORE AREA FIVE. NUMERACY
Factor: number skills
1 Can recognise numbers and place values.
2 Can carry out simple calculations involving whole numbers.
3 Can carry out simple calculations involving decimals, fractions, percentages.
4 Can recognise and apply the calculations required to solve problems.
5 Can solve problems using simple algebraic and logical techniques.
6 Can solve multi-stage problems using various mathematical techniques.

CORE AREA THREE. COMMUNICATIONS
Factor: writing
1 Can write legibly.
2 Can convey straightforward information and ideas in writing.
3 Can select and use an appropriate style and form of writing to maintain confidence of the user.
4 Can compile and write a report.
5 Can originate and organise written material in a style suited to the purpose.

(CPVE Notes for Pilot Schools, 1985)

Are these statements really hierarchical, and would one automatically assume, for example, that if one can solve problems using algebra, one can carry out simple decimals, fractions and percentages? Would an employer, for example, reading the former statement, assume that it also included the latter, given that the final profile will only contain one statement? Or, again, we might ask what has writing legibly to do with any of the other higher order skills. Surely one may possess any of those skills without being able to write legibly?

The profiling procedures proposed for the CPVE highlight a fundamental issue in any large-scale profiling initiative of the kind we are concerned with here. Are these technical pitfalls currently identifiable in the procedure merely content problems which can be refined with experience, or are they structural and fundamental to the whole exercise; in that as soon as we start to give fuller information, and then try to impose limits on what is said, we come up against the problem of saying anything that is really adequate and meaningful?

7 Although core skills (as illustrated above) are explicit in 'introductory' and 'exploratory' modules, in

Name of Student:

PERIOD COVERED BY THIS PROFILE (DATES) START: END: REVIEW NO:

Please complete MAIN ACTIVITIES

MAIN ACTIVITIES:
_____
_____
_____
_____
_____
_____
_____
_____
_____

REVIEW NO: REVIEW DATE:

After discussion (and completing this progress profile), we agree that:

(a) progress has been made in:
_____
_____
_____

(b) the student has done particularly well in:
_____
_____
_____

(c) special attention should be paid (before the next review) to:
_____
_____
_____

SIGNED (Student)... SIGNED (Tutor)...

Figure 7.1: Periodic review sheet for CPVE sixth-form college

the 'preparatory' module assessment is on content rather than process since all the objectives of the module must be covered for a pass to be awarded. Therefore there tends to be a contradiction between formative and summative profiling.

8 The certificates are not very impressive to look at and come too late to be useful.

9 Many students do not understand how the assessment works, the terminology employed or its educational purpose. Also, credit cannot be given for achievement which is more than the minimum for a particular level but insufficient to qualify for the next. Thus some pupils may have little sense of progress. The effect in both cases is to undermine the objective of increasing motivation.

Looking back to the list of key questions on page 117, we can see how the specific issues identified in this particular profiling example relate to this list. Thus the status, location, relative isolation and external constraints of CPVE together preclude any attempt to fit the CPVE approach into the college's other work. Although staff enthusiasm is still high, pupil and parent attitudes have tended to be negative at least at the outset because CPVE is perceived as the least desirable option. Time and resources are insufficient to do the task properly. It is still too early to identify the effects of the scheme on pupils, the institution and the world outside as this may depend as much on the perception of CPVE nationally as on its implementation in any one institution. Nevertheless, it is clear that the formative objectives of profiling are being undermined by the complexity of the scheme and the other operational and technical problems outlined above.

Comment

Those operating a profiling scheme will be aware of the problems they encounter in using it. Those managing it will be aware of other problems of implementation. Still other insights will be available to those outside the school – parents, trainers and employers who have close contact with its effects on young people. It is important that *all* these perspectives be brought together in a regular procedure of review and reflection. Not only will this prevent a potentially dangerous accumulation of worry and resentment. It will also provide the essential basis for a continual process of improvement and refinement of the scheme.

Accreditation

Because of the complexity of skills, achievement and experience that go to make up the typical profile, little attempt has been made to provide external accreditation of individual pupil records on the external examination model. Instead, most schemes concerned with providing an external 'guarantee of quality' are opting for an approach in which it is the institution itself which is 'accredited' by means of external moderation of its courses and procedures.

Schools and colleges involved in such external moderation will be required to extend the kind of internal evaluation described above to take account not only of their own institutional concerns but also those laid down by the external accrediting body. Both the criteria for such external accreditation and the procedure for implementing them are likely to be detailed and extensive. This is well illustrated by the following example taken from the OCEA consortium.

The OCEA accreditation process

The term 'accreditation process' covers the whole set of events from the time an institution decides it wishes to participate in OCEA to the stage when it is able to do so. It also includes a continuing periodic review. Broadly, institutions wishing to participate in OCEA will begin the accreditation process by seeing how far their own educational processes match the OCEA accreditation criteria. Following discussion, an institution will make a submission to the OCEA Accreditation Committee, a submission which indicates how far the institution currently meets the accreditation criteria and what its plans are for meeting those not yet met. Following the validation of this submission by the OCEA Accreditation Committee, the institution can then be accredited as being able to participate in OCEA.

The method for accreditation varies according to the three different components. With regard to the 'P' component, it is strongly felt that the Delegacy should not impose a common framework on all schools, but rather recognise a great variety of practices, all of which are deemed as supporting the accreditation criteria. In this way it is hoped that a balance may be achieved between the development of a credible national standard and the preservation of the freedom of individual schools and colleges to design schemes and curricula which reflect the needs of the local educational environment (p. 9, OCEA handbook).

With regard to the 'G' component, appropriate moderation procedures will be implemented in order to ensure, through moderators, that the 'G' component assessment criteria are being interpreted in an agreed way within and between schools and across LEAs. With regard to the 'E' component, schools and colleges will be asked to try to transmit the appropriate information to the Delegacy.

The basic principle underlying the OCEA accreditation process is that the initiative should come from the school, but be supported by the LEA, where the LEA as a whole is participating. This assumes the establishment of advisory and supportive local arrangements. How this is to be done, e.g. through school consortia, INSET, networks, etc., is to be determined by the LEA. Apart from ensuring national credibility of OCEA, the work of the Accreditation Committee is also designed to facilitate the cross-fertilisation of ideas and good practice. This relationship is an on-going one, in which periodic reports will be submitted to the Accreditation Committee and continuing support and INSET provided by the LEA. Thus an institution from a participating LEA would go through the following steps to get accredited:

1. First, finding out about OCEA from a variety of sources, making the decision to take part, self-evaluation of existing practice against OCEA accreditation criteria, and consultation with interested parties such as staff, parents, governors and LEA personnel. A detailed submission will then be made to include current position, intention and plans, statement of resources and INSET needed, plus a statement from the LEA indicating what support will be forthcoming.
2. Having considered the submission, OCEA will then agree to monitoring arrangements, validate the submission and accredit the institution; the monitoring to be repeated at agreed times until all the criteria are fulfilled, and then once every five years.

The OCEA Accreditation Committee membership has yet to be established, but it is envisaged that it will include LEA, teacher and Delegacy representation.

The accreditation criteria are:

1. The school/college is expected to demonstrate commitment to the main principles underlying OCEA.
2. The institution is expected to provide opportunities for the compilation of records of experience and achievements.
3. The institution is expected to provide opportunities for the preparation and practice of skills and capabilities to equip students to take advantage of the OCEA process.
4. The institution is expected to provide a variety of opportunities for personal and social development and achievement. Furthermore it should demonstrate that it recognises and values the significance to the student of activities and experiences which occur outside the range of the institutional provision.
5. The institution is expected to provide opportunities for reflection on, and appraisal of, the personal record, and the production of a series of summary statements through a process of discussion and review.
6. The institution is expected to design and deliver its curriculum in such a way that students are involved in a constructive planning and reviewing process.
7. The institution is expected to provide opportunities for students to be able to demonstrate their achievement of the 'G' component criteria.
8. The institution is expected to employ a range of assessment techniques which will enable students to demonstrate their achievement of the 'G' component criteria.
9. The institution, supported by the LEA or other appropriate agency, is expected to provide opportunities for teachers to discuss and develop their understanding and application of the 'G' component criteria.

(Based on OCEA handbook)

		INSTITUTION	LEA	REGIONAL	NATIONAL
1	OCEA	Makes submission (through LEA) on how far it meets the criteria and its plans for meeting the rest.	Supports schools by coordinating INSET etc. Has arrangements for forwarding schools' submissions for accreditation.	OCEA Accreditation Committee accredits schools to participate – initial monitoring and 5 yearly reviews – moderation likely to be regional rather than central, with moderating committee reporting to Accreditation Committee.	
2	NPRA Scheme 1	Draws up work units and establishes criteria.	Pre-validating body* acts as a filter to ensure that only units with a strong chance of validation are submitted further. Also coordinates INSET. (* Made up of advisers, heads, teachers, FE, commerce, industry, etc.)	Validating body* ensures criteria are met and validates units. (*Same membership as LEA Validating Body + members + staff of NEA Boards.)	
	Scheme 11	Draws up work units and establishes criteria. A Committee (comprising e.g. teachers, the local inspector, parents, industrialists) pre-validates units.	Ensures criteria are met and validates units.	Samples, validates schemes to ensure standards are maintained.	
3	Gulbenkian	Validating Board established by governing body – validates schools' records.	Local Accrediting Board* which moderates the institutions' records. (* Made up of professional educators.)		Accrediting Council for Education, accredits the local arrangements.

Adapted from Nuttall, 1986

(OCEA – see page 121; NPRA – see page 123; Gulbenkian – see page 123)

Figure 7.2: Some different approaches to accrediting records of achievement

Figure 7.2 compares the OCEA approach described above with two other major profiling initiatives involving external accreditation – both of which were described in detail in Chapter 4. The NPRA is based on a unit credit system and the Gulbenkian Project on individualised, negotiated learning programmes and these major design differences are reflected in differences in the accreditation procedures of the two schemes. Nevertheless, when all three examples shown in Figure 7.2 are compared, it is apparent that certain basic principles are held in common namely:

- It is the programme of work, the quality of the education that is the prime target for scrutiny.
- A more democratic approach to the control of educational quality in which a wide range of educational interests are represented – not just the examination boards who have traditionally held this role.
- Several levels of scrutiny which reflect the different concerns which need to be met in any public certification procedure.

Such external accreditation is still in a very early developmental stage and it is not easy to predict how it will develop. The scale of current initiatives in this respect and the government's commitment to the production of national guidelines for records of achievement by the end of this decade, suggest that provision for external validation of profiling schemes and accreditation of the awarding institutions will become increasingly the norm. Whether this model of accreditation, borrowed largely from higher education, starts to make serious inroads on the more conventional model found in public examinations of moderating individual pupil performance remains to be seen, however. This is certainly one more area in which records of achievement philosophy and practice represents a major challenge to traditional assessment assumptions.

By the same token, profiling schemes which are not externally accredited are likely to become fewer in the future as the value of such an imprimatur becomes apparent. Nevertheless, there will still be many initiatives – perhaps in an individual department or concerned with a younger age level – for which external evaluation is inappropriate. Yet for these schemes too, as this chapter has tried to show, regular 'de-briefing' will be essential if the profiling scheme is to function as effectively as possible.

Such de-briefing, however, is likely to be concerned with the more immediate and visible aspects of profiling. Now that we have covered the basic issues involved in setting up and running a profiling scheme – the reasons for having one, the options available, the approaches to implementation and the need for on-going evaluation – the main aims of this manual have been achieved. There are, however, one or two more general issues about profiling which are not crucial to its implementation. However, they may prove critical to its long term educational effects. They thus provide a fitting postscript to this volume for those with a little time for reflection.

Postscript

In the implementation of profiling, our perspective on its success or otherwise will be very much that of the school, the teacher, the parent or the employer, for these are the people whose support – political and practical – is critical to the enterprise. Those most closely involved and affected by the scheme – the pupils themselves – may not even be consulted. They are certainly unlikely to be members of a working group on the subject. This is of course normal in educational matters. And yet, without the enthusiastic support of pupils and an equal commitment to making the procedure work, it would be hard to justify the staff time and energy involved. This is particularly true of the formative aspect of profiling in which it is the *process* rather than the *product* that is central.

Indeed at the heart of the present movement to introduce records of achievement is the notion of reviewing. In practice this can mean a brief chat about progress, a pastoral interview or a negotiated discussion about past progress and future work plans. As yet we know little about the impact of such reviewing on pupils and their learning and motivation or indeed on teachers and their approach to their work. The DES Policy Statement of 1984 anticipated that the institution of a much greater measure of one to one dialogue as part of recording achievement would result in enhanced pupil motivation. Certainly this would seem to be the case given that such dialogue is likely to encourage pupils to take more responsibility for their own learning, to feel appreciated and respected as an individual by the teacher and to give them the chance to communicate to the teacher their own perceptions of their strengths and weaknesses.

Having said this, however, a number of important questions need to be addressed, both practical and more philosophical ones. First, the notion of equality: how far are we talking about teachers discussing with pupils their progress, needs, etc. and how far are we really talking about teachers relinquishing some control over the learning process itself to the pupils? To what extent can equality between the taught and the teacher ever be achieved without the very nature of teaching being re-interpreted?

Further points arise from this, for example,

1   If negotiation is to be taken seriously by pupils, can teachers avoid submitting themselves to the same process? How can such a role be made compatible with teachers' other roles such as controlling pupils, administering discipline etc.? How can the necessary environment of trust be created in schools at the present time?

2   Are pupils being prepared to take advantage of the opportunity that this situation offers them?

Do they perceive it as a useful exercise because, if they do not, then it is unlikely to bring about the desired effects on motivation and learning. Are some pupils by virtue of their ethnic, gender and class background likely to be better able to take advantage of this opportunity than others, and if so, how may such differences be overcome?

3 Pupil exposure. The notion of negotiation and dialogue has at its heart a much broader conception of education and by the same token a much broader involvement of a pupil in the learning process. In this sense it constitutes a move from a simply instrumental view of the curriculum to a more expressive one where both the affective and cognitive dimensions are seen as important. Whilst highly desirable in many respects, it is also important to consider whether this greater degree of pupil exposure will have the effect of subjecting pupils to greater stereotyping and surveillance than exists at present. Although it is commonly agreed that pupils themselves should keep the record, there are many problems associated with defending the pupil's right to privacy and what to do about disclosures that pupils might come to regret in future. Are such interviews to be equivalent to a medical consultation? In many cases, individual profile information will be kept on disc or stored in a computer. Although personal data can theoretically be safeguarded by the use of personal access cards, these can be relatively easily broken into by keen computer hacks. A detailed ethical code relating to the generation, storage, use and destruction of profile information is urgently required. The term 'sentencing' is creeping into the special vocabulary of profiling to mean the achievement of a particular criterion objective. We need to be sure that the other, more familiar sense of the word has no place in the profiling movement.

Sooner or later, if this is the case, the problem of the relationship between summative and formative recording will need to be addressed since most schemes anticipate that at least some of the recording will become public at some stage.

Secondly, there is considerable research evidence about the extent of stereotyping of pupils which currently goes on and we need to examine actively ways of training teachers to overcome this. The evidence from many research studies that teachers hold, and interact on, the basis of differential expectations of pupils according to factors such as sex, ethnic background, speech, dress, physical appearance and personality should give rise to concern in relation to profiling. One of the main reasons that public examinations have survived for so long despite their well-known disadvantages is that their anonymity guards against the overwhelming power of the social criteria that they were brought in to counteract. How far profiling leads to greater social inequality will need to be carefully watched.

Thirdly, there are the practical problems. While these are not so intractable in the long term, in the short term teachers are likely to see the provision of time, resources, place etc. as a key issue in the success of review procedures. In the current teacher/pupil ratio, it may prove insuperable for some subject teachers to find the necessary time. Schools will certainly have to engage in fairly radical reorganisation to make this possible on a large scale, and this in turn has implications for the nature of teaching more generally. But we need to be sure that reviewing is perceived as a useful exercise by not only the key personnel involved, the pupil and the teacher, but also others associated with the exercise more generally, such as parents or potential users of the certificate. In particular we need to know what aspects of reviewing tend to be successful, and what inhibits this, if we are to justify the time spent on it. Essentially this is a high-risk strategy for which the pay-off is potentially considerable but where the dangers are correspondingly high.

These problems posed by the novel approaches to recording achievement which are now being pioneered are likely to be further exacerbated by the advent of an equally new examination at 16+ being introduced at virtually the same time – the General Certificate of Secondary Education (GCSE). This latter initiative is a powerful and much more lavishly-funded exercise which builds on more than a century of tradition of public examinations at 16+. Thus whilst both GCSE and records of achievement are built upon the same prevailing consensus that:

1 a wider range of achievements should be acknowledged;
2 all pupils should have some testimony to their achievements;
3 certification must be relevant to both the pupils themselves and potential users;
4 pupils' self-esteem and motivation should be enhanced by the provision of achievable goals;
5 certification should support and encourage desirable curriculum change;

there are distinctive characteristics of records of achievement which are not found in GCSE, such as the inclusion of information on personal and social skills and experience in a wide range of activities where comparison between pupils is of little significance. These and other distinctive characteristics of records of achievement which have been discussed at length in this book may thus come to be of little significance beside the more traditionally-certified subject attainments of GCSE. Even with the current moves to provide external accreditation which have been described in this chapter, records of achievement may prove no match against the impact of GCSE.

It is possible that the result of these twin initiatives in certification will be a new and still more desirable assessment hybrid. Alternatively it may make the dangers with which profiles and records of achievement are inherently fraught almost impossible to avoid.

At the heart of profiling initiatives lie some or all of the following objectives:

THE PROMISE OF PROFILING
- The promotion of democratic teacher–pupil relations
- The promotion of a sense of self-worth for each pupil
- The provision of a flexible and negotiated curriculum
- The promotion of pupils' ability to be self-critical
- The promotion of pupils' ability to take responsibility for their own learning
- Encouraging pupils to compete primarily against their own previously achieved standards

It is the promise of profiling that this book is built around. Against it, however, we must set the perils of profiling:

THE PERILS OF PROFILING
- A sense of powerlessness and coercion among pupils
- An even greater intrusiveness of assessment
- Imprisonment in a benign but ubiquitous judgement from which there is no escape

This may seem a sombre and perhaps over-philosophical note on which to end this essentially practical and action-oriented book. It is justified because in the long term, these more philosophical questions will prove the most practical of all. To ask 'can it be done?' is not simply to raise the problems of time and resources, status and currency – as important as these are. It is to ask 'can it be done *well*?', for if profiling cannot be done in such a way that it begins to make a reality of the promise set out above, then it should not be done at all.

References

H. D. Black and P. M. Broadfoot, *Keeping Track of Teaching: The Role of Assessment in the Modern Classroom*, RKP, London, 1982

P. Broadfoot, 'Communication in the Classroom: The Role of Assessment in Motivation', MEd dissertation, University of Edinburgh, unpublished, 1977

P. Broadfoot, 'Pros and Cons of Profiles', *Forum*, Vol. 24, No. 3, 1982

P. Broadfoot (ed.), *Profiles and Records of Achievement*, Holts, Eastbourne, 1986

T. Burgess and E. Adams, *Recording Achievement at 16+*, NFER Nelson, 1986

R. De Groot and J. McNaughton, *PPR Handbook* (lst edition), 1982

EEC, *Policies for Transition. A European Community Action Programme*, Brussels, March, 1984

FEU, *Computer-assisted Profiling*, DES, 1983

FEU, *Microcomputer-assisted Profiling Manual*, FEU Capital Media, London, 1986

C. S. Frith and H. G. Macintosh, *A Teacher's Guide to Assessment*, Stanley Thornes, 1984

D. Garforth, *Profile Assessment: Recording Student Progress*, A School-focussed INSET Workshop Manual, Dorchester, Dorset LEA, 1983

L. Gow and A. McPherson (eds.), *'Tell them from me': Scottish School Leavers Write About School and Life Afterwards*, Aberdeen Univ. Press, Aberdeen, 1980

Gray et al., JEP, Ch. 1, p. 23 in Vol. 1, No. 1 of *Education Policy*, 1986

D. H. Hargreaves, *The Challenge for the Comprehensive School: Culture, Curriculum and Community*, RKP, London, 1982

A. W. Harrison, *Profile Reporting of Examination Results*, Schools Council Examinations Bulletin 43, Methuen Educational, London, 1983

G. Hitchcock, *Profiles*, County of Avon, 1983

G. Hitchcock in P. Broadfoot, op. cit, 1986

Institute of Personnel Management (IPM), *School and The World of Work: What Do Employers Look for in School Leavers?* IPM, London, 1984

B. Law, *Uses and Abuses of Profiling*, Harper and Row, London, 1984

Manpower Services Commission (MSC), *Young People and Work*, Manpower Studies No. 1, London, 1978

MSC, *Making Experience Work*, HMSO, London, 1979

D. Marcus, *Reports and Reporting*, Bosworth Papers No. 3, Bosworth College, Leics, 1980

Scottish Vocational Preparation Unit, *Assessment and Youth Training: Made to Measure?* Jordanhill College, Glasgow, 1982

R. C. Sims, *The Strengths and Weaknesses of Profiles*, University of Bristol, unpublished, 1985

N. Stratton, *Profiling Systems*, CGLI, London, 1985

D. Suggett, *Guidelines for Descriptive Assessment*, VISE, Australia, 1985

T. Wilkes, *Pupil Profiling: Demanding Innovation*, Diploma in Advanced Studies in Education dissertation, University of Bristol, 1985

R. White with David Brockington, *Tales Out of School*, RKP, London, 1983